ME AND MY MOUTH

AUSTIN HEALEY
The Autobiography

Monday Books

A CIP catalogue record for this title is available
from the British Library

ISBN 0-9552854-4-5
(2007 ISBN: 978-0-9552854-4-8)

Typeset by Avon DataSet Ltd, Bidford On Avon,
Warwickshire

Printed and bound by Creative Print & Design Group,
Harmondsworth, Middlesex

www.mondaybooks.com
info@mondaybooks.com

Contents

Foreword

I owe a lot of people a great deal. My mum and dad ferried me everywhere when I was a kid, and have supported me every step of my playing career. My wife Lou has always been there for me, backing me when times were tough, soaking up my frustrations, helping me to succeed. My friends, in and out of rugby, at Leicester, England and beyond, have been immense, too. I'm eternally grateful to all of them; they're too many to name, but they know who they are.

Of course, I owe just as much to the game itself. Without rugby, I'm not sure where I'd have ended up.

I took a lot from the sport – fun and enjoyment, a good living, and the highs and lows that a professional career brings.

In return, rugby has taken a lot from me. On holiday this year, I sat down for dinner – and my knee dislocated. If I'm not careful, it goes when I try to stand up. It hurts, believe me. I've got arthritis in the knee and I can't jog without pain. Eventually, maybe ten years down the line, I'll have to have it replaced – an operation normally reserved for people in their late 60s and 70s. The replacements last around 15 years . . . after that? Who knows. I've done my shoulder, my ankles are knackered and I wake every night with back pain.

Yes, rugby took me to the peak – it allowed me to represent my country on a sports field, and to win doing so. But it also took me to the bottom. If you're as desperate to win as I was, it hurts when you lose, much more even than wrecked knees, dislocated shoulders and a damaged back. I've been depressed and almost suicidal, I've come close to alcoholism and some might say I've flirted with insanity.

For all that, I don't regret a moment of it.

I called this book 'Me And My Mouth' because it's my mouth that many people think of when they think of me. That's a shame, because I reckon I was a pretty useful player. But then I made a second career, almost, out of opening my gob and sticking both feet in. If you want someone to say the wrong thing, at the wrong time, to the wrong person, I'm your man. Equally, if you need the right thing saying when everyone else is keeping their heads down, you know where to come looking. Right or wrong, I didn't always steer the most sensible course. I've fallen out with coaches, other players and even fans along the way. Most of the time, we shook hands later and it was all forgotten. Occasionally we didn't, and that cost me England caps. But life goes on.

I've tried to be as honest as possible in these pages. Sometimes, I don't come out of the stories all that well. There'll be times when you wonder how so much arrogance and attitude can be packed into one melon-sized head. There'll be others when I sound cruel, or juvenile, or spiteful. All I can say is that I'm only human and that, in the dog-eat-dog world of professional rugby, you do what you have to do to survive. Of course, to tell the truth, a lot of it was front.

Anyway, that was me when I was Austin Healey, rugby player.

Now I'm just Austin Healey, husband and dad.

Doing my best to adjust.

Austin Healey, November 2006.

Melon Head

It's not easy for me to admit this, but when I was a kid I was known as Melon Head.

I know what you're thinking, but it was because I had a big forehead, not because I thought I was God's gift to the world – though I did, of course. When you fancy yourself as much as I fancied myself, nobody pays you any compliments, so I paid them to myself. I was good at sport, I was quite clever and I was also, as my under-9s rugby coach was first to point out, a bighead. Humility was a far-off land, many miles from Merseyside. I still haven't quite located it but various events in my life have brought me closer to the region. Almost going to prison for assault and twice being banned for foul play on the rugby field have made me slightly more humble. But at heart I'm still the smart-arse kid they called Melon Head.

It helps to have a bit of arrogance, of the right sort, on a rugby pitch. In professional sport there is no place for self-doubt. You can't afford to let it surface – you end up getting hurt. But if you want to banish doubt, on or off the pitch, you have to work at it. My way was – and is – to put up a curtain of invincibility and bury any weaknesses by way of non-stop banter. If you're good at it, you can almost end up convincing yourself. Plus which, if you spend your whole life talking yourself up, you absolutely have to perform. There's no get-out, it's make or break, win or bust. That's when I'm at my best. It certainly worked for me in rugby. I always felt that if things went wrong in a game, I could put it right. When Leicester were staring at defeat against Stade Français in the final minute of that first Heineken Cup final in Paris, I knew I could win it for us if I got the ball in my hands. Likewise, when the Lions trailed ACT after the hooter on the ill-fated 2001 tour Down Under, I still had hope.

Of course, I've got a vulnerable streak, just like everyone has. I pretend to have all the answers but inside me, behind the bravado, there's a normal person hiding, prone to the same failings as everyone else. It's just that I don't want to be normal, so I don't let him out.

With a name like Austin Healey, most people assume that my mum and dad, Denise and Allan, were car lovers. The truth is, neither mum nor dad cared two hoots about our motor, just so long as it got us from A to B in one piece. It was my granddad, Sidney, who suggested the unusual first name when I was born. He was an offshore powerboat racer who competed all over the world and it was he who fuelled my love of soccer in general and Everton Football Club in particular.

Where I was born, in Wallasey on Merseyside, in October 1973, the sporting choice is a straight one, and it's not soccer or rugby. It's, *Are you blue, or are you red? Everton or Liverpool?* For everyone in my family except my sister Ashley, who supported Liverpool just to annoy us, it was Everton. Trevor Steven, Kevin Radcliffe and Neville Southall were my sporting heroes. The last thing I'd see before I turned my light off at night would be the faces of Trev, Kev and Nev on my bedroom wall; I'd never even heard of Bill Beaumont, Fran Cotton or Clive Woodward.

At the time, Everton were probably the best team in the world, though they got robbed by a lot of shocking referees, and my proudest moment was appearing as a ball boy at Goodison Park, my proudest possession a piece of the pitch

2

I nicked that day. I went to all their home games with my granddad, sitting in the Bullens Road stand. He was a nightmare – he'd spend the afternoon shouting at everyone and starting fights. Even more frightening was the journey to Goodison in his tiny Fiat 126. He'd point out where all the bombs had been dropped during the war and completely ignore the traffic lights. More than once I thought my number was up.

I had these two friends, Mark and Paul Stewart, who lived at the top of Shamrock Road in Claughton Village, and we'd spend all our time in the back alley kicking a football around. Soccer meant everything to us and we played for as many teams as we could fit into a weekend. I captained the district team and averaged a goal a game from defence. I was a sweeper for the county side and played right wing for another team. You know, versatile. I reckon I'd have been a soccer legend, following in the footsteps of all those Everton icons, if I'd kept it up. I know I was good enough.

But then the Stewarts went and switched sports. I can still recall the horror when I called round one Sunday morning. 'Sorry, Austin,' said Mrs Stewart, 'They've gone to play rugby.'

Wallasey was not exactly a hotbed for rugby union, but Birkenhead Park – where the Stewarts had gone – were a pretty decent side at the time and I ended up dragging my feet down there after them the next weekend. I took to it straight away and never really looked back.

Paul and Mark were big lads – by the age of six they must have been about five feet tall. I was around 2ft 2in, and was immediately pigeon-holed as a scrum-half. I hate the way that happens. If you're big and tall, you're put in the forwards, if you're small, you must be a half-back. OK, I had brilliant hands, dazzling pace and incredible vision, but they didn't know that when they first saw me.

Mum ran our home and dad was a self-employed tiler, who had good times and bad. I could tell the difference between the two because it was either a snooker table, a video game and water skis for Christmas, or an orange. They spent half their lives in the car, ferrying me to and from different sports clubs; only once did they fail me, when the car refused to start one freezing morning. I had to run two miles to the pick-up, arriving just as the last car was leaving. Luckily, I was fast even in those days – I broke 11 seconds for the 100 metres whilst I was at secondary school – so I made it in time.

My folks supported me brilliantly. Dad was always quiet on the touchline, but mum, who's from Zambia and has a fiery Zambian temperament, would stand there yelling me on. One time, she took things a bit too far. I was playing for Birkenhead Park Under-12s – I was only nine and we were up against a Rhyl team who were a lot older and massively bigger. I'd scored a couple of tries and was going for my hat-trick when one of their monsters caught me and hammered me into touch. Mum stormed straight onto the pitch – the last thing I remember was her swinging her handbag at this lad. It was possibly the most embarrassing moment of my life.

I scored a fair few tries because I was quick, and my speed had other benefits, too. I was small – I was on the front row of the school photo in my final year at primary school, at the age of 11 – and I was gobby and, naturally, I was an obvious target for the bullies. So unless I was sticking up for my little sister, I spent a lot of time on my toes, running away from confrontations – until my very last day at primary, when a lad called Marvin had a go at me. Normally, I would have legged it but the worm finally turned. I thought, '*Sod it*', and whacked him hard in the face. It felt surprisingly good. For me, that is – I think he cried.

It was a defining moment: I went on to St Anselm's College and, from that point on, I had a fight pretty much every day. If anyone said anything, it usually ended in violence of some sort; I would wait for them to swing and then nail them. The teachers told my parents but I think dad was quite happy that I was starting to stick up for myself. 'If they hit you first, whack them,' he'd say.

By the time I turned 16, I could look after myself and I'd become something of a rugby mercenary, playing for whoever asked me as long as they sorted out the travel. I played for Hoylake before moving onto Birkenhead Park, but I always returned to Hoylake on Friday nights as that was the venue for the weekly disco. My list of conquests is too long to detail, obviously, but suffice it to say that St Anselm's sister school was a convent and what they say about convent girls is completely true. I find it impossible to believe that any of the girls I knew at Upton Convent grew up to be nuns.

I have got a lot to thank religion for but none of it would make the church particularly proud. Although I went to a Catholic school, I wasn't a Catholic: I did consider switching codes, but only because my convent girlfriend of the time had to go to Heswall RC Church every Sunday. We'd stand at the back by the spare hymn books, snogging through the service.

As I say, I was reasonably bright but I didn't try at school – I was always going to be a sportsman. Maths and geography were the only subjects I didn't loathe, and I tended to mess around if I didn't respect the teachers. In Latin and woodwind, the masters would walk into class and say 'Healey out!' before even opening their books. I wasn't allowed into woodwind lessons for three years. But I didn't waste the time I spent outside. I met my good friend Simon McKee and we'd play pitch and toss together. For three years. We became pretty useful. I suppose anyone would in three years.

As a rule of thumb if anything happened in primary school, junior school or senior school I got the blame for it. If there were no suspects, Healey would do. It was that way with the exploding goldfish. I was only eight, for heaven's sake and it was my mate who fed them the polystyrene. They ate it and went pop; it wasn't me, but I took the rap. I had to stand outside the headmaster's office for two days and the school wrote a letter to my parents. Luckily, mum and dad believed my version of events.

I'm actually a footnote in the history of St Anselm's. I was the last boy to get the strap there before corporal punishment was banned. It was the final day of the summer term, and spirits were high. As usual, I'd been told to sit in the corner of my form, away from everyone else. All my classmates shared double desks except me and there was a six-foot exclusion zone around mine for five years because I was, supposedly, 'a disruptive influence'. On the day in question, Mr Johnston – by coincidence, the father of Saracens and England centre Ben, with whom I toured South Africa in 2000 – returned to the classroom just as I was in the process of moving my desk back to its regular position. It was a tricky manoeuvre, sliding it backwards across the wooden floor from the door where I'd driven it. But I was doing pretty well. Mr Johnston declined to acknowledge my skill. Instead, he gave me the strap – a leather thing, half an inch thick, which hurt like mad when it was brought hard on the palm of your hand. I got three swipes but smiled through the pain to wind Mr Johnston up.

Given my attitude, I suppose it was something of a miracle that I emerged with good results – 10 GCSEs, and A levels in theology, statistics and general studies. The one A level I failed was economics, where my teacher was Ted

Rudd, an England wing in the mid-1960s. Sadly, he didn't have any interest in sport at all. He was pre-occupied with supply and demand. I was particularly immature in his class and, shamefully, made fun of his stutter. I am not at all proud of myself for that – he used to send me out all the time for finishing his sentences.

The two teachers to escape my baiting were Joe Green and Martin Regan. Martin had played for England at fly-half in the fifties, while Joe was a huge second row forward with a big loping stride. Although he was a clumsy forward, it was Joe who impressed on me that it was not good enough just spin-passing off my right hand. He also taught me to kick off both feet and was a real inspiration: I would have been suspended a number of times if it hadn't been for Joe suggesting that the school rugby team might have suffered.

The one cloud on my sporting horizon was my asthma. I was rushed to hospital after an attack when I was six and spent a week in an oxygen tent. I developed a pathological fear of needles there: day after day, I watched a nurse walk through the ward with a syringe in her hand and stick it into the lad in the bed next-door. Every time she came near him he screamed the place down. One day I saw her heading our way and assumed she was coming with another injection for that poor kid. But she walked past his bed and stopped at the end of mine. Talk about terror. I developed a horrible phobia from that day on.

Two years later I nearly died after another bad attack on holiday in Romania (why we were holidaying in Romania I have no idea). It hit me on the first day, and my normally-reliable Ventolin inhaler had no effect. For 20 minutes, I struggled for breath . . . one gasp here, one there. We had the doctors out and they gave me an injection of cortisone which probably saved my life. For the remainder of the holiday we had to drive 20 miles, twice a day, to a clinic for more of the same. I had 13 jabs in all and by the time I got home I had a shadow on my lung. My parents always look back to those few days and say they nearly lost me.

In the early days, asthma hindered my sport but the fitter I became the less effect it had. 'Asthma' describes the inability to take in air because the bronchials have contracted – so if you have the ability to work with less oxygen it helps. Nowadays, I control it through breathing techniques and by avoiding what sets it off. Cats are particularly murderous for me. I don't mind dogs, but I've got a deep hatred of our feline friends, who I believe were put on this earth to curse me. A lot of people take it for granted that a little inhaler here and there can cure people, but you still have to be very careful.

Some forms of the condition are more serious than others, mind. I've met a fair few players down the years who have suffered from exercise-induced asthma, which is a slightly different thing. It's called being unfit.

Playing With Tigers

Leicester were the biggest and the best rugby club in the British Isles long before our Heineken Cup triumphs. I know that because Richard Cockerill told me the first time I met him. He also punched me in the face.

It was the summer of 1996 and Cockers, the small and imperfectly-formed Tigers hooker, thought I was a smart arse. I'd just joined the club from Orrell and was taking part in my first training session out of the gym with my new team mates. At least, I thought they were my team mates. My introduction to the lads was a game of touch rugby. My introduction to Cockerill was a knuckle sandwich. I made a half break and touched him and he swivelled round and caught me on the jaw. After I had stopped laughing I asked him what the hell he was doing.

'There are no superstars here,' he yelled, in that over-dramatic way of his.

In his pea-sized forward's mind, he thought he was doing it for the club (he was known as Captain Club Man, because he'd have died for Leicester Tigers). He obviously thought he had to show me the Leicester way. I laughed again.

I didn't want to be immersed in Cockers's idea of the Leicester way. I hadn't moved clubs to change the way I do things on the pitch. I had known from the outset that I was a different person to all the forwards – OK, maybe Neil Back and Martin Johnson might have shared my lateral thinking – and I had no intention of becoming a zombie. I wanted to play with a spark, be a bit different, even if it meant being obnoxious and big-headed at times. I wanted to play for Leicester but I didn't want to become as obsessive and insular as some were at that time, where they couldn't see the wider picture of what was going on around them.

That day at Oval Park was a testing ground for me. Cockers wanted to know how I'd react. I think the other lads expected me to bite back and go for him but when I just stood there laughing I'd passed the initiation test. He used to have a fight in training every single week, without fail. Trouble was, he wasn't quite as hard as he thought he was. I've been hit harder by my little girls.

Don't get me wrong. Like many things at Leicester, Cockers wasn't what he seemed at first. He's actually a really good lad – he and his wife Serge were the first to welcome me into their home when I joined the club and beneath that Deliverance-style exterior lurks a heart of gold.

I'd joined with Will Greenwood, and, being two northern lads with a bit more brain than most of the Leicester old guard, they regarded us with deep suspicion. They thought we were using the club for our own devices, as a stepping stone to playing for England. The ABC Club – the unholy front row union of Cockerill, Graham 'Wig' Rowntree and Darren Garforth – were particularly forthright. In our early days, they'd openly tell us that we were parasites, only at the club for what we could get out of it. That was probably true in Will's case, but I resented it bitterly. It was an attitude that deepened when we did start playing for the national side, and playing well. Eventually, they warmed to me, of course, but they never liked Shaggy much. Good judges of a man, the ABC.

Rugby's full of divisions, and club vs country and forwards vs backs are two of the deepest. It reeks of hypocrisy: a forward gets injured, so he doesn't train and it's all hunky-dory. But if a back picks up a knock and sits out a session, he gets abused. It's like our injuries don't count.

It was an attitude that persisted throughout my career, and – joking aside – it really used to get me down. I can have a moan as well as anyone, and I don't mind people niggling me. But I did lose my patience with, 'Oh, you're saving yourself for England' or 'You're just saving yourself for the Lions tour'. I never did that, ever. I loved my club and I worked my arse off to be fit for the team. Because of the abuse, I often trained when I shouldn't have and, who knows, maybe it shortened my career?

The first thing you need to know about forwards is they're stupid, selfish mutants who usually have no idea what they're talking about. You don't need much up top to play in the front row, after all. Anyone can bend over and push.

It's ironic, then, that the main reason for me choosing Leicester in the first place was that gang of ugly mutes. A decade ago – is it really that long? – Bath were the better side in terms of running rugby, but Leicester had a brilliant pack and, as a scrum-half, that was more important to me. I'd been contacted by Darren Grewcock, then a No9 at the club and now a leading fitness trainer, and asked to come down for a chat. I was very flattered, until I met Tony Russ, the then director of rugby, in December 1995 and heard what Leicester thought I was worth – £10,000 a year. I'd been making more on expenses as an amateur. Even worse was Russ's condescending attitude. The initial plan was that Leicester would sign me, Will and Jim Naylor in a job lot. We played together for the North and had made a pact to stay together. Russ changed all that. Jim met him and promptly decided he would join Newcastle instead. I almost backed out too but happened to speak to Les Cusworth, a Tigers legend whom I knew from the England set-up.

'I can't see me joining Leicester after all, Les,' I said. 'I don't like Tony Russ and he's taking the mickey with his offer.'

It turned out to be a smart move on my part. Cusworth put me in contact with Peter Wheeler, the Tigers' chief executive and a top man; soon after, I met Brace at Leicester Forest East services on the M1. He was charming, sharp and straight: we agreed a £30,000 basic, I'd get a nice Rover 600 Turbo and the chance to play at a top club. I signed in March before flying out to the Hong Kong Sevens. When I returned Russ had been sacked. I haven't seen him since.

I didn't know anyone at Leicester when I arrived that June morning with my fellow new boys, Will and Craig 'Jocky' Joiner, the Scottish international, so I went with an open mind. Initially, Will, Craig and I were housed in the Holiday Inn hotel, where we stayed for almost three months. They were strange, almost surreal times. The club paid for everything, so we were eating carvery every night and just messing around, three young lads having a laugh together. Eventually, the meal bills got too high, so they put a stop to it, but we used to sneak a look at the hotel's list of guests and slip into the restaurant under assumed names.

Eventually, we found a place together and that first year we had an amazing time. We all had girlfriends who came down and stayed at weekends, but the majority of the week it was just men behaving badly, playing indoor golf and generally causing mayhem. Our rented house took a hell of a hammering and so did the local pubs.

I remember one of our first nights out together – I think it was the night that Will first met Caro, now his wife. We got a taxi into town and we had this big thing about not sitting in the front seat – whoever sat there had to pay. Craig had already paid for two and he wasn't too keen to pay for the third. Sadly, Will and I beat him to the cab. He decided he'd drag one of us out and chose me. I was holding the inside of the door closed while he was pulling the outside and between us we pulled it in half: I had hold of the interior and Craig had wrenched the outer part away and off its hinges. Not surprisingly, the taxi driver went absolutely mad; we crapped ourselves and legged it up the street. It certainly showed how much weight training we were doing at the time.

Craig's a cracking guy, and was always very placid and laid back, until he got drunk. Then his alter ego took over and he became 'Angry Graham'. After a certain number of beers, Graham would turn up and before long he'd be chasing you, like Captain Aggressive, intent on causing you serious injury. One night sticks in my mind, when Craig and I spilled out of a nightclub, fighting – except I was fighting with Graham, not Craig, and he was yelling 'I'm goin' tae kill ye,' in his ridiculous Scottish accent. Happy days.

Back at home, I used to do the cooking, Craig would tidy up and Will spent his life on the sofa watching TV, because he's a very selfish person. He would probably say the same about me, but it's not true. Will was in charge of the remote control and was completely obsessed with *Coronation Street*, *Eastenders* and *Friends*. If you turned the TV off when *Friends* was on he would burst out crying, and say things like 'But it's the only thing I want to watch all week.'

So we'd say, 'What about *Corry* and *Eastenders*?'

And he'd just blub a bit more.

'Will,' I'd say, 'there's an excellent documentary on BBC2,' and he'd storm off up to his room and slam the door and me and Craig would collapse laughing.

We were always winding each other up; it was always easy with Will, you just hid the remote, but I think the best wind up I ever got him with was when we got our letters for the 1997 Lions Tour. All those in the preliminary squad of

70 had been told that if we were in the tour party we'd be notified by mail on the morning it was announced.

I got up early on D Day and, there were two letters on the mat – one for me and one for Will.

I heard his door open upstairs, so I slid his under the mat and stood there, ostentatiously reading mine out loud.

' *"Congratulations, you've been picked for the Lions,"* it says here, mate,' I said. 'Fantastic, that, eh?'

I left him on his knees going through all the other post and wandered back five minutes later.

'Have you got one?' I asked.

'No,' he said, looking very glum. 'I'm not in.'

'Oh, mate,' I said. 'I'm really sorry.'

I let him suffer for a few hours. Around lunchtime, I said, 'Will, I've got to go down to the club for a TV thing. Sky are announcing the squad there – apparently, there's six Tigers players in it.'

'Who are the six, then?' he said, puzzled. He counted them off on his fingers: 'Backy, Johnno, Wig, you . . .'

'Eric Miller?' I said.

'Miller . . . that's five. So who's the sixth?'

'Dunno, mate,' I said. 'Anyway, can you do me a favour and give me a lift down there? I'm going to have a few beers to celebrate . . . it'll be a massive night, it's gonna be great. I'll get a taxi back.'

'Yeah,' he said, trying to put a brave face on it. 'No problem.'

We went down to the club and everyone started slapping him on the back and saying, 'Well done, Will.'

'But I wasn't picked,' he said, all bewildered.

As he said that, I pulled the letter out of my back pocket and gave it to him. He was absolutely spewing.

Very, very funny.

I did a little interview with Sky, and they asked me how

I felt to be selected. 'It seems strange,' I said. 'I remember the last Lions squad and remember having great admiration for them. Now Will Greenwood is in a Lions party I have no admiration for them at all.'

My friendship with him dates back to our time together in the North Under-18 side. On the pitch, we both wanted to look for space and run with the ball, which gave us a different perspective on the game to most other English players at that time, most of whom were obsessed with contact and tackling. Big hits are exciting, and a solid defence is an important part of the game, but just going out to smash the opposition doesn't put bums on seats and is ultimately a sterile way to play rugby. Shaggy and I understood what each other was doing on the pitch, too. Off it, we were kindred spirits, and annoying swines. We enjoyed nothing more than taking the mickey out of select Leicester forwards. Guys like Cocker, Wig and Garf couldn't see it half the time, which made it all the more fun. But when they twigged it could get quite nasty.

A classic example was in Italy in 1997, when Leicester beat Milan in the European Cup. Waisale Serevi, our Fijian star, had been absolutely awesome, scoring a stack of tries and famously beating a player four times in one run. Afterwards, Bob Dwyer was asked to nominate a man of the match. It was plainly Serevi, everyone could see that, but he chose Cockerill, who'd thrown eight line-outs not straight and lost one against the head in the scrum. The rest of the lads knew he was having a laugh, but not Cockers. 'Fair play,' he said, all fake modesty and a half-smile. 'I made that little break, did a few other good things . . . blah, blah, blah.'

After the ceremony we all went out and had a drink in the city, and Will got absolutely steaming drunk on wine, port, beer and spirits. We ended up in a nightclub where he was so out of it that he peed down the opposition flanker's leg. Not surprisingly he was chucked out and so I headed back to the hotel with him for a few more drinks. By the way, drinking played a key part in my rugby career. Sometimes it wasn't pretty, or funny, or clever. But we'll get onto that later.

So Will and I are in the hotel and Cockers arrives back with his MOM trophy. Somehow, Will gets his hands on it and starts mucking about with it. That evolves into blatantly taking the p*** out of Cockers. Richard didn't find it amusing, and eventually he snapped and punched Will in the side of the face. I stood up. 'Hey,' I said. 'We're all team mates . . . there's no need for that, he was only having a laugh.'

Cockers was having none of it. 'You and your northern mate can f*** off back where you came from,' he shouted. 'We don't need you here. You're both s***.'

I clapped him, sarcastically, so he turned round and punched me, too. At that, I lost it. I started kicking and hitting him and, like the big-talking forward he was, he started backing away on to the marble floor in the hotel foyer. I ran at him, slipped on the shiny surface as I threw a punch and somehow went over his shoulder and landed on my back with my head wedged against a flower pot. Cockers scuttled off, trophy in hand, to lick his wounds and Shaggy and I went back to the bar and ordered another beer.

There were always lots of scraps at Leicester, though most of it was in training. Banter would fly around, someone would take it too far and the fists would start flying. A lot of noses were broken, and a fair bit of blood spilt, but it never meant anything. When you have thirty blokes all training their backsides off to play a hard contact sport there are going to be flashpoints and you just accepted it. Next morning, we'd all be sitting having breakfast together and laughing about the cuts and bruises.

Like I say, I never saved myself for England, but of

course one of the reasons I joined Leicester was to further my international chances.

Playing for England had been all I ever wanted to do since I'd left round balls for egg-shaped ones.

It is hard to put into words how it felt to pull on an England shirt. I felt a responsibility to the country – to *my* country – and a burning desire to do well. The Celts are passionate about their nationalities but somehow that's frowned on if you're English. Not by me. I'm as proud an Englishman as there is.

In those early days, I remember how winning one cap seemed unlikely, never mind the stack I finished with. I'd first been called up to the A squad when I was playing at Orrell. That was a great feeling – it was being part of the national set up, albeit at a low level. Unfortunately, the coach, Peter Rossborough, kept me on the bench for what seemed like my entire life. I played just one game, against New South Wales, and watched Andy Gomersall get start after start. I've got nothing against Gomers, I just don't think he was ever as good as me, and I couldn't understand why I wasn't making any headway. Maybe some people didn't want me to progress in an England shirt. I've always had a talent for making enemies, after all. One day we were on the team bus playing a game of Trivial Pursuit or something, and Rossborough was getting all the questions right. I got a bit fed up of this, so I piped up from the back of the bus, 'Who played football for Scotland and cricket for England?'

He thought about it for ages before coming up with some name none of us had ever heard of.

'No,' I said. 'Kenny Dalglish and Ian Botham.'

The lads wet themselves laughing but Peter wasn't happy. He shot back. 'Who's going to be the next England scrum-half?'

'I don't know,' I said.

He just put both his hands on Andy Gomersall's shoulders.

At that point, for perhaps the first time in my life, I bit my tongue. I was going to say, 'Who's not going to be the next England coach?', but I didn't. I wish I had now.

I did eventually get the call to the senior squad, when Jack Rowell was the coach. I can still remember the buzz I felt as I drove down to the session at Henley with the England doctor Terry Crystal, who happened to be my GP when I was at college in Leeds. Jack had called a trial match, Probables versus Possibles, and I played for the Possibles. I scored three tries against guys like Bum Chin and Skeletor (sorry, Will Carling and Jerry Guscott) and thought I'd made it.

'I'm going to be picked for England this weekend,' I said to myself. 'I've got to be after that.'

How naive I was back then. I had given it 110%, whereas the established names jogged about in second gear thinking *'Why's this little whippersnapper running around like a blue-arsed fly?'*

Sure enough, when they named the squads I was only on the bench . . . for the A team.

That set a bit of a pattern – I'd keep getting invited back to full England sessions without ever getting picked. But the As were great. We met up on Saturday nights at the Richmond Hill Hotel, after playing for our clubs. We'd have dinner and then the coaches would say, 'Right guys, we've got a really hard training session tomorrow at 9am, so straight to bed, yes?'

We'd all nod and, as soon as they'd left, everyone, to a man, would sneak out, get absolutely destroyed and not come back in until about 5am. They were a great bunch of lads, and we weren't getting paid so we didn't take it too seriously.

I gradually worked out why I wasn't getting any real chances. Orrell weren't a fashionable club, and for the selectors to see me play we either had to be on television or playing away in London. Hence the move to Leicester.

I made the senior bench for the game against Scotland in the 1997 Five Nations but didn't come on, despite the fact that Gomers didn't have a particularly good game. I sat there quietly fuming, and nudging Les Cusworth, urging him to tell Rowell to put me on.

After the game we all trooped back to the Hilton. I'd never really spoken to Jack before then – just a few grunts and the odd nod here and there. We got to the bar and he ordered a bottle of champagne for the bench players on the RFU tab – a traditional way of thanking the subs for working hard in the week and a consolation for not playing. The barmaid asked for his room number so she could put it on his bill.

'1918,' he said.

'She wants your room, not your date of birth, Jack,' I said.

He chuckled, it broke the ice between us and we had a bit of a conversation. I thought I'd maybe have a chance of a start the following week against Ireland . . . but, no, he put me on the bench again.

The night before the game, I played cards with the lads and ended up losing £500 to Jerry Guscott. We were playing three card brag and Jerry was a better bluffer than me. I hoped he'd get slaughtered the next night so I could mug him, but sadly that didn't happen. Because I eventually got my first cap the next day, I developed a superstition that, if I lost at cards the night before, things would go well for me on the pitch. I ended up losing a fair bit of money playing cards with England over the years, but I did have some good games so maybe there was something in it.

That first cap came on 15 February 1997, when I came off the bench for eight minutes at the death. With 25 minutes to go, Les had told me to go and warm up and I remember stretching and jogging about in front of all the Irish fans, with them throwing sweets and drinks and good-natured abuse at me.

I came back, and Jack told me I was going on so I stripped off and stood on the side of the pitch, waiting. It's quite hard to describe that moment: I felt very proud, and slightly numb that something that I'd always dreamt of doing was about to happen. I know it sounds weird, but I could feel the *smiles* of the people I knew who were there, and who were watching at home on TV – I could really sense their smiles. My mum and dad had flown over, just in case I got on, and Lou was there too, and I had a strong feeling that this was not just about me, that there were other people involved, my best mates like Si and Ade, my folks, and extended family and so on. I knew they'd be enjoying it almost as much as I was, and that was pretty cool.

I ran on, Gomers ran off and I thought, *'I don't think you'll be coming back, son'* which was a bit cocky, I guess.

I headed over to the forwards, where we had the put-in to a scrum. The first person to speak to me was Jason Leonard.

'Just keep talking to us,' he said.

'I don't think that will be a problem, Jase,' I said.

The first thing I did was put the ball in and the second was pass the ball to Paul Grayson. Grays had been a team-mate at Waterloo and it was reassuring to see him there; the pass was an absolute shocker, though, and he did brilliantly to pick it up off his bootlaces and clear it about 60 metres down the pitch. If he'd knocked it on, that might have been the sum total of my international experience: consistency of selection wasn't exactly a hallmark of England in those days.

I like to think I made my mark; I made three of the four

tries we scored in the time I was on and we ran out 46-6 winners. *The Rothmans Rugby Union Yearbook* later wrote, 'It was the late arrival of Healey and Guscott which added pace, bite and imagination to the England attack.' At the time, it was Ireland's heaviest-ever championship defeat and our winning margin was our biggest in Five Nations history.

I don't actually remember any of it, mind you. It's almost as though it was someone else running onto the pitch and doing those things: all my memories are from seeing it on TV.

I went back into the changing room where everyone was celebrating the win. There was a lot of banter flying about and I was made to shotgun a couple of cans in front of everyone. I went to see my mum and dad afterwards; they were both tearful and I can imagine what they must have been like in the stand, mum nudging people and saying, 'That's my son, that is.'

We got on the bus and I sang *Molly Malone*. It was a tradition with England that new caps sang on the bus while everyone else booed all the way through, trying to make you give up. I got all three verses out.

We arrived at the dinner, and my dad had wangled his way in somehow and was standing at the bar. Mum and Louise were at the ladies' dinner – in those days you didn't have mixed dinners, which sounds like Victorian stuff. That was where things started to go horribly wrong. Another England tradition said you had to have a drink with everyone in your team. OK, fair enough. Then the Irish players, in particular Keith Wood who wasn't even playing, decided that all the Irish boys should have a drink with me as well. Woody came over with two pints of Cointreau and orange. I don't think there was much Cointreau in his but there was a lot of it in mine. Somewhere I must have let slip that I wasn't very good at drinking red wine. Two bottles of red wine later, I was in bits. The last one to come over was Carling, who gave me a tequila slammer. I did the slammer and lobbed the glass over my head. It landed on the committee table, smashing glasses and everything while they were eating. Fortunately for me, Will went over and apologised to the table, saying he'd thrown it, he'd meant it as a joke and he hoped that everyone was alright. What a nice gesture – it was good of him. We always got on quite well, Will and I. We were both big-heads, so we had something to talk about, I suppose. I remember the first time I played against him, for Orrell against Harlequins. I came off the bench – I was only about 18, and played in the centre in those days. There was a scrum, and I shouted across to him, 'Will!'

He looked across, as if to say, '*Who's that little idiot?*'

I said, 'I'm just going to take you on the outside now, alright? Enjoy it.'

Sure enough, I got the ball and took him on the outside.

Five minutes later, we had another scrum and I shouted to him again. 'Will!'

This time he acknowledged me. 'Yes?'

'I'm going to try and take you on the outside again,' I said. 'I'd get a bit of a head start this time, if I were you.'

He did get a bit of a head start so I stepped him on the inside, which was funny.

Back to My Debut Shame. I'd gone to the toilets and was trying to make myself sick, to get all the booze out before it took effect. It didn't work. I couldn't vomit no matter what I did – I'd never have made a supermodel. So then the alcohol started to kick in, big time. I was placed in the recovery position on a chaise longue behind a screen, just outside the dinner, with the doctor, Terry Crystal, and the rest of the medics coming out to check on me every five minutes. I started puking up into a bucket, so hard that I burst the blood vessels in one eye and turned it bright red.

At some point, Lou arrived from the ladies' dinner, which normally finished early so we could all meet up, but she wouldn't have got a lot of sense out of me. I lay there all night and enjoyed the pleasures of the likes of Cockers coming up to me and punching me in the face. Jerry Guscott peed in my shoes and gave me a couple of slaps around the face for good measure, I seem to recall. The worst part of the whole night was when I'd stopped being sick; the Doc made me drink some water to rehydrate. I got it down but it came straight back up, and it tastes awful second time round.

That was my first cap.

I didn't play against France next up – England lost and Gomers had a shocker – but the following game I got my first start down in Cardiff, where we pummelled Wales 34–13. That was the last game at Cardiff Arms Park, a great occasion and it was an honour to play in it. Being on the pitch, singing the national anthem – that, to me, was really my first cap. I was up against Rob Howley and there was a lot of talk that year about the Lions, and about how Rob would be the scrum-half for the South Africa tour. I was determined to have a good game and I honestly think I had the better of him until the last move of the day. He picked up a loose ball and broke down the middle; I'd heard he was pretty quick, so I covered across and ended up giving his speed too much respect. I overran him, he stepped inside me and scored under the posts, which really soured things for me.

I almost scored myself. My first touch came off a lineout; I passed the ball to Phil de Glanville, who made a half-break and was half-tackled. He popped the ball and it bounced off the floor and into my hands. I broke through and went round Jenkins to go for the corner. I was just about to dive over when I got tap-tackled by Jonathan Davies. Jiffy was a

35-year-old at that point, which just shows how quick he must have been in his prime. I went out for a few drinks with him afterwards – it was his last game.

Those early days with Jack Rowell were interesting. He was somewhat removed from reality at times. I remember a famous team meeting. Rowell had an overhead projector and it looked as though a fly had landed on the white screen. He went up to the screen and tapped it with his pointer. The fly didn't move, so he walked behind and tapped the back of it. At which stage, the guys were in pieces laughing. Mark Regan shouted out 'Village' (idiot), and the whole room erupted. Ronnie shouted again, 'Village . . . it's on the screen.'

A very puzzled Jack started tapping the screen again.

'Not that screen, the projector screen,' said Ronnie, as guys are fighting for breath and falling off chairs.

Jack finally realised that the fly was on the projector and flipped it away.

'Yes guys,' he said. 'Very funny. Graham Rowntree, what are we going to do in the first scrum this weekend?'

Graham opened his mouth – probably to say 'push as hard as we can' – and Jack went, 'Oh never mind . . . I'm not interested anyway,' and walked out of the room.

He could be a funny bugger and – this won't surprise you – we didn't always see eye-to-eye. Before one game, he called me and Mike Catt into his bedroom for a morning meeting with the other coaches. We were the half-backs that day. 'What's the first thing you are going to do today?' he asked me.

'I don't know Jack,' I said. 'I might pass, I might kick, I might run, I might tackle. I don't know.'

'The first thing you will do when you get the ball is kick it,' he said.

I looked at him. 'What if I'm in their 22?'

'You will kick it,' he said. 'The first thing I want you to do is kick for territory.'

'OK,' I said, 'but I don't think I will.'

He looked at me; his face said, *If you want to play, you will.*

He turned to Mike Catt. 'What's the first thing you are going to do when you get the ball?' he asked.

'I'm going to kick it, Jack,' said Mike.

Quick learner, Catty.

Playing for England with Jack Rowell at the helm was hardly going to be inspirational. Fortunately, that was his last season.

oOoOo

There was just one blot on my landscape at that time. Contrary to the impression I sometimes give, I don't dislike all Australians. I actually like the odd one or two. Bob Dwyer is definitely odd, but he's not one of them. He coached at Welford Road for eighteen months between May 1996 and February 1998 and he made my life a misery almost from the day we met.

I knew next to nothing about 'Barbed Wire' until I joined. His appointment was a big story on the English sporting scene and it should have been a fabulous opportunity for an aspiring international like me: Dwyer was, after all, a World Cup-winning coach who'd taken Australia to the pinnacle of the sport in the 1991 final, and working with him ought to have been a dream. But then, my granny could have coached that side – they were a pretty useful set of players, after all – and Bob did nothing for me at all.

Obviously, I was careful with him at first. My initial concern was to settle in at my new club and make a favourable impression on my new coach. The problem was, within a matter of weeks, he'd made an unfavourable impression on me. From the off, Dwyer was very vocal and forceful. We were going be in at 7am every day, five days a week, we'd do things his way and that was that: no arguments, no disagreements, not even any discussion. I suppose that would be fair enough if you were dealing with schoolboys, and Bob did remind us all of a schoolmaster, in much the same way that Graham Henry would on a Lions Tour five years down the line. But at least Henry had the excuse that he used to be a teacher; Dwyer trained as a sparks. Red is live, blue is neutral. Or is it the other way round? I must check with Bob. The thing was, we weren't kids and we weren't altogether useless ourselves. But the opinions of players like Dean Richards and Rory Underwood meant nothing to him. If he'd introduced himself slowly, tried to work his way into the heads of all the boys slowly, tried to earn the respect of players who had themselves been around the block a few times, things might have been different. As it was, he went at it like a bull in a china shop.

The older guys saw through him straight away and dug their heels in, but most of the younger lads kept their heads down and tried to adapt. Unfortunately, I've never been good at keeping my head down and before long I was joining the senior players in questioning his methods. Dwyer wouldn't tolerate the merest hint of dissent, and the seeds were sown for what quickly developed into an acrimonious relationship.

I was in great shape, having spent all summer training like never before ahead of my move, and I'd started with quite a bang. I don't think it would be too arrogant to say that I was clearly a better player than Aadel Kardooni, my rival for the No 9 shirt. But Bob made a point of rotating us, Aadel one week, me the next, and telling everyone that Aadel was as good as, and maybe better than, I was. Just as

I was starting to get overheated by the way he was messing me about, he went back to Australia for a month or so to tie up some unfinished business and Ian 'Dosser' Smith stepped in. The lads really responded to Dosser and we started to play some really good stuff. But all too soon, Bob was back with a new assistant coach, Duncan Hall, and Dosser was out of the door. The way Dwyer forced out a man who'd given his life to the club was scandalous, but Bob had a star-struck board hanging on his every word so he had the power.

All through my first season, he niggled me and I niggled him. There were other dissidents too: Dean, Rory, John Wells to a certain extent, and John Liley, but I think I became the main thorn in his side. I'd question his methods or game-plan and he would call me a smart arse, when I was just putting forward a different point of view. I'd always had a lot of ideas about the game and I was going to go on to get half a century of caps in a variety of positions so I must have had *some* clue as to what I was talking about. Bob wouldn't listen, even if I went into his office quietly. That was my biggest gripe; he didn't have to implement my thoughts, but he should at least have listened.

Instead, we'd get constant reminders of the great Aussies of the past . . . *Nick Farr-Jones did this*, and *Mark Ella did that*. So what? That was then, this is now, Bob. Get over it, the game's moved on.

He was obsessed with targets, another area of conflict between us. His favourite phrase in training was 'tackle the tackler'. Not only were you carrying the ball, you had to smash the defender backwards. That was always going to be hard for me, given my size, but it didn't interest me anyway. Why run into someone and stop the game if you can run around them and keep it alive? I wanted to attack space. My form started to dip and my morale with it. Perhaps if I'd been more receptive to his plans I'd have played better. I accept some of the blame, but I was only 22 and my judgment was clouded by the way he was treating me.

At one point, he asked Johnno whether I was on steroids, because of my mood swings. 'One day he's fine, the next day he's a complete lunatic,' he said. Partly, that's just my personality. I am changeable. But mainly I was up and down because I'd started out at a big new club and I was pretty insecure. I've always set up barriers and stopped people getting past them to the real me; some see through it all, others think I'm just cocky and over-confident. Bob was in the latter camp and his response was to put me down all the time, when all I really needed was a pat on the back every now and then. There were no steroids, by the way, and my build was down to 15 egg whites a day and a hell of a lot of hard work in the gym, before you ask.

He ran us into the ground with work. We were not a lazy team, but we spent half our time complaining about Bob and moaning about the amount of training we had to do. I think the transition between the amateur and professional eras was hitting a few of the older guys quite hard, in particular. For the younger guys it wasn't too bad, but by the end of that first season, I was absolutely destroyed physically. After the Lions tour, Lou and I went to Spain for a holiday for ten days; for the first four days, I didn't get out of bed. I just slept.

For all our differences, it wasn't until the second year that our feuding spilled into the open. Bob would give me so much grief that I was sometimes taking it out on other players in the changing room, and being quite caustic with my banter. This has been a problem for me all my life, certainly as a rugby player; this book isn't called *Me And My Mouth* for nothing. I take the mickey out of people. Sometimes it's a joke, and people get it and fire something back. Sometimes it's a joke, but people *don't* get it and want to kick my head in. And sometimes – very rarely, even back then, and almost never now – it's a bit nastier, a comment with a bit more of an edge. Mainly that would be in matches, when I'd be trying to wind an opponent up, probably someone I actually didn't like. It's a fine line and occasionally I'd get it wrong. It's not great when it's your own team-mates on the receiving end.

Dwyer started trying to get rid of me. The rumour was that he wanted to replace me with Agustin Pichot, Richmond's Argentine scrum-half, and had phoned them and offered them me plus money for Gus. Basically, anything to get me out of the club. He described me as an unstable influence, I think because he couldn't control me. And the more he tried to control me the more resistance I put up.

The pivotal moment came in a row between us on the training ground. He'd picked me on the wing to play against London Irish. No problem. But on the Wednesday, he had a massive go at Leon Lloyd, then one of our younger players and a weedy young strip of a lad who was very prone to tears. Leon had knocked a ball on and Dwyer bollocked him, loudly and openly, in the middle of the session.

It was a stupid thing to do, bound to affect the confidence of a really promising player, and I saw Leon's head drop so I went over to him. 'Look mate,' I said, 'keep your head up and ignore what he said. He's only saying it to try and get a reaction. Just concentrate on your next job and forget about it.'

Andy 'Kiwi' Key, now Head of Rugby Development at the club, overheard what I said, or at least thought he had, and reported it back to Dwyer. Bob said nothing at the time but when I turned up for the team run on the Friday the balloon went up.

We had a move where I had to run round from the wing, then straighten up and offload. I followed orders, went round, took the ball and gave it, only for Bob to shout 'Stop, stop' and bring proceedings to a halt.

'Austin, I want you to run straighter.'

'Okay, no probs.'

So we did it again, and I ran a bit straighter.

'No, no, stop, stop,' Bob yelled again. 'If you can't run in a straight line I'll get someone who bloody well can.'

'What are you on about?' I snapped back.

'I've told you to run a straight line. If I tell you to run straight when you come round the corner, run straight.'

I couldn't believe what I was hearing. 'I'll tell you what, Bob,' I said. 'If you think I can't do it why don't you get someone else?'

'Right, you're dropped.'

'It's Friday afternoon and you're dropping me from the team because you think I didn't run in a straight line?'

'Yeah . . . f*** off.'

'Right, see you later.'

I walked off the training ground, got changed, drove straight to Welford Road and told Peter Wheeler exactly what had happened.

'There's obviously been something going on behind the scenes to wind him up because I didn't do anything today and he just went for me,' I said.

'Kiwi has told us all that you told Leon to ignore everything Bob says,' said Peter.

'That's not true,' I said. 'I was just trying to pick his head up.'

Brace clearly believed me. 'Look,' he said. 'You're on the bench tomorrow – just keep your head down and get on with it.'

The game kicked off, we didn't play well and by half time

the crowd were growing restless. Bob came down to the touchline where I was stretching. 'Mate,' I said. 'I'm keen to get on and try and make a difference.'

He turned and looked at me as though I had three heads. 'You're not going on this pitch, not now, not ever,' he said.

'Oh, right,' I said. 'Fair enough.'

Then he just snapped. There were a load of kids sitting nearby, but he started swearing and ranting at me, effing and blinding in front of these children and their parents. Sure enough, the following day there were complaints about his language. I'd not responded (unusually) but the next day I sought out Peter Tom and David Matthews, both senior figures on the Leicester board, and told them exactly what had gone on. They said they would sort it out.

I went off to England training on the Sunday, resigned to the fact that I might be playing for a different club the following week.

But it was Dwyer who got the boot. By Wednesday, the club had released a statement saying he'd been sacked. It was as though a huge weight had dropped off my shoulders. Deano was announced as his replacement, and he immediately came down to the England team hotel to see the Leicester boys and tell us how things would be changing. It immediately impacted on my performance that weekend for England against Wales. I scored a try and we stuffed them 60–26.

In the early days I'd had bad dreams about Dwyer, crazy thoughts about attacking him and all sorts of stuff. My sleeping patterns were all over the shop. *Why is he dropping me? Why is he not picking me? Why is he playing mind games with me?* But by the end he had tried it on too far and I just had to make a stand. I'm not painting myself as whiter than white; it was me as well. But my occasional gobbiness was (and is) a major part of what makes me *Me*: ever since

I smacked Marvin that day at school, I've always stood up for what I believe and said what I thought. It's not always the best course of action, and it's probably cost me dear over the years, but it's who and what I am.

Officially, his removal was purely a rugby decision: we'd failed to win the league. That was a factor, sure. But Dwyer had lost the respect of the squad – he'd never had much in the first place – and he had to be sacked.

Off he went to join Bristol, and I believe I'm right in saying he didn't exactly win the Premiership with them. (After that, he went to NSW Waratahs and I don't *think* they ever won the Super 12 in his time, either. Is there a pattern here?)

Dean brought Joel Stransky and John Wells in as his assistants, and things were immediately on the up.

By a lovely coincidence, the win which clinched our second Premiership in the two years since Dwyer had been kicked out came at the Memorial Stadium, home of his new team. He didn't like that at all. Afterwards, one of the members of our Board reached down to shake his hand and Bob bit his head off. So the tone had already been set when I saw him down on the pitch, after the stadium emptied and went over to him. He came at me and I actually thought he was going to punch me, so I moved out of the way, squirted some water in his direction and started laughing at him, and that only incensed him more.

I didn't see him until a couple of years later in Sydney, when I watched him defend the indefensible: Duncan McRae's sickening and cowardly attack on Ronan O'Gara during the match against his New South Wales side. Dwyer attempted to justify McRae's eleven unreturned punches. Ludicrous. But then, so is he.

Dean and Wellsy – and Stranners in the brief time he was at the club – were a good team. I had massive respect for

Dean, particularly. As players, no-one had been able to touch them. Dean was unrivalled at No 8, Joel had won a World Cup and in the10 years Wellsy played for the Tigers he lost the ball in contact about three times – or so he'd have you believe. He probably passed the ball about as often in that period, too.

I'd warmed to Dean the moment I met him. In my first week at the club we were sent to conduct a coaching session in Norwich together. We met this guy called Smokie, a real huge bloke. We had a few beers and a curry, then Smokie started challenging people to arm wrestles. I may not be the biggest chap in the world but arm wrestling is my speciality, as Dean had already discovered.

He looked at this Smokie character and said, 'My money's on this little fella Austin beating you. If he does, you can pay for everyone's curry. What do you say?'

Smokie looked at me and laughed. For about five seconds, until I slammed his arm down onto the table and Dean dissolved into hysterics.

I then started winding him up, calling him 'Smoking'.

'My name's Smokie,' he kept saying.

'Okay Smoking, I hear you.'

I kept going until he was at boiling point and Dean had to step in and save me. It was a great night, a brilliant way to break the ice between us and we always got on well from then on, though I can't forgive him for giving me scrum pox during a mass bundle on the team bus when he was sweating like a baboon in the Sahara.

Those early days under Dean will always have a special place in my heart. It was just such an uncompromising environment. Everybody had the same goal: winning, for each other, the club and the fans. There are lots of prima donnas in sport, and they exist in rugby, too. Some people probably put me in that bracket but they don't know me if they do. You couldn't play at the Tigers and be a prima donna, it's that simple: the lads would not have tolerated it. In the 10 years I spent at Welford Road we had some of the biggest names in English rugby playing there, but the club always came first. After an international, the England boys – and internationals from other countries – were always straight back to play for the club. I remember Johnno and I turned out against Sale in the driving rain three days after we'd helped England batter Scotland – not because there was a three-line whip, but because we wanted to. It wasn't like that at all other clubs.

The ethos at the club was to treat every game the same; whether it was a Heineken Cup final or a routine league match, we prepared equally thoroughly. The peer pressure was so great that the management rarely needed to dish out bollockings. The other players would let you know if your standards fell below those expected of you.

Of course, Dean and John had their faults. They'd been such talented players themselves and yet they hated seeing me try different things. I'm sure they thought I was some kind of alien. Taking quick 22s or lineouts to myself, reverse passing from scrums, that sort of stuff. They saw me as a showboater. If I took a tap penalty they'd go ballistic and it took me three years to get that out of them.

Dean's man-management skills weren't to everyone's liking either. He suited me down to the ground: you always knew exactly where you were with him. There was none of Bob Dwyer's snideness, no trying to read between the lines. He said he'd do something and you could stand by that. But not everyone likes that kind of bluntness.

One of his worst traits was around contract renewal time. He would never offer new contracts to players, especially young lads, until right at the very last minute. We lost Craig Joiner because Dean left it two months too late; all he needed to do was call Jocky over and say, 'Craig, you've had a great season . . . do you want to sign for next year?' Craig would have said, 'Yeah,' and that would have been that. He didn't want more money or anything – he just needed the security of knowing where he was going to be working in the immediate future. Not too much to ask, surely? Anyway, Deano messed around, the club lost a good player, and I lost a close mate.

He also liked to keep things close to his chest. He didn't tell the squad about players linked with the club; we'd read in the paper that guys like Josh Kronfeld and Carlos Spencer were on their way, which was poor; the players should have been kept informed.

The problem was, sometimes Dean couldn't see the wood for the trees. All he cared about was Leicester winning games on a Saturday afternoon, and fair enough. But sometimes you need to think about the bigger picture because what might look like minor details are part of the reason you're winning. For instance, if the team was going well, Dean would not change it, regardless of giving other people opportunities. That proved to be Will Greenwood's downfall. When he had a dip in form, as we all do, he was left out and I don't think he was ever given an opportunity to get back. Consequently we lost one of the greatest centres England has produced to Harlequins. Likewise, Glen Gelderbloom never let us down but wasn't particularly well-looked after. Jocky Joiner was another: Craig scored goodness knows how many tries coming off the bench, played really well, was a massive impact player, but never got the opportunity to start even in less-important games. Dean could easily have thrown in what were perceived to be his second choice centres, Will and Craig, they'd have benefited from the experience and the guys they replaced from the rest.

One other thing: I wondered, sometimes, how hard he

pushed the club financially, on behalf of the players. Looking back, I think occasionally our loyalty was taken for granted. We were professionals and should have been paid what we were worth at the biggest club in the UK. There were an awful lot of people getting paid more at lesser clubs, despite our successes. That success wasn't purely down to the coaching, a lot of it was down to the players and I often wondered whether, when we'd stopped playing, a lot of the boys would have much more than great medals, great memories and great mates to show for it.

For all of those gripes, look at what we achieved in Dean's years at the club. Seemingly endless Premiership titles, two European championships, unbeaten at home for years and years . . . he worked wonders, albeit with an extremely strong bunch of players at his disposal.

Our supporters have to take a lot of the credit for our success in those years, too. Which set of fans would you swap for them? Not one. We won games – one or two a season – which we'd have lost without them. The added buzz we got from 16,000 people packed inside Welford Road was fantastic: it spurred you on when you looked beaten, gave you energy and strength and took it from the opposition. I always loved the relationship we had with our supporters, the fact that there were no barriers between us. We had 13 bars at Leicester and after a game you'd always find players sharing a beer and a chat with fans somewhere around the stadium.

We also had a great team spirit. There was a time for working and training, and we were very focused when we needed to be. But when we weren't – watch out.

The nights out at Leicester were legendary. My introduction to R&R at the Tigers started in 1996, when Derek Jelley's stag night coincided with the club's Christmas outing. It was a fancy dress night, and Louise and I turned up as a gorilla and a polar bear respectively. Johnno came as a rapper, complete with blacked-up face, Adidas tracksuit and half a ton of gold around his neck. Rob Liley and his wife came as Hitler and Eva Braun. I don't remember Rob's outfit, but his missus wore a little bra and leather boots up to her knicker line and I do remember her. We drank for England that night, and I ended up getting thrown out of the club we were in after Leon Lloyd got narky when I took a bite of his burger. As I was deposited onto the pavement, this polar bear ran up and punched me in the face. Thanks, Louise.

The stag nights were always scary. Backy's was a belter. He booked a barge on a canal out of Leicester and invited thirty of us along. The evening started off quietly enough, but then Wig started running up and down the side of the boat and the boat driver saw red. He told him to stop or he'd have to turn around and when Graham declined to behave he made a phone call and summoned a bouncer. You should have seen the lad's face when he got on the boat and saw the entire Leicester squad, arms crossed, staring at him. Backy was made to snog a pig's head for 30 seconds, which was harsh on the pig I thought, and then we got off the barge to go to a pub three miles away. Darren Grewcock persuaded 20 of the lads to get into a horsebox, saying he'd hitch it to the back of his Land Rover and tow it to the pub. They climbed in, the fools, and he locked and bolted it and drove off, leaving them there. The boys went absolutely mental and had to kick their way out.

Johnno's stag do was rather more orderly, as you would expect of the England and Lions captain. He took 40 of us to Benidorm for a mini-break before the England tour to South Africa in 2000. We checked into a hotel where everyone else was well over 60; all the other guests spent their evenings playing dominoes and bridge and, after the first night, most of the lads wanted to go home. But we bravely battled on. Dorian West got so drunk on the second day that the police were called. They arrived to find us all chilling out and playing Frisbee on the beach, assumed we'd been the ones causing trouble and tried to arrest us for being 'peesed up'. Meanwhile, Dorian was in a karaoke bar down the sea front attempting to sing *Minnie the Moocher*.

I had three stag nights before tying the knot with Louise: one in Cape Town, one in Newcastle and one in Leicester. Each were wild affairs but perhaps the funniest moment came in the North-East where we piled out of a nightclub in such a bad state that we hopped into four taxis, asked for the Copthorne Hotel, then watched as the convoy did a u-turn, came to a stop on the other side of the road and charged us £5 each. How were we to know it was only fifty yards away?

We were so together it was almost frightening. We played Pau one year, a French bearpit of a place with a ferociously hostile atmosphere. We won, and Deano took us on a lap of honour round the ground, smiling and waving while the furious French fans threw coins and spat at us and Wellsy tried to put his eye back in after being gouged. They were nice as pie at the dinner, weirdly, and we all got pleasantly destroyed together. Afterwards, we went out to a club in Pau and Darren Garforth got up on one of the bars and started singing a song. As he leant back to finish it off, he fell straight onto the tiled floor of the serving area. He disappeared for 15 or 20 seconds, and we all thought he'd killed himself. Then he suddenly popped back up and finished off the song. Typical Garf.

Later, we got on the bus and we had two large inflatable Heineken bottles with us. Me and Dosser Smith I made it to the back seat first and used these inflatables to block the aisle in front so you couldn't get past. The windows got all steamed up, and I started writing 'Cockers is gay' on them.

He was smashed out of his face and going mental but he couldn't get to me because the blow-up bottles were in the way. When we arrived back at the hotel, I jumped out of the fire exits so he couldn't try and kick my head in. Though he couldn't have, to be fair.

That team bus was the real testing ground for us – forget Welford Road and the training pitch at Oval Park.

Every week, World War Three would erupt in the battle for the back seats, which – in those days – were habitually occupied by Messrs Cockerill, Garforth, Rowntree and Johnson. A couple of challengers would make their way to the back and try to kick them out and, more often than not, they'd end up getting battered, with their clothes ripped off and chucked out of the skylight. I could have taken any two of them, possibly three, but the four of them together were a tough call and successes were few and far between. It galls me to admit it, but Pat Howard was one who succeeded, on our pre-season tour to Omagh in 2000. A few of the new boys had tried and failed so the heavy brigade, the likes of Paul Gustard and Adam Balding, went back as a group and got stuck in. As the fur flew, Pat slid along under all the seats and popped up triumphantly at the back. They were all scrapping and hadn't seen him coming. He had all his clothes shredded just the same, but he'd achieved something very few manage. And through brain, not brawn – all forwards, please note.

Deano appreciated that achievement as much as anyone because he regularly tried to take the back seat and, more often than not, he failed too. This was when we were by a long chalk the most successful rugby club in Britain. I suppose our soccer parallels were Manchester United and I love the idea of Sir Alex Ferguson having seven shades kicked out of him by Beckham, Scholes and Giggs on the way back from beating Arsenal. Somehow, I doubt it ever happened. In May 1997, Deano caused a near riot on the bus by stubbing his cigar out on Dorian West. We were on the way back from winning the Pilkington Cup final, and all hell broke loose. One of the tables got ripped off at the back of the bus, exposing a spike, someone landed on top of Dorian, the spike pierced his leg and Nobby needed a heap of stitches, both internally and externally. He also got blood poisoning and a big red hole of a scar in the back of his leg. The club picked up the bill for that one and there were a few more besides for damage to Colin's Coaches, though we had a very tolerant, if completely mad, driver by the name of Tone. Tone was a great guy but he seemed to have a problem with braking distances. The most common chant on away trips was 'Steady, Tone!' as he suddenly slammed on the anchors.

The great thing about Leicester, especially early on, was that it was a real rugby club, firmly rooted in the old amateur ethos, with a great family and team atmosphere. We worked together and socialised together – after matches, there'd be 25 of us all out nightclubbing together. It built great team spirit. Yes, Cockers smacked me in the face the first time I met him, and, yes, the forwards moaned endlessly, but you quickly learned that it was part of the Leicester way. They did it just to check you didn't overreact, that you weren't getting precious, that they could count on you.

Moments Of Madness

As I sat in the cells awaiting sentence, I hated myself as never before. I was scared and alone and I deserved it.

I'd been banged up beneath Leeds Crown Court for five hours waiting for the jury to come back and I just *knew* I was going to prison. Possibly for quite a long time: earlier, I'd pleaded guilty to wounding with intent and I was waiting to be called back up to be sent down.

I looked around the miserable grey cell. Graffiti had been scrawled on the walls by others who'd gone before me, bragging, taunting messages from more hardened men than me. I half-thought of scribbling my own pathetic note to posterity: *Austin Healey: don't want to be here – s****ing my pants*.

A year earlier, I had headbutted a bloke in a Leeds nightclub. I'd been completely hammered and he'd done nothing to deserve it, other than to have looked less than impressed when I tried to dance with his girlfriend.

It had been a week short of my nineteenth birthday, in my first year at Carnegie College in the city. My housemate Robin and I had won the student union raffle and the prize was a crate of Diamond White and another of Castaway, an orange and passion fruit alcopop. Mix the two together, as we did, and you get a Blastaway, a concoction with a kick like an angry mule. We drank our prize before hitting the dance floor.

I was drunk, utterly obnoxious and attempting to make a

move on a girl I'd never seen before when this tall lad came towards me. I thought he was going to chin me, so I got my retaliation in first. Better to ask questions later, I thought. Only I'd got it all wrong. I later found out he was a well-brought-up guy who'd had no intention of hitting me.

My immediate punishment was to be dragged out of the club by three of his mates, pinned against the railings and given the hiding I deserved. I managed to throw one of them down an escalator but I still got a good kicking.

It wasn't until three months later that the law caught up with me, by chance. In the days after the incident, nobody had known my name or where I lived. Like many students, I was in digs off campus so, after getting a few butterfly stitches at hospital, I was out of the way. Which is where I would have stayed had the policeman leading the investigation not been a rugby fan and had I not scored a try in a Waterloo vs Orrell derby. On the telly.

I was asked to come down to the station and held overnight before being interviewed and charged. It took a year for the case to come to court but despite the dark cloud hanging over me I didn't realise how serious the situation was until I arrived for the trial.

My barrister, David Gee, came over. 'How did you get here?' he asked.

'I drove,' I said.

'Well, you should give the keys to your dad.'

'Why?'

'I don't think you'll be driving home.'

Those words, and the sinking feeling they left me with, will haunt me forever.

I sat in the dock while pictures of my victim were shown to the courtroom – pictures I hadn't seen before. They were horrible. The lad had a broken nose, and his face was a right mess. Only then did I realise how badly hurt he was, how much damage I'd done.

The judge didn't look at all impressed.

Now, as I sat in the cell block, drowning in self pity and dreading the sentence he would pass, I thought about how I'd let myself and my family down, how worrying and upsetting this must be for my parents.

I thought about how I had changed as a person – about how I could turn nasty with drink. I swore I'd never let myself get into that position again. I was frightened, but at least I was being honest with myself.

It was about four o'clock when I was called back up. I braced myself for the worst – a year or more inside – but the case put forward by my barrister, and my favourable references, from John Elliott, the England under-21s manager, and Deb Murphy, a QC who was my next-door-neighbour, saved my skin.

'At first I was going to give you a custodial sentence,' explained the judge, a severe-looking man with bundles of gravitas and a razor-sharp brain. 'But I've changed my mind and you will serve 200 hours of community service instead.'

I felt enormous relief, tinged with regret. At no time during the trial had I got the chance to apologise to the lad I'd attacked. I felt as guilty as hell and I wanted to say sorry. I still do.

It was during that stressful time that I first realised Louise really cared for me. We'd been out together for a while but had split up after going through a rocky patch. On the day of my court appearance I went to a morning lecture in a suit while the rest of my so-called mates wore the usual tracksuit. But no-one said anything to me, except Lou. She went out of her way to wish me all the best. When I most needed support she was there for me, and we got back together soon afterwards.

So one good thing came out of all of this: I ended up a wiser man with a girlfriend who would become my wife.

I was back in the same courtroom three months later. For my community service, I'd been assigned to Oxfam in Headingley, near to my college. I had to leaflet houses, asking for old clothes which we'd then sort through in the shop. Two hundred hours felt more like two hundred years. One day we were sent to pick up all the old desks and furniture from the court, which was being relocated to a new building, so they could be sold for charity.

I was teamed up with another lad who had tattoos all over his arms and his neck and who'd also done something bad. It was ironic, and all the more so when the lad dropped a desk on me and cut my leg open, causing a deep gash. I'd expected to leave a pound of flesh here and I ended up leaving a pool of blood.

I was on a short fuse, back then, though mostly on the pitch. Around that time, I got banned for violence in a rugby match, too.

Waterloo, my side at the time, were playing Nottingham and their tubby ginger flanker Dorian West – later a team-mate at Leicester and with England, of course – took it upon himself to give me an eye examination in a ruck. In layman's terms, he gouged me. I'd had a bad game, I was bubbling with frustration and I didn't need much of an excuse to lamp somebody; Nobby gave me the justification I was looking for with his fat little fingers. Something inside me snapped – fortunately not the muscle fibres around my eye – and I rolled over and butted him, twice, following up with a flurry of punches for good measure. We both left the field, Dorian on a stretcher and groaning like a girl. After the game, he followed me into the shower with a big lump on his head and a grin on his face and said, 'What was that for, chief? I was only wiggling your eyeball about.'

I looked at him, snarled and walked out. He'd have laughed his pants off if he'd been wearing any.

Rugby's a violent game but they have to draw the line somewhere and I'd clearly overstepped it. The judges from the Lancashire Rugby Football Union weren't quite so impressive, or daunting, as the man in the wig at Leeds. In fact, they looked like a pub darts team after a night on the ale which was fitting, given that the hearing was held in a boozer in Preston. I told them that Westy had gouged me, that the first butt had been an instinctive reaction and the second to teach him a lesson. Despite that, the panel, all Lancs ties, ruddy cheeks and comb-overs, took a rather dim view. 'We can't have this,' the top man snorted. 'It won't do'. They gave me an eight week ban and by the time it expired I'd left the club for Leicester.

It wasn't the smartest period of my life and I'm not proud of the way I behaved. But at least Nobby had deserved what he'd got – unlike the lad in the nightclub.

It wasn't the last time I'd come up against the rugby authorities for doing something stupid in the heat of the moment, either.

For some reason, it was usually my feet which got me into trouble: rather than use my fists, I tended to lash out with my boots. I remember going for Ben Clarke during one game against Bath, kicking him up the backside. But I always said to myself that I'd never kick anyone in the face. Like biting and gouging, that was a no-no.

So it's hard to explain My Stamping Shame.

It was 1999, and a game at home against London Irish. We were top of the Premiership but they were up to third and on a roll after winning seven straight games. More important-antly, they had twice got away with foul play in the opening minutes of the game. Craig Joiner had been clothes-lined by Brendan Venter and then shoed by someone else. There was a definite edge to it all.

Ten minutes in, I found myself near their scrum-half Kevin Putt. He was on the ground and I was shoved from behind and that gave me an opportunity to let him know he was in a game.

It all happened in a split second. I knew I was going to land on him and I knew that if I slammed my foot down I would inflict serious damage. I honestly didn't want to do that. So I tried to flick my boot in order to minimise any injury but, at the same time, let him know that I *could* have kicked him in the face.

I had no seriously malicious intent: I certainly didn't want to injure him and it definitely wasn't a 'stamp', rightly a serious offence in rugby. Unfortunately, things don't always work out how you intend. As I brought my right foot down I felt Kevin's face under my stud: I could almost feel the flesh tear, and knew I was in trouble. Of course, Kevin was in a worse way: his face was streaming with blood and he had to go off for six stitches to a cut very close to his eye. Thank God it was only 'very close'.

I played the rest of the game like I had concussion. My mind was elsewhere, away from the rugby, pondering the consequences of another moment of madness. The game itself was a blur.

As I walked off the pitch at the end, Dean Richards and Peter Wheeler took me to one side. 'We just watched the incident in the Sky van,' said Peter. 'It looks pretty bad. We don't want you saying anything about it.'

That's not my way – I don't like brushing people off with no comment. I'd apologised to Kevin when he came back onto the field after being sewn up. 'Sorry mate,' I'd said. 'I couldn't put my foot anywhere else.' He laughed. 'I'm not surprised considering the size of my nose,' he'd replied and, between us, the matter was pretty much dealt with there and then.

So if the journalists were going to ask me about what had happened, I'd repeat that apology. They did, and I did.

Obviously, that wasn't going to be the end of it. Stephen Jones, writing in *The Sunday Times*, was one who wanted me dealt with fairly severely. 'Television replays clearly show Healey balancing on one leg and thrusting downwards quite vigorously with his studs pressing into Putt's face,' he wrote. 'He appears to make no effort to avoid Putt, nor does he appear to be off-balance.'

In rugby, the system for punishing players for transgressions is such that if the referee sees an incident and deals with it – via a yellow or even a red card – the case is supposed to be closed. Unfortunately, Graham Hughes, the referee that day, hadn't seen it, which meant I could be 'cited' after the game.

That was fair enough. I'd done something stupid and potentially very dangerous and all players have a responsibility to kids watching, to sponsors and to the game to play it in the right spirit. I'd let the club down and myself and I was prepared for whatever punishment came my way . . . within reason.

Kevin Yates, the Bath prop, had just been banned for four weeks for stamping, recklessly rather than wilfully, on Wasps flanker Paul Volley, who'd needed seven stitches in his forehead. That seemed to be the sort of suspension I would be looking at.

I felt pretty sure Leicester would punish me – partly because it was the right thing to do and partly to take the heat out of the situation. And when Clive Woodward phoned to tell me that I wouldn't be playing for England against Scotland at Twickenham the following weekend that feeling solidified. Sure enough, the club called me to an internal hearing in one of the executive boxes at Welford Road to hear my side of the story. They concluded that there was no wilful intent on my part, that it hadn't been a 'stamp' but that I could have done more to avoid contact with Putt's face. They banned me for three weeks. That ruled me out of the first half of the Five Nations Championship, and meant I would miss the trip to Ireland as well, not to mention a big Tetley's Bitter Cup quarter-final at Richmond. But maybe that was the end of it.

If only.

The Press were on my back. 'Healey has always been a competitive beast,' said *The Daily Telegraph*. 'He is forever pressing, forever annoying the hell out of the opposition. For the most part this is a virtue. On Saturday it wasn't. The fine line is the most important marking on the pitch.'

The Mirror published a close-up of Putt's cut face beside the headline *'Healey gets just 21 days for doing this to an opponent'*, just one of a number of calls for strong action.

What about Kevin Yates getting four-weeks? I muttered to myself. *Why don't they believe me when I say I didn't mean to hurt him?*

The heat was being turned up, and London Irish turned it a notch or two further. They were, naturally enough, very angry about what had happened to their player; they said my explanation was 'unsatisfactory' and that Leicester's action was inadequate. Inevitably, an RFU hearing was called, which was a worry. If I was found guilty of stamping, things would suddenly get a lot more serious: that carried a recommended ban of three months.

As the days passed, I became increasingly frustrated that everyone was discussing the case but there was nothing I could say or do to affect it. Three days before I was due to go before the RFU at the East India Club in London I had finally taken all I could stand. A letter addressed to me had been sent to the club from some loony in Dublin threatening to kill me if I set foot in Ireland.

'Healey, you scum,' wrote this guy. 'When you come over here you're going to get it.'

Fan mail comes with the territory when you are a high profile sportsman. Sometimes, it's a note saying, 'I love you, here are my knickers.' Sometimes it's, 'I hate you, you're rubbish.' I normally take them all with a pinch of salt but I don't like death threats any more than the next man and, coming on top of all the other nonsense I was getting over the episode, it really annoyed me.

At the hearing, we ran through every line of defence we could. We'd even got experts in biomechanics at Leicester and Loughborough Universities to take a close look at the video evidence, and they'd concluded that, far from stamping, I was trying to remove my foot as quickly and as softly as possible.

A lot of good it did me. I got banned for eight weeks.

That was double what Yates had received for his offence, and double what Jason Leonard got for stamping on the chest of Budge Pountney earlier in the season. There was no doubt in my mind that they had made an example out of me. I wanted to scream 'injustice' from the rooftops, and I definitely wanted to appeal. But as I sat on the train back from London I resigned myself to my fate. 'I know it's my fault and I got us into this situation' I told Deano and Wheelbrace. 'If you think it's right to appeal then we can appeal. If you don't then I'll abide by what you think.'

We didn't appeal, but I think Dean and Peter respected me for that: I hadn't sulked like some spoilt brat or spat my dummy out.

I left the ball in their court and went off and trained. My suspension was due to end the day before England played

Wales in the final match of the Five Nations, a match on which the destiny of the Championship, Triple Crown and the Grand Slam could well rest (and did, as it turned out).

That couldn't have been further from my mind: all I was thinking about was getting fitter, faster and stronger than I'd ever been, so I could come back with a bang. I was a man on a mission. I turned to Neil Back for advice. Backy had served a six-month ban in 1996 for pushing over referee Steve Lander at the end of the Pilkington Cup final at Twickenham. He knew what I was going through. 'Stay positive,' was his simple message. He assured me that his enforced rest, if not the circumstances that prompted it, was the best thing that had happened to his rugby career. During his ban he had become turbo-charged, lifting his fitness levels to uncharted heights. I decided to do the same.

Peter Wheeler was a great support to me during this time. He was heading out to Portugal to play in the Henry Cooper Golf Classic and, after hearing that one of the celebrities had pulled out, put my name forward. Not only did I play in the tournament, I joined a week-long training camp with a number of international athletes, by the end of which I was firing as never before. I had lost loads of fat, felt sharp and had a burning desire to get a ball back in my hands.

The following week Clive phoned to say he was picking me on the bench for the Wales game to cover wing and scrum half, following injuries to David Rees and Kyran Bracken. I thought the whole nightmare was over, but I was wrong: not only did I not get onto the pitch, but Scott Gibbs scored in stoppage time to grab victory for Wales and rob us of a Grand Slam. It was an awful end to an unhappy chapter in my life.

These incidents changed me. My approach to rugby remained the same – I always believed you had to play on the edge of the edge if you were going to be any good and I never wanted to be an average player, making up the numbers.

But I learned to rein in my temper. The nightclub incident, and the court case that followed it, particularly, affected me. I started to shy away from violence on the pitch. There have always been fights in rugby matches, punches exchanged, people pushed around, and the culture of the sport says you join in on your mates' side if that happens. From then on, my first instinct was to step away from trouble, not towards it. Unless I saw someone getting a really good kicking, I just wouldn't get involved.

Not out of fear for the repercussions – court action, bans, press scrutiny – but because of what I did to that lad in Leeds.

Laying The Foundations

Clive Woodward took over as England coach from Jack Rowell in 1997, and my caps started to grow in number. He was my type of boss and we got on well: as a player he'd had flair and vision and the bravery to take risks, and he carried that through to his job with England.

The signature development under Clive was that the players' needs were always taken care of. We had lots of specialist coaches, the best back-up and support and we stayed in great hotels. He wanted to make playing for England special, and he did that.

I remember our first training session with him at Bisham Abbey. All week, the newspapers had been full of speculation about who was going to be made England captain. They ran down the odds: Dallaglio 2–1, Johnno 3–1, Jason Leonard 5–1, all the way down to me at 200–1. So I went up to Clive at the start of the very first session.

'Look, Clive,' I said. 'My name's Austin – hi, how do you do? – I don't know if you're aware, but there's a lot of speculation about who the new captain is going to be. I've got really long odds and I've also got £50,000 in the bank. How about you make me captain for the first game, I'll go halves with you and then you can sack me after that and say I was no good?'

He started laughing – I thought it was a flawless plan, but unfortunately he didn't.

We always had that sort of relationship where I felt I was

OK poking fun at him. We played Wales in 1998 – when I scored my first try for England – and I'd noticed Woody had been putting on a bit of weight. So on the Friday before the match I stuffed a pair of tracksuit bottoms down the back of my shorts, another pair up the front of my top and ran around in a pair of glasses with a whistle pretending to be him, telling the lads what to do. He laughed at the time but warned me he'd get me back.

The following week, Leicester were playing Saracens away. I got on the bus after the game and the front row guys were at the back of the bus, all doing their colouring-in and dot-to-dots. I went down there and got a surprisingly hostile reception.

'You think you're funny, do you?' said Cockers.

'What are you on about?' I said, genuinely mystified.

'You think you're funny?'

'What are you talking about, you mutants?'

'Sending letters and a pair of knickers to our wives. Do you think that's funny?'

I goggled at them. 'Do you honestly think I'd send pairs of knickers to your wives?' I said.

Garf scrabbled about in his bag and produced a crumpled up letter which he waved in my face. 'This is a letter from you, signed by you, to my missus,' he said. 'What the hell's going on?'

'Don't be ridiculous,' I said, but I made my way back to the front of the bus, out of harm's way. As I sat down, I turned my mobile on. The first answer phone message was from Clive.

He just said, 'Don't ever mess with me again.'

The second was from Lou, asking me to call her. So I did.

'Austin,' she said. 'What's going on? I've been getting calls all day from all the other girls saying you've sent them all a pair of knickers with '*I Love Austin*' written on the front of them, a signed picture of you scoring your first try for England and membership to some 'Austin Healey Fan Club'. What are you playing at?'

It was probably the funniest prank Clive played, and I am determined, to this day, to get him back. I don't know when or where – it may be at his funeral, but I'll be there and I'll have my revenge.

We had the horrible Tour of Hell Down Under in 1998, which I won't dwell on, and then a pre-World Cup trip to Australia in the summer of 1999. I didn't get selected for that, which really wound me up. I went on holiday with Lou, Martin 'Cozza' Corry, Craig Joiner and their partners and for the first week I was unplayable. Snappy, irritable, the works. Lou took me to one side. 'Look at yourself,' she said. 'Look at the way you're going on. Now look at Cozza. He's had another awesome season, and yet he *never* gets picked. Do you ever hear him whinge like this?'

That brought it home to me that I'd been a complete embarrassment. We all went out to dinner that night and I apologised for my bad attitude. It was a weakness of mine, and luckily I had a strong wife to set me right. She was right, of course.

I found myself back in favour ahead of the World Cup and we arrived at it, as a squad, in decent shape. We weren't one of the tournament favourites, despite Clive inviting the media to judge him on our results in the tournament, but we weren't no-hopers either.

Personally, I was in terrific condition and playing really well. I started the games against Tonga, where I scored a couple of tries, Italy and Fiji. We won all those. The key game was the pool match against New Zealand: win that, and we had an easier route to the final. Lose it, and we had South Africa, defending champions, in the quarters.

Once again, one man loomed large over a World Cup

game against England. Four years after his astonishing performance in 1995, Jonah Lomu did it to us again.

The match was finely balanced at 16–16 when Jonah got the ball and started running from deep. All of a sudden, it was like alarm bells and sirens were going off everywhere. He ran through Jerry Guscott, who didn't even try, and then fixed me in his sights. It was make or break time. '*Knock down Lomu here and you're laughing,*' I told myself. So I put everything I had into hitting him low and just squeezing my arms. Even if I only got one leg, I was determined to hold onto it. I hit him as hard as I could around his right thigh, got my arms linked, which usually means you're going to drag your man down, squeezed as hard as I could and thought to myself '*Job done! I've got him!*'

Next thing I know, his heel hits me in the chin and he's gone.

I looked up, saw Daws come across and grab him by the shorts and start sliding in his wake. Then Dan Luger arrived and jumped on his back and he was still going. By the time Lawrence got to him, he was over the line.

Jonah was immense. Will Carling famously said he was a 'freak' but I think that's a bit strong. 'Gifted' would be more accurate: there's never been anyone like him before and I don't think there will be again.

I tackled him probably three times in my life, and I can assure you it was phenomenally difficult. When you saw him coming, your first instinct was to go low as I did, to try to cut him down and use his high centre of gravity against him. That was probably the worst thing to do, though, because you couldn't get round his legs; he was so strong, and they were so big and thick, and they just kept pumping so you slipped away. If you stood in front of him you had no chance – if he ran straight at you there was only one place you were going and that was backwards, in a heap. Your only chance was to try to get him from the side, round the collar, then round the waist, almost like a lion bringing down a buffalo.

The All Blacks broke clear after his score, we got booted out of the Tournament in Paris by Jannie 'Drop Goal' de Beer in the next round and went home early, feeling pretty sorry for ourselves.

Clive took a lot of stick for that exit but his attention to detail had been awesome. We'd gone out to Australia to train and get into serious shape and then came back and did some teamwork stuff with the Royal Marines at Lympstone, on the moors down south.

In the week leading up to it, Clive had read the Riot Act to us. 'Lads,' he'd said, 'we'll be staying in the Officers' Mess and I want everyone to be on their best behaviour. We are there to work, we are there to do a job, and I want everyone turning up meaning business and looking smart.'

He glanced at me, for some reason. 'That includes you, Austin,' he said. 'No messing about.'

I got into trouble quite quickly, when Daws bet me a quid I couldn't get through the front door of the Mess in an Hawaiian shirt and flip flops carrying my golf clubs while Clive was sat outside talking to a couple of the senior officers.

I wasn't the only one to disgrace myself, though.

The Marines took us to their helicopter survival training base, where they drop a chopper into a swimming pool to simulate a ditching and you have to get out. Clive's big thing was always about The Team: 'Look after the man on your inside,' he'd say, 'look after your team mates generally, and they will look after you.'

I got into the helicopter with Jase, Johnno, Lawrence and Clive. There were two small windows, probably only a couple of feet square, on each side, and we'd have to get out of these once we were submerged. I had Johnno and Lol on my side, and they made very clear I was going out last. I didn't really have a choice in the matter, so I did as I was told and went out last.

On the other side were Jason and Clive. Obviously, they didn't want to put Jase with three people just in case he got stuck. They dropped us in, we all swam out of the window in the pre-arranged order, rose up to the surface, all five of us were there, well done lads, job done.

'Great team work, guys,' said Clive. 'Excellent work. Right, let's get out.'

'Hold on a sec,' said the Marine in charge. 'We normally ditch at night and it normally turns upside down so we really ought to simulate that for you too.'

The lads were dubious. 'I'm not too keen to do that upside down in the pitch black,' said Jase.

'Come on,' said Clive. 'It's all about the team, this, it's what *we're* about – teamwork.'

So we all climbed back in.

It was quite scary, actually: the lights went out, helicopter got dropped and it turned upside down. Still, we managed to get out – though as I swam to what I thought was the surface I hit the bottom of the pool and realised I was going the wrong way, which was interesting. Up top, I could just make out the silhouettes of three other heads bobbing in the water. Then the siren suddenly went off and the helicopter got hauled rapidly out, spinning round the right way up as the lights came back on. There was Jason Leonard, coughing and spluttering inside and looking a bit panicky.

'What happened, Jase?' said Johnno.

'I dunno,' said Jase, shaking his head and spitting water out. 'I banged my head a couple of times somehow.'

'We'll have a look at the video,' said the Marine. 'We've got cameras in there.'

So we wandered over to the monitor and they pressed 'play'.

There we all were, sitting in the aircraft. It plunged into the pool and rolled over, and there was Clive, too: scrambling for the window, elbowing Jase in the face and then kicking him in the head on the way out.

'You know what, Clive,' I said. 'That was great teamwork.'

He had a smile to himself and may have blushed.

We had some very funny moments with him. One of my favourites happened around that time, when Clive had got it into his head that mobile phones were a distraction in team meetings and banned us from having them anywhere except our rooms.

Obviously, the lads ignored that and still took their phones to meetings, but just made sure they had them on silent. Equally obviously, we'd all be phoning each other throughout the meetings to see which mutes had forgotten to turn the ringer off.

One particular day, a phone kept on ringing – two or three rings and it would stop. Clive went mad, and he was really losing it in the end.

'Whose is that bloody phone?' he was saying. 'Come on, own up. Where is it?'

Eventually, he found it – under his desk where I'd Sello-taped it. He saw the joke, though I didn't own up to it at the time. So Clive, if you're reading this . . . that was one of mine.

Despite the 1999 World Cup disappointment, he was firmly on track and slowly but surely built us into a side to be reckoned with. A highpoint shortly afterwards was our 2000 tour to South Africa, a great two-match mini-series which ended in a draw. It should have been 2–0, but we were denied victory by some, er, eccentric video replay decision-making by the, er, South African video ref.

There were downsides – I didn't get on all that well with Andy Robinson, Clive's No 2. Andy's never really liked me. I think it stems from the time I played against Bath for Orrell as a 19-year-old. Robinson took a tap penalty about five metres out from the line and I smashed him, gave him a bloody nose and started laughing at him. I spent the rest of the game reminding him that I was a little teenage back who'd stopped a big international forward within a yard. He didn't appreciate it and he's never forgotten it.

I remember a session around the time that all the lads had started wearing more fashionable boots. I'd just been sent a pair of white ones. I thought I'd better mention it to the management. I took Robbo on one side and said, 'Andy, just so as you know, I'm not trying to make a statement or be a *prima donna*, but I've got these new boots and I'll be wearing them at the weekend if that's alright with you.'

He looked me up and down and glared at the boots. 'Well,' he said, 'as long as it doesn't put you off your game. We're here to play rugby.'

Yeah, I think I sort of gathered that when I started 10 years ago, Andy.

Apart from the clash of personalities – I had one, he didn't – he never really liked my style of play, either. He was very like Wellsy; he didn't like 'show ponies', probably because he saw himself as a back rower who worked 'at the coal-face'. If he took training, you were restricted, shackled, to the point where you didn't dare take any risks or do anything that might be seen as different. He didn't seem to appreciate that the really good teams have all sorts of characters and players, even including show ponies. Look at David Campese – he could turn a game with a moment of magic.

Around that time, I started feeling the effects of a punishing playing schedule for the first time. After the tour ended, I tried to switch off, flying straight to Skiathos for a fortnight with Lou and Cozza and his fiancée (and now wife) Tara. But the time was too short. The aches and niggles from the previous campaign hadn't gone and it still hurt to get out of bed in the morning. Even on holiday I'd normally watch my diet and spend time in the gym but I just couldn't be bothered. I needed the time off, but I started beating myself up for being a slob.

My spirits were down and before I knew it the holiday was over and we were flying back to start pre-season at the Tigers. I pitied myself, I resented rugby and I resented Leicester for calling us back so soon. I wasn't ready. I'd only just finished the previous season and I'd done nothing to get my fitness to the level I expected of myself. There was a lot of hard work to be done but I just couldn't motivate myself to do it. Getting back on the treadmill had no appeal. It was a combination of me being unprofessional and of the unrealistic demands being placed on us. I should have said 'This is my job and I've got to do it.' But I was so worn out that I couldn't. I was tired, angry and bitter.

I always suffered from different forms of depression. The worst was if I was dropped: I couldn't sleep, I'd lie awake, my mind turning in search of an explanation. This was different – a hopeless, forlorn misery springing from boredom. Leicester had just got rid of two of my best mates, in Will and Craig, and I was turning up for training, doing my bit and then going straight back home, where I'd sit down, switch on the television and fall asleep.

I took it out on Louise more than anyone else and our relationship undoubtedly suffered at the time. I was short-tempered about everything. I was not a good husband, to be honest, and that's one of the things I've always tried to be. She knows when I'm annoyed because I take it out on her. She just takes it and then tries to find ways to get me out of it. But ultimately I have to realise myself what's going wrong before I listen to other people.

I'm pretty stubborn at times and have a habit of blaming others for things which are actually down to me, until I get a chance to think clearly for a minute and it clicks. Louise is brilliant with me and my moods but don't get the impression she is a soft touch. If I overstep the mark she tells me. She doesn't put up with any nonsense.

I remember waking up one morning that summer, looking out of the window and thinking, 'It's mid July, there are another 364 days of training and matches until the Lions arrive back from Australia.'

It sounded horrible: that was a lot of bruising, painful punishment. Assuming I was selected to tour – and, injury and form permitting, I was sure to be – that was a full year of rugby. It's bad enough to work for a year in any job without a break, but in ours it was utterly crazy: the campaign stretched out before me like a never-ending road, and I panicked.

To that point, I'd always coped well with the pressures of professional rugby but I wasn't at my best as we were dragged, kicking and screaming, into the longest season we'd ever experienced.

oOoOo

As if I did not have enough mental hurdles to overcome, I was having problems at the club with our Aussie centre Pat Howard. Pat had been with the Tigers for two seasons, in which time we'd won back-to-back Premiership titles, and now that Joel Stransky – a guy I really admired – had moved on, Pat had taken over as our backs coach.

His first conversation with me in his new position had been to inform me that he wanted to use me as an impact player in the coming season. He explained that he wanted to keep his young players happy because he didn't want them leaving. That – and a few other personal niggles – set the tone for our relationship, and it never recovered. I don't know whether non-players really understand it: you'd probably see being put on the bench as something temporary, a tactical decision, nothing to worry about. But imagine it's your livelihood at stake, and imagine you think – in fact, you know – you can do a better job than the guys they're bringing in ahead of you?

'What about keeping your internationals happy?' I said. 'It might be worse to lose an international than a young player.'

Not long afterwards, I read an article in *Rugby World* magazine in which Paddy claimed that he was uncomfortable being a coach because he had been one of the boys the previous season. Rubbish. He was completely *obsessed* by it. At stages through the year he even referred to Leicester as 'my team' and I got the impression he got a power kick out of messing me around. I was all the more annoyed because the previous season I had been consulted about back play. I had been playing 10 and had ended up being voted Player of the Season. To go from that position to turning up at training and being told I was an 'impact player' did my head in. I was under no illusions that I was the finished article – I had a hell of a lot to learn about playing fly-half. But I'd run the plays pretty well and I felt deserved a little more respect from someone with half as many caps as me.

Me being me, I didn't keep my thoughts to myself.

Moaning about it obviously did the trick. Not. In pre-season, they handed the number 10 jersey to Andy Goode and stuck me at scrum-half.

I asked Pat why they were picking Andy instead of me but it got me nowhere. He came out with all sorts of stuff like I didn't take the ball to the line properly and that Goodey's kicking was better than mine. I responded by saying that my defence was better than his and that I could break down defences on one leg better than him. Pat wasn't listening.

To be fair, Andy's a good player, but back then he was just starting out and learning the trade. I didn't feel he was ready to go into the team in the position in which I wanted to play and I thought I was better than he was. Admittedly, I was only looking at it from my point of view. I was better than him as a 10, viewed in isolation, maybe, but was I better than him for the team? Maybe not. The forwards wanted me at scrum-half and Goodey at 10, where his big boot could bang us into field positions from where they could win us games. Not my idea of exciting rugby, but they had a point, I guess. I disagreed and I argued with Dean as well. 'Look,' I said, as the start of the season approached. 'I played 10 for England the other week.' I'd stepped in at short notice for Jonny in the first Test against South Africa, and done OK.

Dean looked at me with that sardonic grin. 'So what?' he said. 'You're back at Leicester now.'

Then he told me to lump it, as only he can, with a grin and a shrug of those Honey Monster shoulders, and we left it at that. Once he'd made his mind up, that was it. I'd thought life would be a cakewalk when he replaced Dwyer. One sentence from Dean changed all that. 'You're on the bench,' he'd said. 'You missed a tackle last week.'

Anyway, thanks to Pat and the No9 shirt in my kitbag, I went through pre-season feeling miserable and unfit. My morale was in a tailspin. I wasn't interested in playing at all. I'd turn up, pass the ball, go home. I went through a long period where I really couldn't care less about playing for Leicester. I was pretty keen to leave.

But a funny thing happened on the very first day of the

season. As so often is the case in sport, one man's misfortune opens the door for another. Andy Goode suffered a broken leg in our Premiership match against Wasps at Loftus Road and, after all that arguing and stress, within minutes of the new season kicking off I was back at fly-half. Better still, I scored two tries, the second of which came with the final move of the match, deep in stoppage time, to nick us victory. All that pre-season depression was washed away on a tide of adrenaline. I felt for Andy but I had to answer two questions: firstly, did I want to play fly-half, and secondly, irrespective of what Deano, Pat and the forwards thought, did I honestly think I was the better player, for the club, in that position? I answered both in the affirmative.

Not that all was rosy. Neil Back and I had decided to carry our pre-season training through to the start of October and consequently I was nowhere near the physical condition I should have been for the first few games. I had basically a five-day training programme which ended with a weights session on Friday afternoon. The club knew about this but didn't like it because it left me tired in matches but I went off and did it just the same.

I also aggravated a hamstring and I had a long-standing problem with one of my ankles which forced me to play with a silicone pad in my boot. My Achilles was dodgy and I was petrified of rupturing it, especially when Thomas Castaignede did his in the warm-up before France took on Australia in November.

I was taking suppositories to play every week and was constantly in the physio room; I probably should have rested but I had to carry on because of the way my contract was structured, with a fair slice of my income, around 30%, dependant on appearances. Maybe it was a mistake signing that deal at that point in my career, as it put too much pressure on me to play when I wasn't right. But in the previous three years I'd been lucky with injuries and had hardly missed any games.

As the weeks went by, I was playing well but my injury worries were becoming an ever larger distraction. I couldn't accelerate flat out because of my Achilles, and I was afraid to do so anyway in case the hamstring went.

The ankle stirred up my depression again. I thought, *'I've got to train, I've got to play, so how am I going to get rid of it?'* It was a vicious circle. On top of that were the financial pressures, which hardly helped. I needed to crash out for a week or two and the chance came in a surprising way.

I'd been playing golf with David Liepins from the Mercedes garage in Leicester. They had given me a brand new CLK 320 to drive for the season, I'd only had it three days and I was driving back from the course when I stopped at a roundabout. All of a sudden, I heard the screech of brakes and I got absolutely smashed from behind.

I'd heard about whiplash before but never thought it was serious. I think differently now. At first I was fine – I just went to the police to report what had occurred and took a cab home. The next day, 24 hours before our first Heineken Cup game against Pau, I was unable to move.

Turning up at Welford Road on the Saturday, everyone thought I was messing about but I couldn't move my head. I ended up having three weeks out and by the time I returned, my neck was fine, my hamstring was healed and I was raring to go.

I was never a good spectator but I was reasonably content to watch us beat Pau and then Glasgow, because I knew I wasn't right. That changed dramatically the following week, when Leicester went down to Pontypridd on a Friday night and were beaten 18–11. As I sat in the stands, powerless to help the boys, I took a load of stick from a section of the crowd around me who seemed to never tire of telling me that Leicester were crap.

Eventually I snapped. 'Let's see what the score is next week when I'm playing,' I yelled. Maybe that was an arrogant statement but I knew we could play better than this and I was fed up with these people rubbishing us. The pressure was now on but our masseur Julie Hayton and physio Craig Mortimer did a cracking job getting me right. The daily combination of two hours massage followed by half an hour in an ice bath at home did the trick and I scored the winning try and a drop goal as we beat Pontypridd 27–19.

Two months in and my season was already resembling a rollercoaster ride. But while my relationship with the Leicester management was far from perfect, I was playing well and the international season was just around the corner. The world champions, Australia, were coming to Twickenham.

I always felt Clive didn't care how well I played for Leicester as long as I didn't let England down. And because I'd played pretty well against South Africa in the summer I took it for granted that I'd get picked against the Wallabies. I'd had a good tour, Clive had been happy with me and the other coaches had given me good feedback. I felt I'd answered the nagging doubts about whether I could cut it against the very best. It said as much in my very positive end-of-tour report. With nothing to worry about, I marked time until the next game, rather than really driving myself on and asking the coaches for more work.

Big mistake. The great thing with Clive's England set-up was that you could phone the guys up in the week and they'd be there at your house in six hours. They'd do video analysis with you, or take you out on the pitch and train you, or advise on any and every little detail of your game. Of course, they also took note of the fact that you were working to improve yourself in your own time. I didn't take advantage of them. I didn't ask Dave Alred to help me with my kicking, and I didn't seek extra defensive work from Phil Larder. I just sat back. Maybe I was tired, maybe I was complacent, maybe both.

The result was that I was dropped back to the bench. The dastardly deed was done at Pennyhill Park, the team hotel in Bagshot, on the Monday of Test week. Everyone was assembling outside the meeting room when I got the nod from Clive. Whenever you got that you knew you weren't in the team. It meant he wanted a private word with you and that in turn could mean only one thing.

He got straight to the point. 'I've decided to . . .'

I finished the sentence: 'Leave me out of the team.'

He explained his strategy, saying that he was looking to use me off the bench to utilise the space and pick up the tempo of the game towards the end. It made sense to a rational mind but my head was spinning. It had come as a complete bolt from the blue, because I'd geared myself mentally to being picked. I was so confident of selection, I had never considered the alternative. I took it badly, stewing in self-pity, staying away from the team room and instead ordering a club sandwich and chips alone in my room.

If I was looking for sympathy, I'd picked the wrong week; the following day came the awful news that Ben Cohen's father, Pete, had died. In an instant, my so-called problems dissolved into nothing. I'd lost my place in a rugby team. Ben had lost his dad. I was struck dumb by the news. I felt desperately for Ben and his family. I'd just left him upstairs standing in front of the cameras with a smile on his face like a Cheshire Cat. It was his day. Having been dropped in South Africa, he'd forced his own way back into the side. He'd been worried about his father, who'd been badly hurt in an attack outside a nightclub in Northampton a month earlier. But we'd all thought Pete was on the mend. Ben had been to see him the previous night and told him about his England recall. He'd been so proud.

For once, the last thing on my mind was that Ben might withdraw and I would get the shirt back. So what? My immediate thought was '*I hope Ben wants to play. I hope he can get through this*'. I'd had a similar experience – albeit not as bad – a couple of years earlier, when my Granddad 'Silver' Sid died on the morning we played Northampton. I was very close to him and I was very upset. He hadn't been well – I'd been to visit him in hospital and he'd looked terrible – but you hope things will turn out OK and it's still a shock when they don't. Dad phoned on the Saturday morning and said, 'I've got some bad news for you... Granddad died last night'. He started crying down the phone and I welled up too. But then Dad said, 'Enough of this. Go and score some tries for him.'

Clive was brilliant with Ben. He took him to one side, broke the news in the best way he could and arranged for him to go home. He told him not to worry about England – if he felt up to playing, the shirt would be waiting for him. As soon as Ben left, we had a team meeting at which Clive told me to be ready to play just in case. That was a really weird position to be in. Of course I wanted to play, but I wanted Ben to play more. There are certain things that are more important even than playing for your country. That was certainly how Ben saw it. He withdrew from the team on the Thursday night.

I didn't see him until he came into the changing room after the game and each of us gave him a hug. I'd wanted him to turn up, as late as Friday, and say he was playing. He would have done so with my best wishes. But by Friday night I was a definite starter and I had to set about building myself up to prove Clive wrong for dropping me in the first place.

For half of the match I was on course. I put in a good hit on Chris Latham, the Wallabies fullback, and when he ran the same line soon after half-time I was confident of nailing him again. But this time he was a decoy runner. Instead of locking onto the ball he left the pass to Joe Roff. I was slightly out of position, went for Roff and went too early, allowing him to brush me off and create a great try.

It got worse. Matt Perry was injured five minutes later and I dropped back to cover at full-back. Roff broke through again down the wing where I would have been. I set myself to hammer him but he stepped me again and I completely missed him. Again it was bad technique, and my own fault for trying to kill him rather than just tackle him.

Twickenham is a big place, but you know exactly where the coaches are sat and when I missed that second tackle it felt like the other 75,000 witnesses had gone, leaving the eyes of Clive, Robbo, Brian Ashton and Phil Larder burning a hole in my back. You hope against hope they haven't seen it – perhaps the whole coaching staff have nipped to the loo or been talking amongst themselves. You hope the TV has missed it too. I particularly hoped they had not seen that I was growling as I threw myself at Roff.

Mike Catt ripped into me for not being in the line on the outside. I pointed out that I'd dropped back for Pezza and he shot me one of his looks. I lost it and told him to sod off. A few minutes later I was subbed for blood, Iain Balshaw came on and set up the winning try for Dan Luger with a little chip kick that Dan ran onto past a turning Aussie defence.

Back then, England beating Australia was a rarity, a big deal, and the drama of Dan's try, with the clock ticking as the video ref played it over and over again, was huge. I was watching on the monitor in the stitches room; it was clear

Danny's career, or certainly his season, had been made in that little passage of play and when I saw him later that night the look on his face said as much. My own expression told a different story – one of misery and despondency, the look of a man who knew he wouldn't be playing for England against Argentina the following week. I'd had a shocker and Ben Cohen would be back in the side without a doubt.

There's no escape when you've had a bad game for England. There is protocol to be observed, formalities to be attended to, so I had to attend the post-match function with my parents and Louise wishing I was somewhere else. I was in an absolutely foul mood. People were asking me for my autograph and I was obliging without so much as acknowledging their presence. My dad tried to talk to me and I told him to leave me alone. Taking things out on my family before I take them out on other people or myself was a really bad side of my character, and it's one I have worked hard to eradicate. They were my biggest supporters but, occasionally, when I'd performed below my own expectations, I abused their devotion by firing cheap shots at them. I hated myself for it.

I was in a particularly foul mood as I went back to the hotel with the team; snappy, extra sarcastic, a pain in the arse generally. The mood improved when Johnno decided we deserved a treat for having beaten Australia and ordered 42 portions of fish, chips and mushy peas from the local chippie. I went down to collect them with him and we arrived back with two big boxes, the hotel supplied the bread and butter and we sat in the team room watching *Match of the Day* and knocking back beers. Well, we had just beaten the world champions.

Midweek, we had all the drama of the strike that never was.

Clive had presided over a sea change in English rugby.

We were on the road to becoming the best team in the world and, as players, we wanted for nothing in our preparation for internationals. Well, almost nothing. A fair contract for the players would have been nice. If the game had stayed amateur, and I'd been lucky enough to represent England, I'd have got the same kick out of it – the honour would have been no less. But I'd have had a 9–5 job in the background, a career which would have been there for me when my rugby days ended. Once the game went professional – and it wasn't the players who made that decision – guys were taken out of the normal world and told they were being paid to play sport. It's a short career, and there are no guarantees. We all had mortgages and we needed to be paid properly to reflect the hours we put in and the sacrifices, in and out of the game, that we'd made and would make in the future. Our pay was partly performance-related. That sounds fine – if you win, you earn more than if you lose. And to an extent, I don't think any of the guys had a problem with that. At issue was the question of how much of our earnings should be weighted towards victory and how much towards appearances. We felt the RFU placed way too much emphasis on victories. We'd beaten Australia in the dying seconds of the game after an interminable video ref decision. Our effort would have been no more and no less if the ref had ruled the other way. And the stadium would still be packed throughout the rest of the autumn internationals, and during the Six Nations, whatever the result, too. The sponsors would still be there. The RFU's income – the income of people like Francis Baron – wouldn't change. Francis drove round in a brand new Aston Martin – we had guys getting absolutely battered in matches who were knocking about in knackered old Ford Mondeos.

We'd raised the issue frequently, and time and again the Union had stalled on it. With Argentina and South Africa coming up, we decided the time was right to act. After a secret ballot, we voted to strike.

It was a weird day or so – players being banned from the team hotel, threats and phone calls flying around – and it was eventually half-resolved after Peter Wheeler drove down to act as an intermediary between us and the RFU. They moved a little on the win bonuses and we went back to work.

It never was sorted properly, though. The RFU recently revealed that they expected to earn £30 million out of the four autumn internationals in 2006 – I wonder how much of that filtered down to the lads getting smashed to pieces on the pitch by the All Blacks, the Springboks and the Pumas? It's all typical of English rugby, where everything gets fudged. The RFU should have got the guys on central contracts when the game went pro. If they 'owned' the players, life would have been much easier. As it is, they take them away from their clubs, see them battered in internationals and then wash their hands: it's like borrowing a mate's car, crashing it and not even fixing it. That's no way to go on – especially when you consider that the game wouldn't even have survived as a professional sport without the huge input of people like Nigel Wray and Keith Barwell. Rugby owes those guys a lot, but you rarely see that acknowledged by the RFU.

On the Wednesday, after the strike had been and gone, I knew for sure I'd been dropped. I had an inkling because during the strike almost every player had a phone call from Clive except me. You didn't have to be Einstein to work it out. Clive broke the news to me and I took it reasonably well as I had half-expected it. It was only then that the real bombshell dropped.

'What positions am I covering?' I asked.

'None. You're not on the bench either.'

The words hit me like a hail of bullets. I was out of the

squad for the first time in goodness knows how long. Apart from the time I had spent under suspension in 1999, I couldn't remember being on the outside. What the hell was I going to do?

Clive said he wanted me to stay around and train all week but Leicester had a match against Harlequins and I was keen to play in that rather than kick my heels. I phoned Dean; he'd already picked the side with Andy Goode at 10 but Goodey agreed to step down which was really good of him, so I borrowed Backy's car and shot up the M1 with my mind a blur. Since being initially dropped for Australia I hadn't been sleeping at all well – I'd been putting loads of lavender on my pillow to help me – and my mind had buzzed with one question. Why?

I knew all the coaches would be at Quins on the eve of the Twickenham international and I was determined to have a really good defensive game. But my luck was out. Early in the match I was kicked on my bad Achilles, and I couldn't run. My tackling was sound but I couldn't spring, make breaks or kick because it was my standing foot. Dean, a top man when the chips were down, did the decent thing by not taking me off. He knew what I was going through and he knew how it would have looked so he moved me out to the wing instead.

The next day England beat the Pumas 19–0 in the pouring rain. It wasn't a classic by any means – when Martin Johnson is named best attacking player you've got to figure something has gone wrong. I was not wholly displeased that it hadn't gone particularly well, although I was pleased that the crowd hadn't booed the players onto the pitch as *The Sun*'s John Sadler had stupidly recommended.

I was at the game doing some corporate work and decided to show my face at the after-match function. Andy Robinson's wife, Sam, saw me and asked whether I wanted to have a go at him for my being dropped. 'It's alright thanks Sam,' I said. 'It's not his fault, it's mine. I'll sort it out.' I think that took Robbo aback. I really don't think he expected to hear me to take responsibility for the situation. But I'd had a little time to think. I'd also had eight double brandy and gingers.

By the time I rejoined the England squad at Pennyhill Park on the Sunday night, to start preparing for the final fixture of the Autumn series against South Africa, I'd got all the bitterness out of my system. I'd not been able to get a straight thought process for a week, which was why I couldn't get to sleep, but the Saturday night spent drinking myself into oblivion had done the trick. I would look at fitness first to get back in. Improve that, I told myself, and everything would be alright.

Twenty four hours later I was back in the doldrums. Clive had told me I was not involved again.

I sat quietly through the media team announcement with a face like a smacked backside, chuntering to myself and generally wondering what the hell I was doing with my life. Peter Jackson of *The Daily Mail* just happened to catch me off guard and I unloaded both barrels. 'I am angry and confused,' I told him. 'I was pretty angry at being left out last week but that was a good opportunity to give others a chance. Against South Africa you have to pick your best 22 and not being in it makes me angry. If I was playing like an idiot and if the other players were better I could understand it, but neither is the case. I'm not playing like an idiot and the other players are not better. I don't really know what more I can do. I'm still the fittest, strongest, quickest back in the squad because the results prove that, so I can't very well train any harder. Nor do I think it's possible for me to make any more sacrifices. Have I done something wrong? Have I said something to upset someone?'

OK, not the smartest thing to say. Me and my mouth again. The rest of the lads read it the next morning and banter was flying, but I don't think any of the coaches were very happy at what I'd said. To be honest, after I read it nor was I. But at the time it was what I was thinking and they all knew I was quite emotional and tended to go off the top board.

Under Clive, the coaches liked to put the onus on the individual to sort his problems out; they respected that. I said I'd stay for the week and train, and I think they realised that in blowing off steam I'd turned the corner. I trained hard and was fully supportive of the other lads. Then at last a break. Mike Catt was injured and doubtful for the game with a popped rib cartilage.

His fitness test involved having to run and tackle Martin Corry ten times. I sneaked down to the pitch and watched from behind the trees, as I didn't want to give the impression that I wanted him to fail. Catty crumpled on the first tackle, Will Greenwood was immediately called into the team and I found myself back in the 22. I'd never felt so good about being on the bench.

England beat South Africa 25–17, Will scored a great try and then had the decency to cramp up, allowing me the last five minutes. It wasn't long but was just enough for me to make a tackle on Japie Mulder and to come away knowing that I was back on track.

My attitude was better and I was being more honest with myself instead of living out a kind of fantasy in my mind that I'm the best player in England, the best back, blah, blah, blah. It took fifty units of alcohol to kill off that fantasy. It was well worth the hangover.

oOoOo

Sport has a habit of turning the tables on you. Dan Luger was the man after scoring the try which beat the world champions in November 2000. Against Australia that day his season was made. Mine was in ruins. Or so I thought.

By the end of the season I'd be forced to revise my assessment. Injury would wreck Dan's ambitions, both with England and the Lions, to the point that he would manage only seven minutes' game time in the Six Nations Championship – having missed the previous year's tournament in its entirety – and two warm-up games for the British Isles in Oz.

At the start of February he was not to know this and neither was I. He remained in pole position while I sat idly in the pits like a spare car at a grand prix. I had at least heard whispers that I was coming back into contention for a wing slot because the coaches had not been satisfied with the way the attack had been going.

You can end up getting hurt if you place your faith in the rumour mill, yet I was feeling a lot more positive about my opportunities and chances to play in the Six Nations, because I felt that while size was a major factor in selection against the southern hemisphere teams, skill was going to be of greater premium against Six Nations opposition. Sure enough, I was called onto the bench for our opener in Wales. I was back in on merit and confident of getting a run. But the eighth minute was certainly sooner than I expected.

Over the Autumn I'd undergone a change in attitude. I was trying hard to listen, to stop acting like I always knew best and show myself willing to learn. I was trying to come to terms with the fact that my inadequacies were actually down to me and not the coaches, helped by the constant reminders of Phil Larder, our minister of defence.

I lost count of the number of times Phil played back my missed tackle on Joe Roff for the benefit of the entire squad, as if he revelled in my humiliation. Whenever an Australia shirt appeared on tape I knew my embarrassment was just around the corner. I felt he overdid it, but Phil liked to beat things into you like that. The fact that my defence against Wales was sharp probably justified his approach, though it pains me to say it.

The build-up to the game was bizarre. Before we journeyed down the M4, Ben Cohen revealed that he had received death threats from some Welsh idiot and then when we got to the Millennium Stadium we found cardboard cut-outs of the entire Wales team waiting to confront us in the away changing room.

The anonymous letter thing was odd. We used to get a lot of this and I never understood it. First off, it's only a game. But if people still want to make threats, why don't they make them to your face, then see what happens? If somebody wants to send me a letter, well, give me your address and I'll send one back. Ben was a young lad who had just lost his father. Whatever nutter sent him those letters was a sick coward. It was a worry Ben could have done without.

The cardboard cut-outs were strange, too. Maybe it was designed to psyche us out? I don't know, but when Matt Dawson started karate-kicking them in the head, the Millennium Stadium Jobsworths quickly agreed to remove them. They might have played better than the actual team. The match was a triumph for my old mate Will Greenwood, who became the first Englishman in more than a century to score a hat-trick of tries in Cardiff. A more interesting statistic, I feel, is that he became the second Englishman to score a hat-trick of tries in the Six Nations Championship. Behind me (against Italy, since you ask).

I was chuffed for him; he'd spent a lot of time out in the cold, with both Leicester and England. He'd bleached his hair and afterwards he claimed this was the deciding factor, which just goes to show how much of his rugby was played in the mind. A lot of people reckon that rugby at the top level is 50% physical, 50% mental. Looking at Will, it's hard to disagree.

In Dan Luger's case, the problems on that day were 100% physical; he took a bang on his neck and his championship was over. Out of the blue, I was given a chance to re-establish myself in the side. We won 44–15, then England's highest score and greatest winning margin in Cardiff, and I played my part.

It had been a good day. Thomas Castaignede and Ieuan Evans both went into print to say that they had just watched the best team in the world in action, and it was not Wales. Ieuan described our performance as 'frightening at times', whilst Thomas went as far as to say, 'I think if a World Cup was played now they (England) would win it.'

Even Graham Henry, the Wales coach bound for bigger if only marginally better things with the Lions, admitted: 'That was as good a performance from a European team as I have seen for a long time.'

Satisfied with life, I returned to the changing room feeling I was part of the team again. The old intimidation factor of playing in Cardiff, a problem for English teams in the past, was long gone. I think the magnificent Millennium Stadium was part of that; it's such an exciting place to play you just have to lift your game.

The Welsh fans were a different matter. On the way back through the city, our team coach was surrounded by a couple of hundred drunken Welshmen chucking kebabs and abuse at the windows; we were not going to be intimidated, so we stood up and yelled back at them, beckoning them over. Some of them began to head-butt the coach and hurl bottles and cans, and then the coach knocked one of them over. Thankfully we were only doing about 10mph, because we had no police escort and we were seriously surrounded. Immediately, we hit the brakes and Clive and Terry Crystal got off to have a look at him. They found a bloke so drunk that he was oblivious to what had happened. He would have a headache in the morning, but he would have had one anyway.

Meanwhile, the yobs surrounded them, hurling more abuse. 'Get out of our country,' seemed to be the favourite. Well, we were trying to lads, but then you started fighting our bus.

It was looking quite nasty and we were all ready to get off and pile in to save Woody from a lynching when three police vans screeched round the corner, a load of coppers jumped out and the confrontation was quickly diffused.

Back at the hotel we jumped off the bus and someone suggested we go out for a drink. I laughed, bearing in mind there was what appeared to be a full scale riot going on in the middle of town.

By comparison, Italy at Twickenham was a mild-mannered affair. For the first time since the previous summer in South Africa, I was selected for the starting line-up, with Jason Robinson called up to make his debut in the match day squad. Jason obviously had bags of natural talent and when he'd switched codes the previous autumn, joining Sale from Wigan, there was little doubt in any of our minds that he would be fast-tracked into the England set-up. Nonetheless there was surprise at the speed with which Clive had brought him in. I didn't see Jase as a massive threat; I was confident that there were things in rugby union I could do that he couldn't, just because he was so new to the game and had yet to start reading it properly. I say that with the greatest of respect to him as a wonderful player.

Clive handed him his first cap all the same, four months after he had crossed the great divide, with 35 minutes left on the clock. He looked a bit lost and didn't receive a single pass, leading to various conspiracy theories being put forward. But there was no anti-League snub, no resentment at the speed with which he had been capped. It was purely and simply that things didn't go his way.

In rugby league, wingers tend to stay quite wide and come in on maybe the second or third tackle to give the forwards a break. Apart from that they don't roam the pitch as much as they do in union. On a few occasions that day I came across from the opposite wing and got inside the pass before Jase. That was not done on purpose, to maroon him out on the touchline, it was simply that I knew where the ball was going. But he was a quick learner and the following game against Scotland, just a fortnight later, he was popping up at the base of rucks and mauls and beating about eight people with every run he made.

Of course, he wasn't the only major England legend to have crossed codes. I flirted with League myself in my younger days. My mate Dave Thompson, now a professional golfer, was from Widnes and he arranged for me to go over there and train. They gave me a couple of games – I played under a fake name, Keith something – because back then you'd be banned from playing Union if you got caught, as David Pears found out. I enjoyed my brief period there, and even scored a couple of tries against Salford as a winger. But the training was a real eye-opener, working alongside people like Martin Offiah, Jonathan Davis, Kurt Sorenson, the Myler brothers . . . my training partner was Andy Currier, a 100-try a season legend for the club. I couldn't believe how fit these guys were. I was quick, but these guys were quicker than me and miles fitter: I learned that it was one thing to have some ability but if you didn't work hard, and train yourself up to be as fit as you could, you were just wasting it.

For the second year running we beat Italy by an emphatic scoreline, our 80–23 victory constituting the highest score and biggest winning margin in championship history. Jonny Wilkinson also made the record books for his 35-point haul and I was pleased to add two tries to my hat-trick in Rome the previous year. But there was still work to be done as for the second year running Italy had enjoyed the better of the first quarter before our fitness and structure told.

It did us no harm that our next opponents were Scotland because we owed them one from a year earlier when we'd blown up at Murrayfield and lost another Grand Slam chance, and all of us were well up for the game. Catty, Will and Iain Balshaw all had points to prove after coming in for criticism from former Scotland captain Finlay Calder in the build-up. Those three were outstanding, Scotland didn't manage a try and were sent home tae think again about a painful 43–3 hammering.

The Ireland game, though, was postponed because of the foot and mouth outbreak. We'd have beaten them, I'm sure, with the momentum we had, but as it was we had a month off Six Nations duty waiting for France to come to Twickenham in the April. We stayed focused, assembling for an extra couple of days training with England in the gap week. Having blown two Grand Slams in as many years we didn't want to risk wasting another great campaign. Ian Jones, the former All Blacks lock playing for Gloucester, had said before the championship kicked off that England must win the Grand Slam to be taken seriously in the southern hemisphere, and he was right.

Nevertheless when the time to play France finally arrived, we struggled to get back in the groove. We'd played mind games in the build-up, mentally rehearsing the playing of the match with the aim of developing our concentration. The idea is that you should eventually be able to visualise and play the whole thing perfectly in your mind. We obviously still had some way to go with that one because for 40 minutes we were pretty dire, while they reproduced some of the dazzling stuff which had accounted for New Zealand on the same pitch in the semi-finals of the 1999 World Cup. They played very wide, very quick, we didn't handle it particularly well; I think everyone in the team missed a tackle in the first half, which was almost unheard of.

But we had a growing confidence, such that we felt we could overcome whatever was thrown at us and were convinced that we were not going to lose, that it was just a question of how we were going to win, not if. That's what it felt like, at least. People called it arrogance, but I don't think it was. It was just a confidence that everything behind the scenes was right. All the coaching was sorted out, every fine detail looked at. Nothing was left to chance or overlooked. And when you got to the games you knew you had this armoury of moves, structures or patterns that we could flexibly adapt to. We'd had it for the previous two seasons, but hadn't been able to switch it between one game and another. Now people were so rehearsed that we could change at the flick of a switch.

Sure enough, when we came out after half-time we were a completely different side and we destroyed them. Jonny Wilkinson kicked 18 points to overtake Rob Andrew and become England's leading points scorer and I was pleased to have executed an overhead kick which put Mike Catt in for a try under the sticks. Geordan Murphy had tried it for Leicester in a Heineken Cup game against Swansea but it hadn't come off. That's no slight on Geordie, who's one of the most talented guys I've played with – it's a hard thing to get right and it's mostly luck if you do. We won 48–19, a record victory for the fixture, as it had been against Wales, Italy and Scotland.

With the Ireland match rearranged for October, there was a strange feeling in the camp. According to the calendar, France were our last opponents. The championship should have been over and we should have had the Grand Slam, the Six Nations Trophy and the Triple Crown safely under lock and key. We had none of them.

I was back in the team but I hadn't been particularly overjoyed with my performances in the Six Nations, save for my second half against the French. I could have given a little bit more but had instead done just enough to stay in. If I was to keep my place next year I was going to have to work harder: improve my defence, improve my ball carrying, make more breaks and be stronger and quicker.

The main lesson I took from the campaign was that if I left a pitch breathing I hadn't played particularly well. If it took me 15 minutes to get my breath back, I'd done alright. I was shattered after the French game and that stats told the tale; I'd had 18 ball carries in the second half and about 14 offloads. I think I'd done alright.

oOoOo

Back at the club, my relationship with Pat Howard was really breaking down. Now I was also not speaking to Andy Goode. We'd had a fight earlier on in the season and I'd had enough of what I perceived to be his misplaced arrogance. He would say things to me in training like 'You just concentrate on making sure you get the ball in my hands.' Bearing in mind I'd played international rugby for several seasons and been on a Lions tour, this stuck in my craw a bit.

Andy would do it quite cleverly, so that no-one else could hear, but I'd just gob off back at him in front of everyone. So I got tended to get it in the neck.

A recurring theme in my life has been opening my gob at

the wrong moment, or just saying the wrong thing, or saying the right thing but to the wrong person, or saying it tactlessly, or too loud, or any combination of these faults and related ones. If I can find a way of fitting my size eight boots into my mouth, I'll do it, usually while simultaneously cutting off my nose to spite my face.

Our scrap had occurred in training back in August and it ended with him needing hospital treatment. It was just a flare-up, of the type that happened every week. He was trying to strangle me to get the ball off me, I couldn't get him off, so I punched him in the face. Paul Gustard came over and grabbed both my arms and Goodey, bless him, slugged me back in the face.

So now I wouldn't talk to the fly-half or the inside centre. I wouldn't even talk to Goodey when I was putting the ball into the scrum, which is less than ideal if you're the scrum-half. Our childish feud went on until we played away at Northampton in March. We stopped off at a pub on the way back and I said, 'Look, it's time we buried the hatchet. Let's just get on for the sake of the team.' We would have shaken hands but we were both having a wee at the time. The following week we beat Newcastle at home to clinch a hat-trick of Premiership titles.

That, too, was unsatisfactory. Unlike the Six Nations, there was a trophy to collect but due to Sky's scheduling we had to kick our heels all afternoon waiting to hear how Wasps, the only side who could catch us, fared at Bath in a later kick-off. You've got to admire Sky for pumping money into the sport but we should have played both matches at the same time. Then there would have been 16,000 people at Leicester to see us lift the hub cap, sorry the Premiership Shield, instead of the 2,000 who'd hung around. Nonetheless, it was great to win it for a third successive year and the team picture was a hoot as my dad almost gatecrashed his way into it. Freddie Tuilagi didn't even get that close. He'd got his timings wrong, gone home to change for the presentation, and not made it back in time. Fortunately there was a lifesize cardboard cut-out of him in the club shop so we roped that in instead.

Despite our high spirits, we emerged from the league campaign with plenty still to play for at the end of this never-ending season.

We were through to the final of the Heineken Cup.

Kings Of Europe

Parc des Princes, Paris, 19th May 2001

As you know, I was often accused of selfishly using Leicester to further my own ambitions with England and the Lions.

That thought briefly crossed my mind as I stood on halfway at the Parc des Princes, with the Tigers trailing Stade Français 30–27, a minute left in the final of the Heineken Cup and only seven days until I was due to join up with the Lions for Graham Henry's Australia tour.

I had come into the game with an injury to my right knee, an injury which I really should not have risked. One bang, and I could kiss my Lions tour goodbye. It might not even have needed a bang: it could have gone if I'd simply turned too sharply. After 79 minutes it was hurting. Really hurting. I had so many painkillers inside me that I rattled when I ran. Still, I could feel the throbbing beneath the strapping which clung to my damaged medial ligaments.

For a second, I thought of all those 'parasite' jibes I had taken down the years from certain forwards at Leicester.

We were in a deep hole, with this one last lineout, surely the last play of the match, our only chance to snatch a victory.

All week, I'd imagined this moment. As I lay on the physio's bench, first in Leicester, then at the team hotel in Versailles, as I worked with the massage machine in the pool, as I took one suppository after another to try to dull the pain. Last minute of the European Cup final, Leicester down a score, Healey gets the ball . . . he races clear . . . it's a wonder try! Just because we're (almost) grown-ups doesn't mean professional players don't still daydream.

The move was a pre-arranged one – we called it the 'Double Suck Option' – which was designed specifically to unlock a drift defence of the type Stade were operating. The idea was I would take the ball and feed Tim Stimpson on the crash. But the lineout didn't go to plan. The ball was tapped back, it bounced on the floor and Neil Back threw it behind me.

I took a step back, caught it and set off at three-quarter pace, trying to pull the defence forward. I did a dummy scissor with Pat Howard, another with Glen Gelderbloom and noticed that David Venditti, their replacement centre, had already set off onto Stimmo, clearly thinking I was going to hit him. My shoulders were facing Tim, so it looked likely. Venditti over-committed himself ever so slightly so I adjusted and shot through the gap.

I knew their fly-half Diego Dominguez wouldn't have the speed to get to me, but I was still concerned about Venditti. If I'd been fit I would have been away and gone, but as I tried to put the accelerator down, to go from three-quarters to full speed, I started to cramp up just below my right knee. If I'd had time to think, I might have thought of my Lions tour going down the pan. More likely, though, I would have reminded myself of a pledge I took before kick-off. That whatever happened in the game I wouldn't use my knee as an excuse.

Contrary to what some of my team mates thought down the years, playing for Leicester meant a great deal to me. Yes, representing England was my ultimate high, but when I pulled on a Tigers shirt I held absolutely nothing back.

Especially when it was the biggest match in the history of a club with a history of playing big matches. Of course I was concerned about the possibility of injury ruling me out of the Lions tour, but it was a chance I wanted to take. I'd been on a Lions tour before, but I'd never won a European Cup and nor had Leicester. I'd rather win this match than go Down Under, if there was a choice to be made. I could cope with having eight weeks' holiday. What I couldn't cope with was seeing Stade lift the Heineken Cup.

So as I felt my leg begin to seize, I took a deep breath. I kept going as hard as I could and managed to get away from Venditti. Ahead of me was Christophe Dominici... but he wasn't really looking at me, which meant Leon Lloyd must be steaming up on the outside. I later learned he was screaming at the top of his voice to let me know he was there, but there were 47,000 people doing the same and it was impossible to hear him. Just in time, I caught Leon out of the corner of my eye. I waited and waited, so Dominici didn't know whether I was going to try to beat him on the inside or give it. Just as he committed himself to tackle me, I threw a pass out as far in front of Leon as I could. He ran onto it, somehow caught it and as I hit the deck and rolled over I looked up to see him dive into the corner.

We were ahead by two points, but we'd led twice before in the game and not managed to press home our advantage. And as Dominguez had already smashed the tournament record by kicking 30 points, from nine penalties and a drop goal, none of us were under any illusions that the game was far from won.

Unless Stimmo could convert from the right touchline. It was a hell of a kick, but on his day Stimmo was a hell of a kicker. And this was his day.

He'd already landed six out of seven when he struck the ball. 'I knew what it meant,' he said later. 'You put all the self-hatred through your head in case you miss before you line it up, so that if you do miss you've already been through it.' But he didn't miss. As the ball sailed between the posts Graham Rowntree turned to the crowd and started playing with his ears, which was always a good sign. We led by four points and we knew we could stop them from scoring a try, no matter what – even if it meant someone diving over and biting the ball – because that was our bread and butter in training sessions. We didn't give our team mates an inch, so why should we give one to a bunch of Frenchmen?

The feeling of euphoria that washed over me as the touch judges' flags went up to signal the kick was good was immense. I'd played in some great games for Leicester, some big occasions, but what happened in Paris that day blew everything else out of the water completely.

The European Cup had been our obsession for almost as long as we could remember. Certainly since we'd faced another French club in the 1997 final. That day is ingrained in my memory because we were humiliated by Brive in a game we'd thought we couldn't lose. We were arrogant and complacent in equal measure and every mention of Europe thereafter triggered nightmare images of another Frenchman running in another try.

The Brive match was as low as I ever felt in a Leicester shirt. I remember knocking on a tapped penalty and missing a try-saving tackle which I would have made nine times out of ten. Nightmare memories. The whole game went so quickly it was just impossible to get into it.

It had gone wrong from the start, from the build-up, Bob Dwyer's masterplan. The week began with us doing different photo calls for this and that – basically, for any Johnny-come-lately sponsor who wanted to come in and buy a piece of the final from us. We went down to Cardiff, where the game was to be played, and had to do a live link from the team hotel to East Midlands TV on the Friday night. There was loads of joking around and messing about when we should have been focusing. We hadn't really watched any videos of Brive during the week. We hadn't analysed them. Bob hadn't spoken about a gameplan or anything like that.

On the day of the match, he announced that we were going for a walk. It was 10 o'clock: we walked out of our hotel in our tracksuits, turned right, walked round the town, back down the high street where all the fans were gathering, and back into the hotel. I turned to the lads and said 'What the hell have we done that for?'

The game kicked off and the Brive boys laid into us with a ferocity that none of our players were used to, even the internationals, and we were smashed 28–9, four tries to nil. The whole episode was born out of arrogance. In the semi-finals we'd stuffed Toulouse 37–11, and they'd previously beaten Brive by God knows how many points. So the final had to be a walk in the park, surely? Sadly not. We should have been the first English side to lift the European Cup, not Bath, but our own complacency – and a great performance by Brive – denied us.

So when we arrived in Paris four years later – not even in a position to become the first side in the East Midlands to win it, thanks to Northampton's victory in 2000 – we were desperate for redemption, for the chance to erase that awful memory for the five of us who had played in the starting line-up in Cardiff that day.

The Heineken campaign had begun with question marks placed over our ability to do the business away from Welford Road. We had crashed out in the pool stages a year earlier, beaten by Glasgow and Stade and we'd also lost at home to Leinster for the only time in a competitive match since December 1997. We had everything to prove.

We started badly, losing our second game on the road at Pontypridd which meant our final trip, to Pau, would be a quarter-final eliminator. The game could not have come at a much worse time. For one thing we had been beaten by Harlequins in the Tetley's Bitter Cup semi-finals a week earlier – Quins turned into a Cup bogey team for us – and for another Johnno was suspended.

After the Quins game we'd had the riot act read to us. 'Let's show how much this hurts,' yelled Neil Back, standing in at skipper in Johnno's absence. 'Let's go the rest of the season unbeaten.' We did precisely that, save for a solitary league loss at Gloucester when the Premiership title had already been won and our international contingent were on day off. Sixteen games in all, of which 15 were won, including two quarter-finals, two semis and two finals.

The tone was set in Pau where we produced a textbook performance in what was a very dirty game. My opposite number was Philippe Carbonneau, a player who never lets you down if you want a fight. He stamped on me early on but I kept my cool, an episode which proved a microcosm of the day's proceedings, and we won at a canter, 20–3. We scrum-halves are a strange breed: if you don't like fighting other scrum-halves you've got no chance. Remember Robert Jones and Nick Farr-Jones on the '89 Lions tour? The Wallabies certainly do. What a classic. Two scrum-halves at war.

Our quarter-final against Swansea was a joke. We expected a really hard game, after seeing them beat Stade Français, and I actually thought they were live contenders to go all the way, but we just completely destroyed them 41–10 and they'd given up at half-time.

That left Gloucester standing between us and the final. We were shocking, Gloucester played one of their best games of the season and we came pretty close to losing. Had

Martin Corry not stolen the ball on our line in a maul I think we would have.

Again, we'd been our own worst enemies. Just like at Harlequins three months earlier, we'd felt we were the better team but weren't prepared to put in the work to prove it. As a result, nobody played outside themselves, no-one had even a half decent game except perhaps Stimmo and Lloydy. You'd have thought we had lost at the end, so quiet was our changing room. When we win an away game we normally stop off for fish and chips as a treat on the way home. But there was no celebration this time, even though we'd just won through to the European Cup final. We knew we had to do better, much better.

As we'd left the changing room deep in the bowels of Parc des Princes, that thought had still been fresh in our minds. I also had the worry about my knee to contend with. Five days earlier I'd been in pieces, unable to walk after injuring myself at Twickenham during our easy win over Bath in the Zurich Championship final; the second leg of our treble. The next day, after 12 hours of physio, I could bend my knee but medical opinion was still that I had no chance of playing. Jamie Hamilton was prepared to play and he must have been gutted when I declared myself fit on the Friday night. All credit to Jamie, he never showed it. He was a great club man, an awesome bloke: guys like him were the backbone of Leicester. Don't look at the internationals as the reason for the club's success, look at guys like Jamie, the boys who kept the banter flying, who were always around and having a laugh.

It was a showpiece occasion, the bear pit was packed and, as with a major international, the two teams had been supposed to walk out together. We waited in the tunnel underneath, me in my usual position at the back of the line, because I liked to turn the afterburners on for a quick burst as I hit the field. But Stade were time-wasting, so after a minute or so I shouted, 'Stuff them, let's run out,' and we did. We got into our usual huddle on the pitch, pulling each other tight and sucking in the atmosphere, and still there was no sign of Stade. Eventually, they walked out and started heading towards us. We broke from our huddle and advanced on them, ready to tear them apart if they started anything. I was convinced it was going to kick off but David McHugh, the referee, got between us and pushed us apart. That set the tone for the day. Intimidation is a big part of the game in France, and we knew if we let them think they'd got the upper hand, physically or mentally, they would have taken massive encouragement. They'd misjudged us badly.

We're Leicester Tigers, boys. Bring it on.

At that moment I think they realised they had an almighty fight on their hands.

Once the game kicked off, I never thought we would lose. Even when Dominguez dropped a goal two minutes from time to put them three points ahead. I didn't even bother trying to charge it down, partly because I was so knackered, partly because I knew we had the character to pull through. I'd seen the way we'd reacted when Johnno was sin-binned for punching their number eight, Christophe Juillet, soon after half-time. It was a good punch which caught Juillet right in the face, but Johnno would have been pretty sick if we'd lost the game while he was off. At least Juillet saw it coming. Johnno hadn't had that luxury when he'd been punched from behind by Richard Pool-Jones earlier in the game. Johnno had come round the side of a ruck and maybe accidentally stood on him. But play had continued and he'd thought nothing of it. Then . . . wallop! It's totally out of order to get whacked from behind like that.

But Stade didn't even look like scoring a try against us, even when we were down to 14 men. The rest of us lifted our game and snuffed them out. We often played our best rugby when someone was binned. The remaining players would step up a gear and we'd move the set-pieces and rucks quicker. So while Johnno was not the easiest person to lose we held firm.

The first half was like a game of chess, both sides jostling for position. Our gameplan was nothing fancy. Kick our way downfield and then steal a lineout if we could. But their lineouts went very well and we didn't steal more than one all game so we had to change tack. Instead of kicking away possession, we kept hold of it and started to build through the phases – four, five, six, waiting for the holes to appear. We just had to stay patient and keep our discipline. But at the turnaround we trailed 15–9, Dominguez having kicked five out of five penalties for them. He was brilliant on the day but I would say Tim Stimpson was even better.

I used to wonder about Stimmo. If he could have got his mind right for every game he would have been one of the best rugby players of all time, I honestly believe that. Physically he had everything, but sometimes his mind seemed to wander. When he was motivated, he was awesome. I remember a game against Northampton, shortly after he had joined from Newcastle. One of his relations had died the previous day but his family were keen for him to play. He went out and played like I've never seen a full-back play. Ever. He was incredible, making tries all over the place, kicking all of his goals. Just brilliant. It was a similar story against Stade Français. He seemed to pick out three or four games a season where he was simply unbelievable and then had lapses of concentration in other games which hurt his reputation.

Leon Lloyd was another with bags of talent and he too shone like a star for us that day. It was his try, 30 seconds after half-time following great work by Pat Howard and Geordan Murphy, which got us back in the contest. And of course it was his second score, right at the death, which won us the game. I was voted man of the match, but I'd have given it to Lloydy. He had a brilliant game and was – still is – a player who was cruelly under-used by England. Leon had the potential to be a major figure in the England team, in my opinion. OK, he's been a bit volatile at times but that shows he has fire in his belly and he's prepared to put it about for the lads. His form dipped, mainly through injury, a year or two back but he's been right back to his best recently and I can't understand why he's been ignored.

The noise from our fans when Leon crossed for the decisive try, and when Stimmo's kick went over, was unbelievable. International rugby is great but stadiums can be full of home fans, the atmosphere one-sided, and the rivalry between supporters which brings football grounds to life is missing. This time, despite the best efforts of the tournament organisers to hand Stade home advantage, the split was far more even, the atmosphere electric, quite stunning. It was as though the entire population of Leicester was there. I didn't endear myself to European Rugby Cup Ltd afterwards by taking them to task for picking Parc des Princes as a neutral venue, but somebody had to say something as it was an outrageous decision. And better I thought to say so in victory rather than defeat. We were 50 yards from Stade's home ground for goodness' sake.

Johnno had spoken in the build-up to the game about how this occasion was personal, about how, for all the things some of us had been lucky enough to win with England and the Lions, this was for our city, our fans and the guys with whom we lived and breathed rugby, day in day out. It was a great speech and I was in tears as I mounted the podium after the match. Though that may have been because Johnno sent Backy and Darren Garforth up to lift the cup when I wanted to do it.

The other two trophies we'd won – the Premiership and Championship – we could bin for all the lads cared at that particular moment. The fact we had won the big one meant everything. Climbing up those stairs and seeing all the fans and the support staff and the alickadoos down on the pitch below, cheering and clapping, was so satisfying: people like Peter Tom, Bob Beeson, Peter Wheeler, David Matthews, their faces all lit up. They had been involved in the club for more than 30 years waiting for a day like this one. To a man they were all very emotional.

In our moment of glory, I thought it might be a good time to press my case for a new contract, so I mentioned to the press that, having won everything club rugby had to offer, I was going to reassess my career. It might be difficult to regain my enthusiasm and motivation after this, I said, and since Louise and I are both from the north, and were planning to start a family, we might move back up there one day. Knowing Dean's preferred method of contractual negotiation is to play a waiting game, I wanted to give him a nudge and to gently persuade him to offer me a new contract sooner rather than later. If I was worth anything, it had to be after that game. It was probably the only time I would ever have the upper hand. Any other time Dean would tell me to get lost.

Happily, he didn't as chants of 'Tigers, Tigers' echoed around Paris. He was too busy gasping for breath after having been ridden across the pitch at the end of the game by Backy. Both were deliriously happy, as they milked the acclaim of the red, white and green hordes in the far corner of the stadium. So much so that Backy went on local radio moments later without his usual composure.

'Neil, it must feel great for someone of your age, coming towards the end of your career, to win a trophy like this?' said the interviewer, excitely.

Big mistake. 'Age doesn't f***ing come into it, mate,' Backy replied.

'Neil, this is actually a live interview,' said the guy.

'Well, we'll f***ing end it there then, shall we?' said Backy. You see, it's not always me.

I was on a high for a good week afterwards. The Lions tour was fast approaching but I did not want to let this occasion go. From the moment I grabbed the microphone on the pitch at the end to thank our army of supporters, until I packed up the car a week later to head for the tour hotel, I was full of it. I clearly wasn't alone. The response in Leicester was unbelievable. There were hundreds of fans waiting for us at East Midlands airport on our return and thousands more at Welford Road where we paraded the trophy. People came up to you in the gym, or beeped their horns in the street, or stopped you at the paper shop. They weren't asking for autographs, they just wanted to say how happy they were to have been there or how amazing it was to watch it on the TV. Even Leicestershire's county cricketers and the boys from Leicester City had been thrilled. Everywhere you went, there was enormous pride in what we'd achieved.

Even hangovers don't feel as bad when you've won. It was quite hard to take in at first because I thought of the flip side. Had I given in to the pain of my knee, had I not made that break, had we not scored that try and instead lost by three points . . . how would we have felt? It had been an unbelievable team effort, yet we were only two minutes away from losing. It makes you realise how fine the line is between success and failure.

Living With Lions

The Lions is the pinnacle of your rugby career, or so everyone always says.

Sorry, but I just never quite saw it that way. Yes, it's big, very big, but, for me, the white of England has always been the colour. I am English first, British second: whenever I'm asked on landing cards and other forms to write my nationality, I write 'English'. The Scots, Welsh and Irish all have such passion about being who they are but somehow English pride isn't allowed. Our nation seems to have lost its identity for some, but never for me. Playing for England meant the world and I never had ambitions to play for the Lions. I didn't want to play *with* the Celts, I wanted to play against them and I wanted to beat them.

All that said, I was obviously pleased to be selected for the South Africa Tour in 1997. I went as a scrum-half, with Rob Howley and Matt Dawson, and while I never made the Test team it was a fantastic trip. That was the last ever amateur/professional tour – the game had only just gone pro, and everyone in the group had been playing for expenses a year or two before and knew what the spirit and soul of rugby was all about. It was full of guys who wanted to work and have fun at the same time.

The work ethic was great, we were very professional and we trained every single day, but often it was with a hangover. The boys went out most nights and had a few beers together but everyone knew that if you got drunk you'd still be there, out on the park, next day. Paul Wallace, the Irish prop, sticks in my mind: he reeked of booze most mornings but he trained his absolute nuts off, was a legend and deservedly made the Test front row.

Fran Cotton got the balance between enjoying yourself and working hard for the games just right. We set our own rules – the first time a team had done that. One of them was that nobody was allowed to drink for 48 hours before a game, even if they weren't playing. That meant Wednesday nights were pretty big.

There were loads of characters on the trip – not just five or six, but 20 or 25 guys who had you in fits the whole time. One guy who sticks in my mind was Eric Miller, the Ireland (and, for a while, Leicester) back rower. I remember we went for our medicals before we left the UK. We had to get weighed, we'd just been training and our big, heavy training tops were soaked with sweat.

The doctor said, 'Eric; you've got to get undressed for your weigh-in.'

Eric took his top off and stood on the scales, still holding it in his hand.

The doctor said, 'You've got to drop it, Eric.'

Eric said, 'Sure, I've taken it off, what does it matter?'

He wasn't the sharpest tool in the box, and the Eric stories are legion. My favourite is the time he told everyone he'd been to the supermarket, bought a load of spuds, baked them in their jackets and then put them in the freezer for later.

South Africa were massive favourites in the eyes of many. They still had a huge mystique, which has largely gone now, they very rarely lost at home to anyone, and certainly not to European teams. In the squad, we were always quietly confident. We had some real quality players, we had a strong and imposing captain in Martin Johnson and we had two great leaders, Ian McGeechan and Jim Telfer.

I rarely got motivated by people speaking, but they were both remarkable and inspiring men. I'll never forget two of their pre-match speeches. Jim gave one before we played Orange Free State, in which he spoke about how tight the squad was, about how together we were and how we couldn't be broken apart. It sent shivers down my spine and really did galvanise everyone.

Even better was the brief couple of sentences that Geech came out with ahead of the second test in Durban. Whatever you do today, he said, *you need to be proud of yourself, because in 15, 20 or 30 years' time you'll be walking down the road, or you'll go to some event, and you'll see someone else from this changing room today and you'll be able to look them in the eye and, without saying a word, you will know what you each achieved today*.

Everyone started looking around the room at each other and a sort of steely passion developed in front of your eyes. It was uncanny, especially since this was a group of players who didn't normally play together. I've seen it a few times with England and, most notably, before Leicester's first European Cup victory in Paris, but that was the first time and, under the circumstances, perhaps the most amazing.

Ian was right about the future, too: a bond did develop between the guys who toured South Africa together and you do have that momentary recognition when you meet again.

We won the first Test in Cape Town against the odds and the media predictions, thanks to Matthew Dawson's lucky try, and the boys went crazy afterwards. Keith Wood grabbed a load of tequila bottles in a bar and was pouring it straight into your mouth. When Keith Wood is forcing booze down your neck you have no choice but to drink it, as I've found out to my cost on several occasions. The whole party was completely shattered with booze.

We won the second with Jerry Guscott's drop goal and Neil Jenkins' astonishing boot, plus a heroic pack that refused to be beaten and a group of backs, led by the likes of Scotty Gibbs, who took the Springboks on, and recorded an historic series victory on what remains the most famous and talked-about Lions tour of them all.

Had Fran, Geech and Jim gone to Australia in 2001, I don't think there is any doubt that we would have won that series, too. Unfortunately the powers that be chose someone else.

Graham Henry's appointment as coach of the British and Irish Lions had been greeted with disbelief by England's players. We'd won the Six Nations Championship and, at the time, we were on our way to a share of a Test series against the Springboks in South Africa – a very rare thing for European sides back then. For the first time in years, a Six Nations team was causing the Big Three of Australia, New Zealand and South Africa to sit up and take notice. Clive Woodward, for my money, should have at least been offered the job. He was a British Lion, after all.

I had no problem with Henry, personally speaking, at the outset. He seemed a really nice guy. But he's not British and that matters. I have Irish blood and I'd been approached to play for Ireland some years before. I'd asked myself, '*Could I sit in an Irish changing room at Twickenham and say 'Let's smash these English b******s?*' The simple answer was no, I couldn't.

As I looked ahead to that Australia trip, I struggled to find the sense of excitement and inspiration people talked about. Maybe it was partly to do with the irritation I'd felt at not making the Test starting line-up last time around, maybe it was more down to the English/British way I feel inside.

For all that, a wave of relief swept over me when the contract arrived.

It was recognition for the way I'd been playing for Leicester and England, and it meant – hopefully – I could stop having bloody dreams about the Lions.

For three or four nights prior to the squad announcement I tossed and turned, flashbacks of key moments in recent Lions history running through my mind . . . David Campese gifting the series-winning try to Ieuan Evans in 1989, Jerry Guscott scoring in Brisbane and, of course, Daws' jammy fluke against South Africa last time round.

There was no guarantee I'd get the chance to emulate him. I was listed at scrum-half, number three in the eyes of many, notably Jerry Guscott, behind Rob and Matt. I met Jerry at a Pro-Celebrity golf day.

'Have you sorted your reading list out?' he asked.

'What?' I said.

'For the tour. Have you sorted your reading list out? Because you ain't going to be playing much rugby are you?'

A few days later Leicester destroyed Bath at Twickenham in the final of the Zurich Championship, I played pretty well and I happened to bump into Jerry afterwards.

'About that reading list,' I said. 'I've just halved it. After that performance I reckon I might get a couple of games.'

A week later he was watching us win the European Cup final against Stade Français, where I made the break for the winning try and then picked up the Man of the Match trophy.

'Jerry,' I said. 'I've decided not to take any books at all.'

Behind all the joking I knew he had a point. I was seen by many as cover for scrum-half, fly-half and wing. It was the curse of my bloody 'versatility'. It sounds great but it labels you as a jack of all trades and master of none and you end up spending your life on the bench. I always believed I had the ability to play each position – scrum-half, fly-half and wing – to international standard and to be worth any of those shirts on merit. I was hoping to prove that on tour and when Graham Henry revealed that he thought I could be the surprise package of the party, I felt good. He went as far as to predict that I would stamp myself on the tour. Maybe he had a crystal ball.

There were few surprises when the squad was named, and one thing that surprised no-one was the appointment of Martin Johnson as captain. I'd certainly been expecting it, after playing mind games with him the day before the announcement. He'd walked into training smiling and I'd said, 'I know something about you.'

'What do you know?' he'd asked.

'A little bird told me.'

'Told you what?' he'd said.

'You know very well.'

He'd caved in. 'Yeah, I got the call last night, I'm captain.'

'So am I vice-captain, then?' I'd said.

Johnno is a good mate and I was really pleased for him. He is one of the best captains of all time and I knew what an honour this was for him. The way he led Leicester was nothing short of inspirational, he was the same with England and had been the same, in 1997, with the Lions.

Neil Back was the third Tiger selected; I couldn't help feeling for Martin Corry, Dorian West and Tim Stimpson. I was gutted for Cozza, particularly: he'd enjoyed another great season after living in the shadow of Lawrence Dallaglio for a good few years.

I finished our season strongly. I could relax and let my game flow. I was on the Lions tour, and Louise was expecting our first child. All was right with the world.

oOoOo

Saying goodbye to Lou had not been easy, more so than usual because of her pregnancy, and on the trip south to meet up with the other Lions there was added apprehension. We were being thrown together with people who, just weeks before, we'd wanted to hurt and humiliate in games. I shouldn't have worried. Take, Robin McBryde, the Llanelli hooker, who for some reason I was a bit concerned about. I'd had this preconception that he was some sort of psychopath. I couldn't have been more wrong. He turned out to be one of the nicest, funniest guys on the trip. The same was true of Rob Henderson, who I roomed with. Hendo smoked like a chimney and snored like a blocked up one, when he was actually asleep. Which wasn't often. But he was a top guy, as almost all of them were.

We'd met up at Tylney Hall, an 18th century mansion-turned-hospital-turned-school-turned-pricey hotel. Lovely place for a blind date, and meeting up with the 2001 Lions for the first time was a bit like that. I knew the England lads, of course, and those Celts I'd toured with in 1997. But I didn't know the boss.

From an early stage, I didn't believe in the way Henry coached us. I was much more about space, expression and playing what you see; Henry was big on structure and a lot of his philosophy was based around targets – attacking people rather than gaps. From our first training sessions, I felt that organisation and attention to detail were missing, too.

Henry had set the tone for the way he'd treat the players on Day One, and it continued in Australia. A light jog was scheduled as our first session but the management changed their minds and the gentle runout became two full contact sessions. It was as though we hadn't just finished a nine or ten month season and flown halfway round the world. We needed a day or so to recover, but Henry didn't seem to understand that.

Right from our arrival Down Under, strange things started to happen. Out in Perth, ahead of the Western Australia game that kicked the series off, I'd just been out to buy some popcorn – I always had the stuff the night before games – and had not long been back in the hotel when there was a knock on my door. I opened it to find two blondes, with big boobs and long legs in very skimpy clothes.

'Hi,' said one, with a dazzling *Baywatch* smile. 'We just wondered if you had any tickets for the game?'

'You might get some downstairs,' I replied, cautiously.

But that wasn't what they wanted to hear. 'Can we come in and watch *Big Brother* on your TV?'

'Nah,' I said. 'Sorry. I'm a bit busy. But there's a TV in reception.'

'OK,' said the other girl. 'We'll go to the bar and wait until you come down and we can have a drink together.'

'Look, girls,' I said. 'I'm going to bed. But thanks.'

'That's a shame,' she replied. 'You have really nice legs.'

I shut the door. From my window, I watched them stalk across the road where a man in a white BMW was waiting. A honey trap. Unbelievable.

Waiting for that first game was boring: nothing to do but be flogged in training, watch TV and take money off Iain Balshaw at cards. Well, I had to teach my monkey a lesson to make him behave.

I decided to keep a diary.

SUNDAY
Neil Jenkins needs ten stitches after Jeremy 'Dangerous Brain' Davidson tried to run over him. I stepped in at fly-half in Team Two. Went quite well, not bad with a dodgy knee. Crawled back to the hotel for another profitable game of cards.

MONDAY
Day Two was worse. As bad as Day One but without the rest, fun or cards. Someone asked Donal the difference between this and the 1997 tour. 'We've been together three and a half days and haven't even been to the pub,' he said. The gag has quickly worn thin. The boys have joked about ringing the bell and travelling around Australia backpacking. Phoned home and spoke to Louise, who was suffering with morning sickness. I hate being away when people are sick at home, ever since my gran, Lil Healey, died while I was on tour in Australia with England under-21s in 1993. My parents didn't tell me until later because they didn't want it to distract me.

TUESDAY
Only been with the Lions for eleven days (including Tylney) and already I need a break. Given the day off by our medical team to help my knee recover properly. Watched the session and came away convinced that the team was starting to take shape. Away from training, we swim in the hotel pool, play cards or computer games and use our squad video camera, mimicking John 'Bentos' Bentley, who made a big a name for himself in 1997 with the *Living with the Lions* video. Bentos spent half the trip pointing the camera in our faces, or indeed at his own, and talking gibberish.

Funny story from the '97 tour: thanks to Bentos, I became known as 'Mr X the Invisible W****r'. Being on tour for eight weeks, you get a bit frustrated so I was spending a bit of quality time in the bathroom with the door locked when all of a sudden it sprang open – Bentos had picked the lock from the outside – and before I knew what was happening I had a camera filming me. By the time I had put myself away he'd scarpered down the corridor and three other lads grabbed me so I couldn't catch him. He went straight down to lunch and announced to the rest of the squad that there would be a special screening later on. I had to think quickly. I broke into his room, turned the place upside down, eventually found the video camera, blacked out the offending footage, rebuilt his room, then put the camera back. Half an hour later he had got the whole squad together. They'd all heard about it and were winding me up big time. Then Bentos started the video. You see him sneaking into my room, whispering 'I know he's in here somewhere, I'm going to catch him out.' As he opened the door the screen went black. I wet myself laughing and Bentos went ape.

We could do with some laughs like that now.

I've been named on the bench for the Western Australia match. Destroy Will Greenwood on the games at the local arcade over lunch, then head to the gym with Dallaglio. Pass some of the lads in a burger bar on the way back.

WEDNESDAY

Newspaper column day. I'm appearing in The Guardian on Friday and The Observer on Sunday. I meet Eddie Butler, the Observer's rugby correspondent, and he puts words to my thoughts. I have the right of veto. Eddie seems a decent enough guy but I'm slightly concerned that he turns up for our interview with neither a notebook nor a tape recorder. Still, the columns have been amusing.

Not that there is any controversy around, just sweat and knackered bodies. It is all about hitting tackle bags, hitting scrum machines and then hitting the sack to try and grab enough shut eye to get you through the following day which you are pretty safe to assume will be spent hitting tackle bags and more scrum machines.

THURSDAY
Shocking warm-up. Team run at the WACA first thing and
Steve Black, our fitness advisor, had people running around
all over the place. He claimed to have choreographed our
movements. I think he made it up as he went along. Blackie
is a nice bloke and a good motivator but not in the same
league as Dave Reddin (the England fitness coach). Have
the feeling that the pace and width of our game will have to
go some to catch up with England. (Sorry non-English
Lions fans, there I go again). Suspect that both Phil Larder
and Dave Alred have noticed this but I don't know what they
can do to change it. It has to come from the head coach. I am
convinced that pounding forwards and big backs with
territory will not be enough to beat the Aussies. I really hope
I'm wrong.

Phil Greening twisted his knee today and is probably out
of the tour. Lot of talk about who would come out. Both
Johnno and I made a case for Dorian West, but Backy seems
to know it will be Gordon Bulloch.

FRIDAY
Last night was a shocker. I had an asthma attack, only a mild
one but I got no sleep. Probably the result of coughing up
phlegm, dust and the dreaded air conditioning. I overdosed
on Ventolin. I went to breakfast and on to the team walk-
through but I still couldn't breathe at all well. I had been
confident that a dose of exercise would bring me out the
other side of the attack. It didn't. I was still very short of
breath.

Thank God for Dr James Robson. The doc gave me a
vibration massage to get the phlegm off my lungs and
bronchials. Then a Salbutamol nebuliser sent me way out
there on a relaxed scale. Unless you have asthma you can't
understand how horrible the tightness in your chest,

shoulders and throat makes you feel. Underwent the treatment at 1 o'clock. Thirty minutes later I felt like a human being again.

Western Australia 10. British and Irish Lions 116

Everyone looks forward to the first game on a tour, but never more than this one.

Biggest victory in Lions history, 18 tries a record, too. All in spite of a quite extraordinary speech by Graham Henry beforehand. He said that down here they don't think we're skilful enough, don't think we're athletic enough and don't think we're committed enough. 'And I should know, because I'm one of them.'

No better in the changing room, when Blackie started gobbing off and shouting out instructions. Most of the guys couldn't be bothered to even listen. Rugby changing rooms should be quiet, so you can chill out, concentrate and focus.

Every player prepares differently. Some listen to a Walkman, some (like Jenks) are sick, some bang their heads, others get changed straight away and go out and warm up and have a proper stretch. I go in, clean my boots, sit down, read the programme for a bit, go and check the pitch, then get changed, put Deep Heat on my calves, have a stretch and go back out and warm up.

I didn't feel nervous, strangely, nor any honour or pride about playing for the Lions in the first game. That will change later on, I'm sure, when the opposition is better.

Great to get off the bench and score the try which brought up the century. Bit of a no-win situation but you have to play well to score 116 points against anyone.

Phil Larder was seething that we'd conceded two tries and Simon Taylor discovered he'd torn his ACL. We all felt sick for him. He's a nice lad and a good player. A load of us went out for pasta, I had two beers and headed back for half a dose of the nebuliser and a state of unconsciousness.

SATURDAY

Early morning training so the main part of the day would be spent in the air, travelling to Townsville on the north east corner of Australia, five and a half hours away. Fair enough, as long as the flight wasn't delayed.

Chucked a bowl of cereal down my throat and headed out to the local pitch for a quick 90-minute session. It was memorable for Andy Robinson coaching support lines and angles and having a go at me about my depth and timing. He may be a good forwards coach but come on! Raced back to the hotel to pack and arrived at the airport to find the plane was screwed. Got another plane after we'd sat around for hours.

Martin Corry has been called up from Canada.

SUNDAY

I've swapped my monkey Balsh for Jenks. He's a top man. Tells a funny story about the time he shared with Jerry Guscott on the '97 Lions tour and started to try and chat with him. Jerry peered over the top of his book and said, 'Look, if you want to talk, phone up one of your Welsh mates.'

Jenks is a true legend, the nicest bloke you could ask to meet. Very proud of his 'little Viking', his 17-month-old daughter Georgia, and showed me some lovely pictures of her. She looks like him, especially dressed in her Wales shirt. Made me think about the baby Lou and I are expecting. Jenks says it's hard to tour when they're so young, that he really misses her and that it hurts him to miss any part of her infancy. Hopefully I'll have a healthy six-month old baby this time next year. I bet I feel the same as Jenks.

MONDAY

Named on the bench for the game against Queensland Presidents XV tomorrow and the game against the Super 12 franchise Queensland Reds on Saturday. This is turning into a nightmare.

Had a team run at Dairy Farmer's Stadium, the 30,000-capacity venue for tomorrow's match and then trained with the squad to play Queensland.

Full on again – the only saving grace for me was that I got to wear the green bib so nobody was allowed to touch me. Still knackered when I got back to the hotel and slept for two hours. Then it was off to Dai Young's team meeting. Dai is captain of the midweek side and a top fella. He spoke well but I can't look at him because I know it will make us both burst out laughing.

Went in search of popcorn at the local cinema. Despite my popcorn habit I'm not superstitious, I just have a routine. Popcorn and Dyoralite in water (to try and get some electrolytes into my calf muscles) the night before, then on match day I shave to try and freshen myself up. Also eat as much as I can – like to have bacon butties but have struggled over here because there only seems to be streaky bacon. Everything about my day is organised in advance. I have trainers, an undervest, a tee shirt, a pair of shorts and socks which I always wear on matchdays so that I don't have any unimportant decisions to make that will distract my focus. I like to avoid surprises. Unfortunately the Lions management have been running into them, one after another. Henry had a beer thrown over him as he gave a television interview in Perth, which was embarrassing for the Aussies. Mayor of Townsville failed to turn up to a reception billed as the 'Mayor's official welcome to the teams'. Beat Matt Dawson at table tennis table, 27–25, 21–19. I just step it up against Daws when I get to the big points.

TUESDAY
With England, I'm always the first player up because I like

to get in two meals before kick-off. But England play in the afternoon whereas the Lions play at night, so there is no rush. My typical match day food is Special K with strawberries, a bowl of fruit, four bacon butties and beans, six pieces of toast with organic jam and a couple of muffins. My other rule is that I stay awake in the five hours before kick-off to make sure my brain is alert, and constantly sip Lucozade.

Queensland President's XV 6, British and Irish Lions 83

Poor first half, which we were lucky to lead 10–6. Problems with continuity, guys playing as 15 individuals not a team. Hard for everyone to get a fair crack of the whip, with a 37-man squad on a very short tour, so understandably people look to make the most of their time on the ball.

Second half was plain sailing. Early try through Colin Charvis and five more in the next 17 minutes. I came on at fly-half with 25 minutes to go. Hendo told me to kick it, but I told him to shut up. We want to score tries. The next thing he knows he's scored underneath the posts. I just laughed and said 'I bet you're happy we didn't kick it now, aren't you?'

Any time you score 73 unanswered points in a single half, you've done well. Jason Robinson scored five tries on his Lions debut, so got all the headlines and fair enough.

We went out for a beer in Townsville, but too many Lions fans for us to relax. Support is unlike anything you experience anywhere else. Got back with Shaggy and Daws at 3am.

WEDNESDAY

Townsville (Hicksville to the boys) has a tropical climate and the Great Barrier Reef just off the coast. Nice place for a holiday but we're on a treadmill.

Excused contact at training because I popped a rib and knee was sore but did the lunchtime press conference. Asked if I'm annoyed to be substitute again? No, I said, you get used to it. I was seething inside. Henry has said I will definitely start next Tuesday against Australia A. I'd better, because if they change their minds I'm out of here.

THURSDAY
Woke at 10 o'clock to learn that I'd missed the biggest night of the tour so far. A large group of lads had escaped. No names, obviously, but they came back at 6.30am pretty drunk. A quiet beer turned into a shot-necking night. Just as well for them that they took their fun while they could get it because there was bad news waiting for us all at breakfast. Supposed to be a day off but two training sessions have been scheduled for the non-Queensland squad and we have an analysis session at 4.30pm. Shocker. Too much training and too much chat on this tour, while the lads just want to chill out and play rugby. Bit of a wedge appearing between coaches and players.

I'm sharing with Daws, so if someone wants a moan they know where to come.

Ahead of our 4.30, we headed to the Sunshine Coast where Neil Back, Richard Hill, Jonny Wilkinson and Martin Corry were going to swim in a shark tank. The sharks looked very scary. The lads were told not to touch them – you don't say! I asked the staff to drop some food into the tank first and they explained that the sharks would also eat the boys. Nice.

FRIDAY
What the hell is going on? Team run at Brisbane Grammar School ground today lasted two and a half hours, the day before a game.

Boys not involved tomorrow got beasted and then had an afternoon session. It's depressing for the squad, a lot of the boys are walking zombies.

I sat in the hotel foyer trying to make sense of it all. I'm at the top of my game but not getting picked, so why am I here? They don't need to coach us in how to win rucks and mauls. The same thing with tackling technique. We're international players. It's mindless. Five different coaches each saying 'I need 20 minutes doing this.' That's 100 minutes. It's too much. Henry could be a good coach but he sees targets and patterns and doesn't look for space. We have been told that our gameplan is to attack 10 and 12.

Thought about my mates out in Ayia Napa on holiday, drinking and partying, and wondered what I was doing out here. I'm a professional sportsman, and this is my job, but sometimes you would like to be normal.

The only thing that keeps me going through the low times is the fact that all my family have saved up to come over here. Had they not been coming, I probably would have said 'That's it, see you later,' left my kit in the room, taken a few clothes to travel round Australia and gone. Might have lived to regret it, obviously.

Had a senior players' committee meeting the other day and they decided that we should train once a day. The following day we trained twice. I don't think there's any point having a senior players' committee.

SATURDAY

Lads prepared well in training, the team run looked good and I got my lucky popcorn, albeit after an hour-long search.

Queensland Reds 8, British and Irish Lions 42

I was convinced we were going to give them a spanking. As it turned out I almost got one first from my new room mate, Cozza. Typical forward: bossy, likes his sleep and always wants to be in control of the TV remote. I nicked the remote and turned the ballet on and it almost ended in death. He's 18 stone and 6ft 6in and I didn't want to have to hurt him before his big game so I gave in.

Queensland tried it on up front, big mistake. Johnno, Danny Grewcock and the other forwards stood their ground and then took total control, mainly from Queensland mistakes.

Game was won by half-time and they scored one try when Matt Dawson had a kick charged down. Afterwards quite a few of the boys went out and got hammered. I had nothing to celebrate so had a lemonade and an early night. The post-match food was rubbish, as it has been all along. I'm losing weight and putting on fat.

SUNDAY

I hate travel days. Living out of a suitcase does my head in. Flight to Sydney was OK. The England netball team were on board and they asked us for our autographs which I found a bit strange.

Graham Henry, speaking before the game, denied we had a split camp. 'It's not just the 15 on the track who are going to win the Test matches. It will be the whole tour party of 50 pulling together.'

For once on this tour I was in total agreement with my coach. It won't last of course.

MONDAY

Manly's awesome when the sun shines and the surf's up. It almost makes you feel pleased to be on tour. Sadly, training was a complete joke. Travelling on Sunday and playing on Tuesday makes adequate preparation impossible. Monday is the day before the game so the midweek team has been going into games diabolically under-prepared (ironically, given all the moans about too much coaching). Today we had 20 minutes as a team with most of the session running plays against the Saturday side preparing to play New South Wales. The split between the Saturday and Tuesday teams is very evident. Midweek boys now known as Dai's Driftwood.

Why don't we name the Tuesday team before Saturday night so we can get through a little bit of work? Surprised no-one has thought of this. The announcement is so late that players have to go to two training sessions not only with no firm idea of what position they're going to be playing but without knowing whether they're going to be playing at all. Our lineouts were awful and we're up against a side containing ten Wallabies who have been in camp for 12 days preparing specifically for this game.

Catty has been fighting a losing battle against injury, is desperate to play but is at least 10 metres off the pace. Jenks is struggling with a swollen knee. I don't think one person on this trip is 100% fit. Had two hours' sleep this afternoon before watching a motivational video. Looked at Daws while it was on and both of us burst out laughing. Purchased popcorn from Manly cinema, beat Daws at table tennis again then went to bed.

TUESDAY
Australia 'A' 28, British and Irish Lions 25
My first start. Amazing. Best player on the tour and I only start the fourth game. Remarkable. Unfortunate too. The Lions hadn't lost a non-Test in Australia for thirty years. Build-up was shocking. I was focused, looking forward to the game, my first chance at scrum-half. But I was nervous about the forwards. Our line out wasn't going well and not all the forwards knew all the calls. Jenks was struggling and I knew I'd have to be very accurate with my passing because he wouldn't be able to reach any 60–40 balls.

Eddie Jones, the opposition coach, had gone into the Press to accuse the Lions of foul play against Queensland. Completely out of order and rejected by Donal. Come the game we were pinged 24 times.

We got absolutely blitzed for the first 20 minutes. They'd picked a huge team – their pack was massive and so were their backs. Our defence had to be awesome. Lineout was all at sea and we lost Catty.

I was knee-dropped and left with a dead bum which meant I couldn't sprint at top speed. I upper-cut one of their flankers for stamping on Will after he fell on the wrong side at a ruck. You expect a shoeing but not being kicked in the top of the head. Some guy called Justin Harrison got involved and I ran towards the touchline, inviting him to hit me in front of the touch judge. It was a stupid thing to do, the way the decisions were going.

They scored on the hour and Daws appeared on the touchline as a sub. As I was running off, he yelled 'You're playing 10, they're taking Jenks off.' We had Rog on the bench, a specialist, and I felt for him. He's a top guy and a good player and it's a shame he hasn't had many opportunities to show it. Made a conscious decision to take the ball on myself and try to win some quick possession and we started to get some pattern going with our forwards running into their backs. Mark Taylor went over for us, then Matt Perry, then Jason Robinson. Had I given a diagonal kick to Ben Cohen slightly more weight the result could have been different. But it needed another five yards and with their fly-half kicking almost everything we finished three points short.

We were gutted. We felt responsible for the whole 37, not just the 15 that were playing. Not used to losing. Leicester and England don't make a habit of it. Donal weighed in with his disapproval, saying we hadn't performed properly as a

Lions team and we were a disgrace. A few of the lads came pretty close to snapping. We'd given everything and only been beaten by different interpretations of the tackle law.

The after-match function was dire. Australians patting themselves on the back everywhere you looked.

WEDNESDAY

Woke in pain. I'm a physical wreck. My body is sore and battered and so's my ego. I need to relax, yet last night's team have to help prepare the Saturday side and I'm on the bench again. Two hours of training – another 'short' session. Dan Luger suffered a fractured eye socket in clash of heads with Backy. A huge loss to the tour and to our prospects of winning the Test series. Suggested to the Stiffs that we head into Sydney, a big group of 20 of us. We started at Doyle's restaurant in the Harbour and then went on to The Establishment, where I started buying 'Dr Peppers' for everyone: half lager, half coke and a depth charge of amaretto. I was quite tipsy by the time I decided to call it a night around 1.30am. Donal was at the hotel bar. The alcohol had freed up my inhibitions.

'Donal, this tour is crap. When are we going to have some fun? It's been rubbish so far. Nowhere near as good as the last one. We haven't had a team day out together yet.'

He looked at me quizzically.

'We want to have some fun. When you went on tour with the Lions in 1989 and captained Donal's Donuts midweek team, you got slaughtered loads of times and had a cracking laugh. I think we need to knock the training on the head a bit, relax and have a bit of a laugh and get some smiles on people's faces.'

He looked at me, said 'Goodnight', and went to bed.

THURSDAY

Had the morning off. Played golf with Mark Taylor, Lol and

Shaggy. Walking back, we bumped into the forwards coming out of the hotel for their line-out session. Andy Robinson looked at me as if to say *Where have you been?*, then said 'We're at Manly Oval'. I didn't see the wind-up and I walked all the way there to do nothing. One-nil to Robbo.

Team meal at Doyles but most boys don't eat seafood so we splintered off into cliques. No-one had a good word to say about Henry, who I now call 'Emperor Ming'.

Good bunch of fellas but a lot of lads just want to go home. Catty's replacement Scott Gibbs has arrived.

FRIDAY
Bob Dwyer has joined the chorus of Wallaby whingers after Eddie Jones accused us of foul play against Queensland. Barbed Wire says we do 'a lot of illegal things' at the breakdown. And my relationship with Ming has plumbed new depths. He doesn't talk to me any more. I'm run down, with scrum pox on my face and if my family weren't coming out I'd be with Catty, Phyllis (Greening) and Luges having the time of my life. I just want to get going on my two-year plan for the next World Cup. I'm all rugby-ed out.

SATURDAY
New South Wales 24, British and Irish Lions 41
Ronan O'Gara's battered mug will be on the back of every newspaper tomorrow. His left eye was beaten to a pulp by Duncan McRae, and he needed eight stitches to stop the bleeding and close the wound. Rog tried to clean McRae out at a ruck, perfectly legally, and McRae went berserk. Rog was pinned down and McRae punched him 11 times. Completely over the top, disgusting and showed what a coward McRae is. A few of the boys were quite keen to go and sort him out after the game. McRae has Small Man Syndrome and needs to get himself sorted out. I saw him at

the post-match do and abused him. I was amazed he had the front to show his face.

Bob Dwyer blamed Danny Grewcock for starting the trouble, claimed the Lions had thrown more punches and that McRae was retaliating to a swinging arm. I don't think the press could believe what they were hearing. NSW tried to rattle us and dominate us. There's an agenda out here to rough us up a bit and you may see the old '99' call come back. What happened tonight has galvanised us as a squad and we will all feel a lot tighter.

Match went pretty well but we're still playing too structured a game which doesn't allow us to utilise or visualise opportunities and space. Several overlaps went begging. Ball retention was shocking and while our defence was relatively strong there is room for improvement.

Pezza may have played himself back into Test contention and Jason Robinson played very well. He's a great natural talent. Dafydd James played alright and seems to be in the Test team already. Remarkable. He's a good player and a nice fella, but I've not been considered on the wing at all, not even in training, which upsets me bearing in mind I've got more caps than all the other wings left here put together. Johnno and Grewy were very physical and seem to be the driving forces in the team at the moment. Scott Quinnell played very well, as did Backy, but Lol's tour ended after he hurt his knee which is another big blow to the squad. We've now lost five players – eight is the Lions record – and we're still a week away from the first Test. Guys are trying to play injured. After the game ice, ice, ice for everyone. Donal made a very good 'backs to the wall' speech.

SUNDAY
McRae got seven weeks and the Lions were totally exonerated. Spent the morning trying to fathom how my

stamp on Kevin Putt two years ago was more serious than McRae's offence.

Flew to Coffs Harbour, another Hicksville town. Played cribbage with Daws on plane, 10p a point, ended up £1.70 down. Sat in front of management, listening. Henry ignores everyone. Robbo made good suggestions and was ignored. I gave my sandwiches to Donal and said I didn't want it to affect selection.

I'm now sharing with Backy, who is so tidy it's scary.

Balsh named at 15 in the side to play NSW Country Cockatoos to give him confidence. He doesn't need confidence, he needs someone to distribute the ball to him and a team which agrees with the gameplan. What gameplan? We only have structure. No heads-up rugby. Attack space, create space. Henry can't spell space.

MONDAY

What an unbelievable day. Ming has completely given up on the Tuesday team. This morning's training session was supposed to be our team run-through. Henry called over Dai Young, our captain, and asked him to rehearse some of the first Test lineout options against the Test team. Dai brought the Stiffs together and said, 'We'll do our stuff first, then the Australian lineouts that Graham wants.' Henry came over and told Dai to do them immediately. We then played all of Australia's options against the Test squad in full speed touch for 30 minutes – we scored two tries and, to be fair, tore them apart. Then Henry stopped the session, so we had no chance to do any of our own stuff. The team to play NSW Country tomorrow left the pitch in a state of complete disbelief, thoroughly hacked off. What is our motivation to play this game if they can't be bothered to put any effort into our preparation? What the hell is the point of the midweek team?

For Henry to do that to players' morale is a disgrace. He

has now said publicly that he has given up on the Tuesday games and is concentrating on the Tests and has destroyed the squad spirit.

At this point I don't see how we can win the Test on Saturday because of the gameplan and because the boys are out on their feet from over-training.

Aussie press have implicated me in a sledging row. They claim I moaned about being sledged in the Queensland match. Apparently, I claimed Michael Foley said, 'You Poms are useless, you shouldn't even be on this pitch with us.' Then they got Foley to slag me off for it. One major problem is I said nothing of the sort, it was Backy in his *Mirror* column. I was seething that I was being accused of starting a war or words. Decided I needed to get away and relax so played golf with Daws against OD and Rob, the cameraman and producer of the Lions' fly-on-the-wall documentary. We played an awesome course and Daws and I played some awesome golf. We had four birdies and an eagle and took $350 off them each. Great laugh with the guys and our troubles dissolved for a while. Then – a bombshell. Got a call from one of the lads telling me that Anton Toia, our ARU liaison officer, had died while swimming in the ocean outside our team hotel. I just couldn't believe it. Anton was a good fella, the lads really got on with him and he worked his arse off for us.

I feel like this tour is cursed. It's certainly going off the rails. The only positive is that Dorian has been called out which should be a breath of fresh air to the squad.

TUESDAY
NSW Country 3, British and Irish Lions 46
My backside is still very sore and it didn't help when I sat around doing nothing waiting for our meeting to start as most of the other boys were twenty minutes late. Time-

keeping on this trip has been shocking – another detail the management has neglected. Even worse, Jerry Davidson pulled away my chair and I landed smack bang on the bruised part of my bum. The pain was severe and I had a real go at him. Upshot was that I couldn't do the walk-through on the morning of the game. Instead I had treatment from the doc, and an injection to stop the pain and reduce the inflammation. First time I'd ever had a jab to play – strange, when the game meant nothing to me.

Dreadful game, too, even though I scored one of our six tries. No passion in our performance, despite tremendous support. Stadium was small, opposition were poor, home referee was diabolical and we were de-motivated by the path the tour has taken. When Steve Black stood up in the changing room beforehand and admitted the coaches had let the midweek boys down, it was impossible to disagree. He said that we didn't owe them anything but we owed it to the Lions shirt to go out and do the business. Henry stood behind Blackie and made some glib remark. He gave the impression he was immune to all criticism.

It's amazing how bored players get in small towns where there is nothing to do. Tonight we played corridor bowls with golf balls for more than an hour and a half before Hendo claimed a victory of sorts. Went back to my room to find Backy had been ruled out of the Test with pulled oblique muscles. This is his last Lions tour and he was bitterly disappointed.

WEDNESDAY
First Test squad announced today. My prospects of a start are bleak. I haven't been given an opportunity to play on the wing, Jonny's the goal kicker so I can't play 10 and Howley's playing at 9 and he was picked before we left England. Hard to stay positive.

Suspense was minimal. Majority of the boys knew they didn't have a chance of making the 22 because they hadn't been given any opportunity to stake their claim. Will Greenwood and I correctly picked the 22 last night, starting with me on the bench. Not difficult once we knew Backy was out. Cozza is in and deserves his chance. Phil Larder stood up and told us that this team was better equipped to beat Australia than England had been in November last year. I got the distinct impression that the management are nervous. Later, I asked him if he truly believed what he had said. He said he thought the squad needed a bit more confidence. I took that as a 'No'.

I was unable to train because my backside is still killing me. We left Coffs Harbour for Brisbane without me having seen any part of the place – typical of modern touring, you go to somewhere nice and see nothing but the training pitch and the hotel.

Louise is flying in and hopefully having her around will relax me. I was going to try and be more positive before Donal stood up on the bus ride from the airport into Brisbane. 'You've got the day off tomorrow lads,' he said. 'Relax, play golf, whatever you want.' Great. But then he added: 'But at 3.30 there will be a team meeting, followed by a run-through,'

The lads stormed off the bus spewing – none of us can believe our day off has been broken up. I went out with Daws, my sister Ashley and JP O'Reilly, one of my Leicester team-mates, for a couple of quiet ones to try to cool down.

THURSDAY
Astonishing. We were taken to train in the Botanical Gardens – with the Australian team hotel right across the road, so they can watch us going through our secret moves. Surely Henry knew they were staying there?

Later I went to the casino and lost money. A great day it wasn't. Bed. I can't take much more of this.

FRIDAY
The day before the first Test and I finally lost it with Henry. We were at Ballymore preparing for a three-hour training session and had just had the warm-up when we came together in a huddle, with Ming in the middle.

'Are you ready then, lads?' he said.

Everyone replied. 'Yeah, let's go.'

He then turned to me and said, 'Austin?'

'Yeah, I'm ready.'

'About f***ing time.'

It came completely out of the blue and none of the lads could believe what he'd said. So I turned on him.

'Who do you think you're talking to, you idiot?'

There was a pause. He looked at me and I looked at him. Then he spoke.

'Right then, let's go.'

He is the coach, he's not my schoolteacher or my dad. Some of the players and coaches later told me to stay cool but I reached the point two weeks ago where it wouldn't bother me if I was sent off tour. I left training totally disillusioned and convinced Henry has got it in for me. Louise came round to the team hotel and I told her what Henry had said in training. She told me to keep my mouth shut and to get on with it.

The Captain's Meeting was scheduled for 6.15pm and, frankly, I wasn't in the mood. But Johnno spoke well, he's a real leader, and we watched a good motivational video with some stirring action highlights and that lifted me. In an instant, the tour started to almost feel important again and I found myself almost looking forward to the game and almost desperate to play.

Returned to my room to be greeted by a note from Blackie asking each of us to write a 'positive motivational message' to each of the other players in the Test match 22. 'A short statement will suffice, it can be about anything you want,' he wrote. 'Just let your colleagues know how much they are valued and respected.' I screwed it up and threw it at Daws, my Brisbane roomy, and then we chatted about his Tour Diary which is being published in *The Daily Telegraph* tomorrow. He read it to me and I have to say I thought there were a few risky comments about the management, given that it was coming out on the day of the first Test. But he only said what a lot of people are thinking.

SATURDAY
Australia 13, British and Irish Lions 29
It needed to be something special to get me excited about being a 2001 Lion and Willie John McBride provided it with his pre-match speech, that and seeing thousands upon thousands of Lions fans at the Gabba today. Everyone in the ground seemed to be wearing a red jersey. It was awesome. Maybe I've been wrong to have such a downer on this tour? A brilliant performance by the lads, against all the odds, and look at the passion of the fans who've travelled so far to support us. I stand by every criticism I have made of Henry, his coaching philosophy and his management style, but the reaction of even my friends back home, who are totally excited by what's going on, has shown me how big a deal this is for people.

Was pessimistic about our chances because of the structure we'd been coached to play but the lads completely ignored the gameplan for the first 25 minutes of each half. They got the ball wide to Jason Robinson and Dafydd James and we saw some exhilarating play from 15 obviously very talented players. It was great to watch.

I sat in the stand for the first ten minutes to try and get more of a bird's eye view of the game and see where the space was on the field. I was minding my own business when some jobsworth steward came up to me and said I couldn't sit on the steps. I told him I wouldn't leave until he got the police, so he went off to find them. I left rather than cause a scene. As I got to the bottom and jumped over the barrier an Australian said, 'You're scared, Healey'. We were already 5–0 up, Robbo scoring a fabulous try with his first touch. When it got to 29–3 – Daf, Brian O'Driscoll and Scotty Quinnell having followed him over – I went back to the barrier to have a little stretch and to look up that loud-mouthed Aussie. 'Who's scared now?' I asked. 'You ought to be scared we don't get 50, mate.' The Lions fans around him liked that.

Hardly anyone had a bad game and my only regret was not getting on to share in the win – I thought they could have done with some fresh legs.

Being 1–0 up, after all the propaganda in the Press about how dirty we are, how we cheat, even how we play boring rugby, it was sweet to silence all the bleating. I feel a bit weird towards the tour now. Have I been wrong about Henry all this time? Has my depression coloured my judgement? All I've done so far is slag him off. He has behaved like a bit of a d**k at times but maybe his planning has worked. Wait a minute, the Aussies were woeful. I don't think this is over yet.

Most of the boys went out but I arranged to have a quiet drink with Johnno. Went up to my room to get changed and Daws was in there with his agent. All hell had broken loose about his diary in *The Telegraph*. I thought it best to give them a bit of space so I had a couple with Johnno then went to Lou's hotel and stayed there for a quiet night. It had been one hell of a day.

SUNDAY
We'd beaten the world champions in their own backyard yet we spent the morning in recrimination mode over Daws' diary. Donal was spewing and Daws was made to apologise to the squad. We sat in a semi-circle with Matt in the middle and he stood there and said he was not apologising for what he had written but for its timing. He had his serious face on and I desperately tried to keep a straight face. I couldn't see what need there was for him to apologise. Everyone thought he was right and none of the players had a problem with what he'd said. The diary had appeared under the headline 'Harsh regime tears us apart'. Not too much exaggeration there. He spoke of 'mindless coaching', of players being 'flogged' and 'treated like children'. All true.

When he sat down Donal said 'Right, has anyone got anything to say?' Everyone went quiet but I put my hand up. 'Yes Austin?'

'Does that mean the public stoning is cancelled for tomorrow?' I asked. 'Because I've already bought a bag of gravel and two flat rocks.'

We flew to Canberra, an unreal place, a huge city with no-one in it, like everyone has been locked in their cellars. Shame it's not like that in every Australian town. Backy and I rooming together again. Two guys with one goal. To get in the Test team this coming Saturday. Coaches are now making a big deal of our match against the ACT Brumbies on Tuesday. Confidence is high for the second Test and I think I've been picked on the wing which means I'll finally get the chance to play in my main international position and start a Lions Test. But first The Brumbies. They're the Super 12 champions and Tuesday's game is the one the midweek side has been waiting for all tour. Balsh, Ben and I are playing together for the first time and I'm really looking forward to the game, a chance to show I should be in the Test team. I'll be as close to full fitness as I can be, considering it will be the 50th time this season I've been in a match day 22.

MONDAY

Woke up full of determination and the team run went well for me. I even kicked quite well. We're up for this game. The team meeting was good and Dai spoke well. We all want a bit of glory for ourselves. Call it selfishness but we want some of the praise the Test team got – a team a number of us believe we should be in. We want to make a statement to that effect.

I spent the evening gambling against local card sharks at the poker table. Some fella tried to abuse me. 'We do it to put you off your game,' he said. Oh well, if those are the house rules... I called him a few choice names, he was duly put off and I won the next few hands. Thanks for the tip, mate. Then to really annoy him I left the table. He wanted me to carry on playing so he could win his money back but I grinned and waved goodbye.

TUESDAY

ACT Brumbies 28, British and Irish Lions 30

Had a bad night's kip so I got up early and went on the nebuliser. Spent the rest of the day chilling out, hydrating and gambling in the casino, losing more and more money. The England boys believe that the more money you lose before a game the better you play. Maybe this was a good omen.

The team's preparation was OK but not great – we hadn't had seven days to prepare like the Test squad gets. But the lineout was better with the arrival of Dorian West, who is obsessed with lineouts. Wonder how his wife Claire feels? They'd literally only been in Spain for ten minutes on their annual holiday; they were still at the airport when Nobby informed her that he was turning round and flying to Australia.

Game was full of niggle especially from Justin Harrison, my mate from the Australia A game. He was constantly patting our players on the head if they lost the ball in the tackle or gave away a penalty. We started doing it to him and he couldn't take it, snapped and started to throw punches.

We made a shocking start, missing God knows how many first-up tackles and conceding three inside the first 25 minutes to go 19–3 down. The second was a complete joke – their winger was a good six inches in touch, the touch judge must have seen it and he completely ignored it. Symptomatic of the problems we have had with officials. Surely there are enough of them in the world to have neutrals?

I intercepted a pass from Pat Howard [then playing for ACT after leaving Leicester at the end of the previous season] just before half-time, anticipating where he was going to throw it, going flat and managing to get an outstretched hand to it so I could trot it in from 50 metres out. I turned round on the way, thinking the ref had blown up for offside which wouldn't have come as any great surprise on this tour, and I saw Paddy, pointed to him and grinned a thank you. That idiot Harrison ran 50 yards to bump into me with his chest. What a waste of energy, what a complete fool. 'That's only one try, you prick,' he said. 'You're still losing.'

We went in trailing 22–10 and got a bollocking from Henry, who said we'd no pride in the shirt. There was silence. It was like being back at school, and a pretty poor way to be spoken to. We didn't go down on purpose. So I got up and started shouting, trying to get the rest of the lads up on their feet and motivated to go back out.

We knew we had re-start with a bang and that's exactly

what we did. They kicked off, we won the ball and took it up the field for David Wallace to go over. Daws converted and added a penalty and the deficit was down to two points. There was then a bit of scrapping with their openside, who had a quality Afro on him. Nugget caught him with a good punch after he'd thrown a few. Then Balsh high-tackled their fullback and Harrison went after him. He seems to pick on the small guys but never has a go at the big guys. He wants to pick on someone his own size. Anyway, Balsh was sin-binned and ACT pulled five points clear again.

They still led by that margin when the hooter went after eight minutes of stoppage time but the ball has to go dead before the game ends and I never doubted that we would score. When the ball came out to me from Balsh no-one was going to stop me. I sidestepped inside a couple of defenders and went over. As I got the ball down, I was knee-dropped and given a dead leg. Predictably Harrison was in my face, again bumping into me with his chest – goodness, what a chest he's got – and hurling his scrumcap at me. It was my turn to give him a mouthful: 'That's two tries mate . . . and you've lost.' Luckily, Daws kicked the extras, and everyone went mad. It was a great feeling, a great way to win a game, especially against so many guys who'd beaten us playing for Australia 'A'. It was good to get one over on Pat Howard, too. Pat was a decent club player but at Test level he lacked a yard or two of speed.

WEDNESDAY
Woke at 5.30am unable to sleep because my leg was too sore from the knee drop. Hobbled into physio for icing and oxygen and a go with the nebuliser. Picked up a copy of The Australian newspaper and saw a photo of a glowering Henry beneath the headline, 'Lions remain divided: Healey'. In fact, my *Observer* column hadn't said any such thing. I'd just

said we were happy we'd won on Saturday and that the midweek boys would have to grin and bear it. The Aussie Press just took this out of context. Big surprise.

My leg was worrying me. Johnno and Henry both emphasised I must do everything to make myself available for the second Test. It sounded like I was maybe going to start the game, but I felt time was against me. Two ice baths, a compression bandage on the flight to Melbourne, and another ice bath when we arrived. Sang 'One man went to mow' to keep myself in as long as possible and managed nine and a half minutes.

THURSDAY

Woke early for another icy plunge and managed ten minutes. Nobby couldn't stop laughing but I got him in a good stranglehold, one that he couldn't break. He's got a broken finger, I've got a dead leg so we're basically playing off the same handicap.

Henry tried to delay his team announcement until tomorrow evening to give me the maximum chance to be fit, but he was told that there was a 48-hour rule. So he named a 22 with me on the bench, and privately led me to believe that I would play on the right wing if I could run. Went with some of the lads to visit the studios of *Neighbours* and arrived just as Harold and Lou were shooting a scene. Bumped into Flick, the only remotely fit girl in the show. A very nice, normal person and I had a photo taken with her. Well, it's not every day she gets to meet an international rugby star. A couple of Press lads were with us. One of them suggested I give Flick a kiss for the cameras. 'Don't be stupid,' I said. 'I'm married to a very hormonal, pregnant woman. How would she feel seeing me kiss one of *FHM* Magazine's top ten beauties on *Channel* 9 tonight? Anyway, I'd be tempted to stick my tongue in.'

A few more of the cast came out. I didn't really recognise any of them which is a sign of the times. Ten years ago I probably could have named them all.

FRIDAY

The Test is tomorrow and it's looking bleak for me though I've not given up hope. I couldn't cross the road let alone jog. The dead leg has been so bad that I've had to admit to some of the lads I'm not positive about playing. Shaggy has started to call me Lazarus. Went to training today but could do nothing. Colonial Stadium is cool, with a retractable roof, and the atmosphere tomorrow night will be awesome. But I fear I'll be a spectator and I came back feeling mega depressed. Went to the casino with Daws to try to lift my spirits but we couldn't relax; too many supporters telling us to get to bed. Moved to a quieter part of the casino and won heavily on pontoon. Bad sign. Winning at cards, losing at rugby.

SATURDAY
Australia 35, British and Irish Lions 14

Woke at 7.30am and lasted 11 minutes in the ice bath. Met the doc at breakfast and went outside to a local park. My leg was still numb and I managed to jog without pain. For a couple of seconds I thought my prayers had been answered. But when I tried to accelerate I couldn't even get out of first gear. No option but to pull me out of the match and draft Jenks in on the bench. Totally gutted, I limped back to the hotel and refilled my wallet in the casino. By the way, I don't have a gambling problem. I only do it on trips like this to relieve the tedium and I always set myself a leaving time whether I'm up or down.

Changed into a tie and blazer for the bus ride to the stadium. Unbelievable atmosphere – 57,000 fans in, and the place was bouncing, so noisy I couldn't hear myself think. More Aussies there than at Brisbane, and the ARU had spent thousands kitting them out in gold shirts and scarves to try and make it look as though it wasn't another home game for us. The Lions fans chanted 'Freebies' at the Wallaby supporters, which I thought was quality.

For virtually the whole of the first half, it seemed the lads had picked up from where they left off. Daf broke up the middle and narrowly failed to get the scoring pass out to Robbo. Scott time and again punched holes in their midfield defence and Woody, Johnno and Hilly all got to stretch their legs. When Backy went over for a try to put us 11-3 ahead I thought the series was over. But then it all started to go wrong. Hilly was caught in the face by Nathan Grey's elbow and left concussed. Then a minute after half-time Jonny threw a pass which Joe Roff intercepted and ran back. Matt Burke's kick tied up the scores. Had we finished off a couple more chances, had Roff not been so alert, things would have been different, I'm sure. Without that try they had nothing. They weren't going anywhere. As it was they saw a way out and took it. Roff and Burke added further tries and we were beaten. But by fatigue more than anything. Chances went begging that we would have finished a week earlier. The regime we'd worked under caught up with us at the crucial time. There was nothing left.

There were bodies lying all over the changing room afterwards and all the physio beds were full. Hilly was out of the tour, so too Rob Howley with bust ribs and Jonny's leg looked really bad. He had been stretchered off and I thought it was broken. But the mood remained defiant. We have not blown the series. There's still next week.

SUNDAY

I'm motivated now. I feel needed and am sure I'll be in the Test team on Saturday. My chin is up. I no longer feel I'm just making up the numbers, wasting precious holiday time before the new season comes around.

We now have 16 players on the injured list. Last night's game took a serious toll. The mood is quiet and subdued. The boys are truly exhausted. No word on Jonny as we flew to Sydney on the final leg, only that he would not be travelling with us. The doc decided it would be best for him, Jonny, Hilly and Rob to travel independently. What effect that will have on team selection is anyone's guess but it certainly means that their understudies will have to take the lead this week. Daws, Cozza and maybe me.

I feel I'm going to be in the team. Whether instead of Jonny or in place of Dafydd, I don't know. Perhaps even at scrum-half if they decide not to go with Daws. You never know with Henry. A lot of players came up to me after the game and wished me luck. One said, 'The script has been written for you to come in and save us.' I think he was taking the mickey.

Returned to my room after breakfast. Louise was still in bed. Dorian gave me a bit of chat about how he and Lou were 'busy' and could I come back in 20 minutes? I told him he was a fat, ginger waster, then got on top of him and put him in a choker hold. He knows he's my bitch. Lou asked me not to hurt him, but she was too late. When he regained consciousness he apologised and I told him to get us all a coffee and get my bags down to the concierge by 11am. He blew it by putting half a teaspoon of sugar too much in my coffee. I'll get the gimp mask out for him.

Lou and I went for a spot of lunch only to run into more abuse, this time from a Lions fan, or rather some idiot masquerading as one in a Lions jersey. He yelled 'loser' at me, which I thought strange. For one thing I hadn't played, for another if he thinks like that perhaps he shouldn't have come to Australia. And for another, could he do any better for Britain and Ireland? It was pouring with rain as we left the restaurant and I said goodbye to Lou. Things will look better at brekkie on the beachfront in Manly.

Had my second bust-up of the day on the bus to the airport – with Keith Wood. He was annoying me and hitting me on the head and I bit my lip and made it bleed. So I picked up newspaper, opened it and pretended to show a particular article to Jason Leonard, who was sat in front of Woody. As I passed it to him, I punched my fist through the paper into Woody's face. He chased me down the bus but before he could lay a hand on me Ronan started chanting 'Can't take it' at him, everyone joined in and he ended up walking back to his seat without touching me.

Good to be back in Manly after a fortnight away from the coast. All pretty positive now, no doubt we'll win. Blackie made an early start by posting a sheet under our doors entitled 'Why we will win', with a subheading of 'Believe it . . . No doubts'. He listed three 'facts'.

(1) We are better than Australia – when we are both fresh and at our best.

(2) We are stronger, more powerful, faster and have better game breakers than Australia – when we are both fresh and at our best.

(3) We are better defenders than Australia – when we are both fresh and at our best.

There was a lot of other stuff, all of which boiled down to us just needing to find the mental strength to win. It made a lot of sense.

MONDAY

Breakfast, and several dozen surfers were out catching the early morning waves. We had the day off so a few of the lads decided to give it a go. My leg was still too sore for such physical exertion so I watched from the hotel. They clearly found it a struggle getting out to the big waves, though Darren Morris looked like he was used to being in the water. Jonny's leg is nowhere near as bad as first thought. Never mind, I'll just have to try and get into another position!

Spent the rest of the day with the medics. I also had a massage from Richard Wegrzyk, whose career has taken him from the Vatican, where he was once an altar boy, to masseur for England and the Lions. He put suction glasses on my leg to help get the bruising out. The pain was considerable and I repaid him with a sly dig on the way out. He's a top boy, Rich.

First squad meal out together at a restaurant called Ribs and Rump. That's right – our first . . . with five days of the tour left. It's good to get a chance to start bonding like this! Awesome food and we put away loads of it. Daws spilt a full glass of water on me but left with a spare rib sticking out of each of his huge ears. There was a vicious lot of banter. Everyone got it in the neck, and I mean everyone. The best line of the night went as follows:

Phil does defence, Dave likes to punt.
But what have we learned off that Kiwi, er, runt?

Returned to camp via the arcade, where Shaggy, Daws, Balsh, Charvis and I battled it out on the Daytona 2000 driving game. I bought some chips on the walk back along the oceanfront purely to throw at Rog and Brian O'Driscoll so that they would be bombarded by hundreds of hungry seagulls. It was hilarious. Hitchcock would have approved.

TUESDAY

Confirmation that I will play on the right wing on Saturday. Well, that only took six weeks! My leg was still sore from the knee drop on me in Canberra and I couldn't finish our training session because it cramped up. Worried that one knock on my quad could finish my tour. Also worried about the amount of people with video cameras watching our workout. Had to use a public pitch and there must have been 250 people watching, many wearing hats with corks dangling from the brim. Maybe, just maybe, we should have had this session behind closed doors. Henry made us rehearse all our lineout moves and back plays in full view.

I'm delighted to be in the Test team but still feel our preparation could be better, more precise. The standards set by Henry off the pitch have been poor, with no attention to detail. He has been consistently late for meetings, he's busy writing his own tour diary and more than once he's shown signs of strain.

Got back to the hotel for lunch and couldn't help but notice that the surf was huge. A load of us decided to give it a go. You have to respect the guys who surf those monster waves. Saw the Sky boys, Mark Durden-Smith and Myles Harrison, carrying boards. It must be a real drag working for Sky, what with the surfing, the shopping and the sightseeing during the day, rounded off with a nice bottle of something vintage at night. Took the mickey out of Durders for a bit, then he started to get feisty and said he wanted to wrestle. Three seconds later I was on top of him, pressing his face into the sand whilst talking to Johnno. Stick to presenting, Durders, or get on a serious weights programme.

Dinner was with the usual group – Daws, Balsh, Hendo, Rog and Ben Cohen – and was again out in town, as we are all disillusioned with the food. It has been terrible most of the tour – another failure of attention to detail which the management should have picked up on.

WEDNESDAY

Just when I thought my luck had changed for the better I pulled a muscle in my back during training. A night of incessant rain had forced us to drive for an hour to find a pitch that wasn't waterlogged. Wish we hadn't bothered now. Mind you, it doesn't feel like anything more than a stitch and it should be fine. As long as my leg doesn't regress I'll be there in the Olympic Stadium to start my first ever Test match as a Lion.

Headed into Sydney on the Manly Jetcat to pass on tickets to my family for the game. We get two complimentaries and can buy a further six. It's amazing that a player has to buy at least one ticket if his mum, dad and wife all want to come to the game, yet loads of the blazers get free tickets. Come the next big game, maybe I'll sit on the pitch and watch them tackle a bag of sweets. Walked around the shops for a bit but my mind was spinning with thoughts about Saturday's game so I caught the Cat back to Manly, arriving at the hotel to find 500 shirts set out on tables waiting to be signed, 200 of which were for the Australian Rugby Union. I asked the liaison guy specifically who they were for and he said an injured players' fund. No problems then, other than the timing of it all. Three days before a major international we shouldn't have these distractions. It should have been done on Monday. I personally think the commercial access to the players on this trip has been too great and has detracted from the rugby.

THURSDAY

Disaster. That slight pull from yesterday wasn't slight and it wasn't stitch. I think my back has really gone. We went to the Olympic Stadium today, a place I hoped would forever have a place in my heart after Saturday's game. I stood there thinking about all the sporting legends that had performed there in the 2000 Games, like Maurice Greene, Haile Gebresalassie, Jan Zelezney and Cathy Freeman and I conjured a vision of adding my name to the roll of honour with the series-winning try for the Lions. I thought about how far our supporters had come and I told myself that no matter how hard and how unhappy the tour had been, we could win on Saturday.

I was really motivated and looking forward to the game. I did some mental rehearsal on my own. Running: quickly, balanced, elusive. Passing: accurate, dummying, off-loading. Tackling: hit Joe Roff low, squeeze, drive. Trigger words, key thoughts. But most of all I was picturing the game, looking for space, feeling the space, attacking with the space. What I didn't foresee was my dream evaporating.

Training started and I was bubbling around, trying to get involved in everything. Hendo told me to get back on my wing. I'd never played outside him before so I forgave his cheek. My back seemed OK, a bit stiff but I thought it would run off.

Henry's plan is for us to kick possession inside our own 40 deep into their half, using my right foot and Jonny's left boot. We'll need complete dominance in the set piece but I know we have the players to achieve that.

The session went well, except that the pain in my back wasn't going and, with one of my last kicks, I felt it wrench a bit. I stopped, iced it and thought no more of it. But by the time we stopped at a roadside restaurant for lunch on the way back, it was completely knackered. I was suffering one spasm after another. I hoped and prayed it was just a pulled muscle and after treatment at the hotel it did feel slightly better and I felt a lot more positive again.

I walked out of the team room into a barrage of waiting journalists. I said how proud I was to be picked, how I would do my best and how I would dearly love to beat the Aussies in their own backyard. I was asked how I felt physically. I said that my tongue was OK so I'd try and talk Joe Roff to the floor. All meant in jest. Then I got dragged away by our media guy Alex Broun, who told me that Donal and Henry didn't want me talking to the Press. How stupid can you get?

I told the Press lads I had nothing else to say and found Eddie Butler to do my *Guardian* column. We disappeared into a quiet corner, and did our normal thing. He still doesn't take any notes, just gets a feel for what I'm thinking. I told him how keen I was that we won the game because of all the anti-Lions propaganda, all the abuse I'd been subjected to, and because I would have the last laugh on that 'plank' Justin Harrison – not that he had any involvement in Saturday's game at that stage.

FRIDAY

Friday the 13th. Every waking hour I spent in pain. I slept on a hot vibration massage pad and when I woke up it felt like someone had Superglued my shoulder blades half way up my back and my muscles were fighting to separate them. I called the doc and, after extensive treatment, stayed in bed until 2.30pm, when I went for a massage. Unbeknown to me my *Guardian* column was stirring up a hornet's nest back home. Harrison had also been drafted into the Wallaby side after David Giffin did his hamstring.

I was getting desperate now and had acupuncture, despite my fear of needles. I'd have tried anything, and I did feel slightly better afterwards. Decided to go out and get some fresh air, crossed the road outside the hotel and walked down to the beach wall, stopping a few times for photos and autographs. Then . . . BANG! I was hit by a massive spasm.

I collapsed to my knees in severe pain and broke into a cold sweat. A passer-by helped me to my feet and I turned back towards the hotel, walking like an ironing board on legs, desperate for painkillers. I just reached the entrance when another supporter asked for an autograph. I said to her, 'Sorry, I'm absolutely desperate to get some medical attention. If I'm better later I'll come out and do it,' and kept walking. Some guy who'd seen me refuse her shouted, 'Healey, you w*****!'

In excruciating pain, angry that I probably wouldn't be able to realise my goal of starting a Lion's Test match, I turned and barked back, 'Shut the f*** up.'

By far my lowest point of the tour so far – having hated being here, then hearing Willie John and feeling a sense of urgency to come back on board and get in the team, then getting picked, then getting injured and now being insulted whilst fighting unbelievable discomfort to get to some pain killers . . . had I been physically able, I would have snapped and something bad would have happened to that guy.

The doc dosed me up with painkillers and gave me treatment for four hours, with me unable to move. I need a miracle now to make the game. Managed to get to the captain's meeting where Johnno simply told us all to come prepared. 'Make sure you're as ready as you've ever been,' he said. Chance would be a fine thing.

Took a last gobful of abuse, this time from the taxi driver taking me to the cinema to pick up my lucky popcorn. Hoping against hope. My crime was to be English. Even if I don't play tomorrow I desperately want the lads to win.

Finally called it quits late on when I failed a fitness test and a scan showed I had a bulging disc. I was trying to come to terms with that when I saw the newspaper billboard. 'Rogue Lion - Up Yours Aussies'. I'd never regarded myself as a 'rogue Lion', but alarm bells started ringing. Asked the driver if he had a copy of *The Australian*, my favourite paper, and he passed it back. The headline read, 'Healey finishes tour in low gear' and it started quoting me. 'Up yours' I was supposed to have said to the inhabitants of the 'Back-end of the world'. My lanky, ugly old mate Justin Harrison was an 'ape'. I hadn't said anything like that to anyone. I was furious.

Back at the hotel, I walked through reception and found Alex, the media guy. 'What the hell is this?' I said. 'Once again I've been misquoted.' Alex said nothing. I felt a cold sweat come over me. 'Oh no . . . Eddie.' I turned and headed across to the internet room and called up my *Guardian* column. Oh my God! I couldn't believe what Eddie had written. He'd really given it both barrels this time and with the worst timing possible.

It's worth reprinting the column.

The Guardian, Friday July 13
"They call me one of the trouble-makers. Matt Dawson and me, the lip machines. Matt says this, I say that; what's going on? Anything we say comes back to this back-end of the world with a whole lot of spin. Well, spin this, you Aussies: up yours. Is that enough to get into the Sydney Morning Sun Telegraph Herald Load of Shite? If ever I wanted to do something, it was beat you lot. There, that's better. Now calm down, Ozzer. Two weeks ago I sat on a table reserved for the replacements and watched the press go by. It was a bit different yesterday. There must have been 20 journalists around me. What were they on about? Would I swap my Leicester European Cup medal for this? Was this better than England at Twickenham for the Grand Slam? How would I know? Is that part of the deal, anyway? I answered the questions as best I could. But, to be honest, what do I really know? This is the big unknown, the great rugby mystery.

Blah, blah, blah. And then I saw there were a couple of Aussie journalists hovering, writing down, Blah, blah, blah. No comment, I said. Spin that, babes. No comment. To be honestly honest – and, look, I've given you everything bar the mutiny scoop – I said it was just great to be here in the team at last. It is. But I can't help feeling for Dafydd James. He's out and I'm in. It's not as if he's done anything wrong, really. You know this hasn't been a bundle of laughs, this tour. Just imagine what it must be like if you get to the final match and find yourself dropped. Still, I think I might have been in with a shout of a place for the second Test. But then I was injured in the ACT game. Something else I have to thank my mate Justin Harrison for. I thought it was that flanker Peter Ryan who clouted me, but, no, there it is on video, my old pal, the plod from the second row. And what do you know, he's in the team to face us. Me and the plank. Do you think one of us will have the final say? I'll say so. The leg's fine now. I've been trying to relax this week. A few of us got some belly-boards and went out surfing. The weather's been lousy here in Sydney, so the surf was really big. I went out among the big waves and got thrown all over the shop. Thank you very much, I said, and went straight back to dry land. I'll take on the ape Harrison but not Mother Nature. Did I say the weather has been crap? Just another Australian thing to get up your nose. What is it with this country? The females and children are fine, and seem to be perfectly normal human beings, but what are we going to do with this thing called the Aussie male? Look, it got so bad I found myself agreeing with Graham Henry the other day. He said he didn't mind them being the best in the world at this or that, but why did they have to rub our faces in it the whole time? It doesn't half make you want to beat them. I tell you, I don't even know where Croatia is exactly, but did I cheer for old Goran Ivanwhatsit in the Wimbledon final, or what?

Come on, you Balkans. And then the Aussies built Pat Rafter into this super-hero loser. What is this place like? I'm trying to concentrate on the game now. But there may still be a twist or two. I'm down to play wing, so I'm thinking wing play, wing play . . . and marking Joe Roff. The journos asked me if it meant anything that he'd been round me a couple of times in the past. I said the only thing that isn't completely knackered at the end of this tour is my tongue, so maybe I can talk him to a standstill. 'Come back, Joe, I haven't finished with you yet . . .' No, of course, it means something. It means I'm going to have to play out of my skin to stop another Aussie bloke rubbing my nose in it. I can't wait. But, then, if Jonny Wilkinson hadn't been fit, I'd have had to go to fly-half. So I might have had to think fly-half, fly-half. And knowing Matt Dawson, he'll probably have had to go and write a special final Test supplement to his diary and get sent home, and I'd end up at scrum-half. That's where I was chosen in the first place. Funny, isn't it? Here I am on the wing. Maybe it's my turn to say something and be sent home. Like, here's to stuffing it up your so-called macho jacksie. What? I'm out of here."

I found Eddie and told him what he'd written seemed a bit close to the bone. 'It's all meant to be tongue-in-cheek,' he said. I thought 'foot in mouth' would have been better. They were my words but they hadn't come out of my mouth. And whatever the mitigating circumstances, it was my name on it, my picture above it, my responsibility.

The repercussions weren't as serious as Matt Dawson's diary, because my criticisms were directed outside the squad, but it was still bad. However, because I was still in pain I couldn't dwell on it. I headed off to get some valium, hoping none of the lads had read it. They hadn't, but Emperor Ming had. Apparently he was in a pretty chipper mood when he bumped into a couple of journos and asked if there was anything in the Aussie papers. Two minutes later he went off like a bag of fireworks and wanted to kill me.

Did I feel I'd let the lads down with that column? No, the game had enough psychological edge to it as it was. Our forwards and our team were so psyched up that it didn't matter what was said in the papers. Bombs could have been going off outside the stadium and the team would still have been completely focused on their jobs. I'm sure it was the same for the Aussies.

I saw the lads before they left and they looked fantastic. I was convinced we would win but now I could only watch and hope. I made a point of going up to Dafydd and wishing him luck.

The stadium and the highly charged atmosphere was everything I thought it would be and more. They obviously had a few fireworks left from the Olympics and put on a fantastic show but my thoughts were down in the changing rooms with the lads. Johnno had spoken really well on the eve of the battle and I was sure his words would have a big bearing on how things went. It was only a short talk but he struck just the right chord, as Willie John had in Brisbane. The lads were ready, I was sure of that. They were unbelievably motivated. No external factors counted any more.

oOoOo

The Decider – Australia 29, British and Irish Lions 23
First thing I saw was Justin Harrison in his horrible orange scrumcap, which made me angry since he was playing and I wasn't.

We led twice and moments after Jonny went over the Wallabies line to add to Jason Robinson's early try, three minutes into the second half, I thought we'd got it in the bag. We led 20-16 and they opted for a lineout when awarded a penalty inside our 22. They wanted to make a statement that they could deal with our pack. Only they couldn't. They tried to roll a maul over our line and we stopped them in their tracks. There was a massive cheer from the Lions fans at either end of the stadium.

Then it all began to go wrong. Daniel Herbert went over for his second try and our lineout ball dried up. That was bad enough, but what made it worse for me was that Harrison was becoming increasingly influential. Jonny levelled the scores again at 23–23 from the penalty spot after Herbert had been sin-binned for a high tackle on Brian, but he then missed a chance to put us back in the lead and Matt Burke made us pay with two late goals. The final indignity was when Harrison nicked a lineout ball off Johnno at the front on our own put-in. The whistle went and it was over. Seven weeks of effort and we'd fallen just short.

The disappointment was overwhelming for the lads but I'd been on valium all day so was pretty much out of it by then. As the valium started to wear off, I started on the beer – three litres of that and the pain was under control again. I was wandering around the emptying stadium when Harrison came in to our changing room and asked for Johnno's shirt. Johnno apologised and explained that he'd already agreed with John Eales that he'd swap with him, but he said he was sure that Grewy would swap. Harrison continued, telling Johnno he was a legend, it was his first game for Australia and would he please do him the honour. Johnno again explained that he couldn't because he'd promised Ealesy. Then somebody yelled, 'Look, just get lost.'

The post-match function was my idea of hell. Australians patting themselves on the back whichever way you turned. They are very good winners aren't they? (Call me a bad loser if you like. I am.) So I headed for the team bus on which a number of players' parents, wives and girlfriends were already sitting. I sat near the back with Louise and her identical twin sister. Hang on a minute, she hasn't got an identical twin sister. It must have been the cocktail of beer, a bottle of wine I'd also had and the valium.

We headed into Sydney and I escorted Lou back to her hotel before going into town with the lads to drown our sorrows in The Establishment. I was well away on Dr Peppers and champagne when I decided to turn my tour blazer inside out. Daws and Cozza then ripped off a sleeve each to create a rather trendy tank top. The action moved to another bar called Jacksons, where I started arm wrestling for Sambuca. Some big Aussie came over and challenged me. Daws said I'd do it for a $500 bet (Daws was on 50% commission). He agreed and I put him in a body bag in less than a second. He paid up and walked off, by which time I was too far gone to speak. Luckily I had written the name of Lou's hotel on my hand, because I couldn't even remember my name. Eventually I found her at 6.30am, just in time to change out of my tank top and leave with her for the airport to meet Johnno and his wife Kay. The four of us were off to Hawaii for a holiday.

We had an agreement that we wouldn't talk about rugby while we were there. Neither of us wanted to. We were going there to relax, not to reflect. Dodging the newspapers piled up in the departure lounge, we boarded the plane and I slept all the way to paradise.

There are many beautiful things about Hawaii, and not the least of them is that my mobile phone couldn't pick up a signal there. So while my character was being assassinated in the Press at home and in Australia, I lay in blissful ignorance on a beach under a palm tree. It was hard to settle down and relax straight away because I was dogged by worry and doubt . . . should I have gone straight to Factor 30, or was Factor 15 the right way forward?

We'd left behind a horrible Australian press reaction.

'Healey the real monkey,' screamed the *Australian Sunday Telegraph*.

'Hey Austin, shut up and slink home,' said *The Sun-Herald*, adding, 'Don't come back. Ever.'

There was more, but I won't bore you with it. I was – and still am – sick and tired of one nation being allowed to say what they think and the other just having to take it. Almost since the day we arrived, they said whatever they wanted about us. We were cheats, we played dirty and we had asked for the 11-punch assault on Ronan. They didn't mention the honey traps, the sly knee-drops, the sledging on the field and the insults off it. Whenever we went out and tried to relax we were subjected to some barb from a complete stranger. We couldn't walk down the street without someone leaning out of his car window and shouting 'You're going to get your heads kicked in tomorrow night.' We couldn't have a normal night just relaxing and switching off from rugby. Yet when we had a go back, you'd have thought we'd broken into their houses, raped their wives and stolen their silver. It's a two-way street, lads. You can't give somebody stick and then complain when you get a bit back.

Anyway, all I did was tell things as they were. I guess you have to admire their press for the way they support their teams; as soon as we lost the knives came out straight away, and most went into my back. There are some people you can rely upon in the British Press and there are others who are just there to sensationalise everything.

This was a tour like none I'd experienced, though on reflection I'm still glad I went on it. There were low moments and we all worked our arses off, but we'd still have preferred to be there than watching it on the TV back at home.

I should have had two Tests starts, but my body let me down – and by the time the 2005 trip to New Zealand came around, it had gone completely.

I made the long list and received my Bangle – Clive sent out about 90 of these things to people with a chance of touring. I was surprised to get one, to be honest, because I wasn't playing for England at the time. All the guys turned up to Lions training with their bangles on, but I'd thought I wouldn't bother. Then we had two days off and I wore it when we reconvened. Of course, the lads started saying I must have phoned Woody up and begged for one, and a letter of invitation. But as we got closer to the tour, I was actually playing quite well and I started thinking Clive might take me, for banter reasons as much as anything. Of course, he didn't and he took some other crap players instead.

The Guardian and *The Observer* hit on a good idea – they'd take me down there as a journalist. The idea was, I'd go to the press conferences and interview Clive and Graham Henry and generally make a nuisance of myself, but they wouldn't authorise my press pass so that got knocked on the head.

So it was back to Eddie Butler and a new load of columns, which were very enjoyable – though, don't tell anyone, I actually wrote them from my holiday in Spain, not New Zealand. I think my favourite line was, '*Have you heard the latest from the lions camp? Clive's sending Andy Robinson to a fancy dress party tonight. He's going as a pumpkin, they're hoping when it gets to midnight he'll turn into a real coach!*'

Not sure how that would have gone down with Robbo. Sense of humour failure time, I'd think.

I was sad the way the tour went, obviously. Mostly I was sad for Clive – he didn't deserve to see his rugby career come to a close (for the time being) like that. I think he became a victim of his own success. For me, Clive was at his best when he coached England almost as a supporter. In his early days with us, he'd be the first man to jump out of his seat when we scored a try, he'd be punching the air and cheering and shouting; as players, we'd see that and think, *'That's fantastic, this guy is really behind the team . . . he's inspired by us.'* That inspired us in return. By the time the Lions came round, he had a knighthood, he had all the baggage of the 2003 World Cup win and it just didn't look the same, to me. I remember seeing him on the telly at some Lions thing, and he was sat at the back of the room looking a bit distant and I just felt a bit for him.

He made mistakes, as we all do, and he'd be the first to admit to them. Take the Alistair Campbell thing. You go on tour to play rugby, you don't go on tour to stop stories getting out. There was just no need for Campbell to be there. Rugby is rugby, it's not politics. It's not that big. If something bad happens on the pitch, guys are usually mature enough to shake hands and say, Sorry, let's move on.

In the wake of the Brian O'Driscoll tackle, for instance, I think the whole media explosion probably got in the way. It was a bad injury, and Brian may have been targeted, but most good players are targeted and it's a sign of respect. I'm sure Tana Umaga would have phoned him up the next day and apologised but the whole thing went too far.

A lot of questions are being asked about Lions tours in the future – *'Should they happen at all?'* being the main one.

I don't know. The Lions have a great history but that's not enough. It has become far too commercial, to my mind. For most rugby players, it used to be the pinnacle of their careers, and you think back to the great amateur tours in '71 and '74, the Australia trip in '89, and even our 1997 South Africa series and, yes, that's what it was all about. Now it's just another opportunity to make more money, another chance to get another commercial contract.

The ethos of the Lions isn't what it was.

Munster Munch

AFTER the highs and, mostly, lows of the Australia 2001 Lions Tour, it was back to the relative normality of Leicester, and contract negotiations with Deano. I say 'negotiations': Dean's devious brain worked on the basis of stringing you out as long as possible so that it got closer and closer to the start of the season and, eventually, you'd be left with nowhere else to go and no option but to sign whatever he put in front of you.

Not that he ever actually put anything in front of me, either – everything was always done on a handshake, which was interesting. It would have been funny to see what would have happened if one of our arguments had escalated and I'd really annoyed him.

What the Reg didn't know was that Stade Français were very keen for me to sign for them and that, while he messed around, they had started to offer me serious cash. It was tempting – who wouldn't like the idea of playing in Paris? – and a difficult decision to make, on paper. But we don't live on paper: Lou was pregnant at the time, she was happy in the area and it had become our home. Everything was good at the club, too. We were reigning European champions . . . did I really want to leave to join the team we'd just beaten? Plus I got on well with all the guys. Pat Howard had left to go back to Oz at the end of the last season, so I had space for some niggle but there wasn't even any of that on the horizon. His replacement, Rod Kafer, was on his way over from

Australia, and I've had my troubles with Aussies so that could have been a problem. But I'd met Rod out there on the tour and quickly found he was a top bloke. He'd made the effort to come over to me before the ACT game and say Hello, and that he was looking forward to joining us, and from that moment I realised that the Tug Boat, the big old guy, was going to be a great signing.

So all in all, while the money was important, I wasn't holding a very strong hand. I pushed Deano as hard as I could but in the end I was in no doubt that I wanted to stay and he must have known that. He did his usual thing of turning up in the club car park with the contract and changing a couple of the clauses at the last minute. So I didn't sign, we shook hands on it anyway and he wandered off, grinning.

Pre-season we went to Northern Ireland, staying in some barracks in Omagh, which were unbelievable: memories of that terrible IRA bomb in the town were everywhere and you really felt the oppression and fear of The Troubles. I shared a room in the Officers' Mess with Cozza, and we decided that we'd try to lose a lot of fat, quickly. That's the best way to get your speed up – fat is just dead weight. We didn't eat any carbohydrates at all for the first three weeks of pre-season, which wasn't the best idea we'd ever had. Breakfast was 20 boiled eggs each with some bacon and a protein shake. Mid-morning we'd have a protein shake, lunch the same, and more of the same at dinner. It was boring and hard and we were both knackered by the end of each day after training. But the fat really dropped off: I'd had about 12% fat, and wanted to drop down to 8%, and achieved it.

The postponed 2001 Six Nations game against Ireland came along in the Autumn. I was recovering from a groin injury which I'd been carrying for a few weeks but I was back to pretty much full fitness, so I was surprised when

With my sister Ashley - I was a good looking lad even then.

Mum and Dad at my degree ceremony.

Enjoying a summer break
from the game with Louise
- at Lake Louise in Canada.

Elvis and Wonder Woman
enjoy another Leicester
night out.

Celebrating our first Heineken Cup win over Stade Français in Paris in 2001 - a great day.

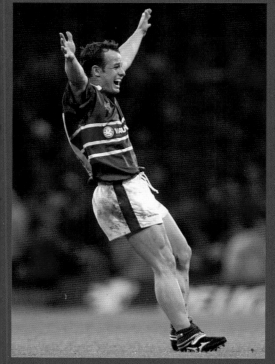

Arms aloft as the whistle goes and we beat Munster at the Millennium Stadium the following year.

Passing from the base of the scrum in my last game, against Sale at Twickenham in the 2005/6 Guinness Premiership Final. I hated finishing but I knew it was the right thing to do. I miss playing and I miss the guys... even Andy Robinson's gimp.

England celebrate a win in South Africa - a really big deal in those days, when we were only just coming to terms with the Southern Hemisphere giants.

Happy days with England - here I celebrate our autumn 2001 win over the Wallabies with Jonny Wilkinson. I doubt there's been a more unlucky player than Wilko, whose career has been stalled by a succession of injuries.

Lifting the trophy with some big ugly forward after England's 80 minute brawl with South Africa in 2002. We won, 53-3.

Clive Woodward's had his detractors but you can't argue with his results. Here he begs me to take on the captaincy - I agreed but Martin Johnson started crying so I let him keep it.

I was always a good wet weather player.

I reminded me a lot of Lomu - it always took at least two to stop me. Here it's Brian O'Driscoll and Girvan Dempsey's turn to attempt the near impossible. We won this one, too, and should have won the Grand Slam.

Celebrating after scoring against Italy. Their introduction to the Six Nations has been a great success, and Rome is a great place to play or watch.

Will Greenwood tries to wrestle the ball off me in Lions training, but his puny physique is no match for my massive upper body strength. A rare light moment in a pretty disappointing tour.

The final curtain: about to tackle Fabien Galthie in what turned out to be my last game for England. I missed out on the World Cup through injury, which plunged me into a deep depression for more than a year.

Clive put me on the bench, and I found it hard to take. I'd played well earlier in the year, and done OK during the rest of the Six Nations, and I'd started well with the club, too. But there was nothing I could do about it.

It was obviously going to be a huge game, in front of a passionate, noisy Dublin crowd, and Dave Alred gave a psychology talk about how to block them out: we'd all build a mental wall around the stadium and play within it, so we couldn't hear the Irish fans. Or something. Well, that didn't work so well.

I came off the bench and scored a try but a bit later I knocked on a Mike Catt pass that was dipping slightly and we lost the momentum we'd built. Dan Luger was tap-tackled when almost clear near the end, but the Irish held out and – for the third year running – we lost a Grand Slam that really ought to have been ours.

It was a serious downer but there's an amusing footnote to Dublin. Terry Crystal and Kevin Murphy, the team physio and doctor, were retiring and this was to be their last game. They'd been part of the England set-up since the early 1980s, were legendary guys and well-liked and respected by the players, so during the week I approached Clive and asked if we could have the RFU credit card to go and buy them farewell gifts on behalf of the squad. He handed it over and Daws and I went into Dublin, found the most expensive jeweller's we could and bought two watches – a Breitling and a Zenith. Beautiful, they were, and not cheap, so we had them engraved so that Clive couldn't make us take them back. Johnno presented the watches to the guys after the match and the following week Clive phoned me. He was hopping mad. 'Austin,' he shouted, 'what the hell's going on? I've got my credit card statement here and it says you spent £8,500 on those bloody watches!'

'Clive,' I said, 'they've been part of England for 20

years . . . that's £400 a year for their troubles. Don't be ridiculous.'

'Well, you're all going to have to pay it back out of your wages,' he said.

'I'll ask Johnno next time we get together,' I replied.

I asked Johnno. He put it to the team. Clive got his answer. We'd pay our share if everyone else who'd played for England during Terry and Murph's time dipped their hands in their pockets too. That included Clive. We didn't hear about it again.

The autumn internationals started weirdly, because we played Australia first and my old friend The Plank was in their team. There was a lot of chat in the papers before the game speculating on how it would all go, and wondering whether the big lummox was going to kick my head in. Yeah, right.

I played, we won and after the match I was accosted by an Aussie woman in her 50s. 'You don't know who I am do you?' she asked.

I had to admit I didn't.

She said: 'I'm The Plank's mum . . . can you sign this?'

It was a photo of me. 'Have you got a darts board at home?' I said.

'No,' she said, laughing. 'It's just that you've made my son more famous in Australia than his rugby ability ever could have and I'd like a memento.'

I had to smile.

We beat Romania 134–0 and put together an excellent 29–9 defeat of South Africa, which rounded off a good autumn, the Ireland game apart.

As Christmas approached, Lou got closer to giving birth and things developed dramatically when we entertained London Irish at home on December 8. I played pretty well, scored a couple of tries and was trudging off at the end of game when the Tannoy sparked up, announcing that I had to go straight to Leicester Royal Infirmary because she had gone into labour. I ran off the pitch, jumped over the barrier in my full kit and boots and ran to the hospital, which is luckily fairly close to the ground. When I got there, it transpired that she wasn't in labour at all, so I felt a bit daft. But two days later, we were back there for the real thing. It hadn't been the easiest pregnancy and the birth wasn't straightforward, either. We got there in the morning, Lou was induced and ended up having an epidural. She was knackered, so she slept for the rest of the day and I spent five or six hours kicking my heels and watching daytime TV.

At 7.15pm, Ellie Mae finally arrived. As soon as she came out, in those few moments, my life changed, totally and forever. It was weird. From rugby being the most important thing in my life, suddenly it didn't matter as much. In two or three amazing minutes, I lost my edge, the edge for the game that I'd had for the previous six years.

I wouldn't ask for that back at any stage for what I got in return. Becoming a dad was the best thing that ever happened to me.

I stayed with Lou and my new baby daughter until I was absolutely exhausted, and finally went home in the early hours and fell asleep in an armchair. Both sets of parents were at our house and I remember them waking me up and making me go to bed. Next morning I got up full of adrenaline, wide-eyed and feeling like I'd had about 12 hours' sleep. I went into town to buy Lou some flowers and fruit, smiling like a loon at everyone I met, wanting them to ask me why I was so happy just so that I could tell them. I felt like standing on top of a mountain and shouting about what had just happened.

We had a family Christmas and I carried on playing. The

rugby was pretty good for a while, and then I started to suffer with Post Natal Depression.

You don't hear about men suffering with PND very often but I happens and, believe me, it's not nice. From early January onwards, I'd get around an hour's sleep a night. We'd got Ellie sleeping in our room and I'd lie there, wide awake, straining to hear her breathing. If I could just make out those tiny little breaths, I might nod off for a bit. But then I'd suddenly wake up, heart pounding, thinking she had stopped. Other times, I'd just toss and turn, my mind full of negative thoughts and fears for her. I was really struggling, going to bed completely exhausted and waking up no better. It started affecting me at training and obviously everyone at the club was tremendously sympathetic. Everyone, that is, except the players, who delighted in winding me up. A few of them really got to me and I snapped more than once or twice. They thought it was hilarious but I actually got quite down about it all and it started to affect my rugby.

I staggered on through February and must have picked myself up because I was back in the England side for the 2002 Six Nations.

We stuffed Scotland at home – Jason Robinson scored twice and I played with a pain-killing jab, after twisting my ankle in the European Cup game against Leinster the week before – and then beat Ireland 45–11 to go to Number One in the World Rankings. That was, for me, Jonny Wilkinson's best game in an England shirt. Forget the World Cup final and all the times he won matches for us with his boot, this was a brilliant all-round display of fly-half play. I kept encouraging him to go wide – in his early days, especially, Wilko could take too much on himself and end up going for the safe option. Here he opened the scoring and spent the afternoon putting people into space with brilliant passing and clever kicks.

We went to Paris for what was, effectively, the Grand Slam decider. Our build-up wasn't helped by all the fuss surrounding a farcical incident involving Martin Johnson and the Saracens' hooker, Robbie Russell. There'd been a bit of handbags in our Premiership match, Johnno had swung at him and caught him near the eye. Russell was left with a little nick which needed three or four stitches and Martin was sin-binned – despite the fact that it wasn't even his punch which did the damage, it was a flurry of digs from Darren Garforth that the ref hadn't seen. It's a little known fact that Johnno can't punch his way out of a paper bag, despite spending his playing career being written up as the hardest man in rugby. He's a good wrestler but, unlike Garf, he hits like a girl.

Whatever, under our citing system, as I've said, he'd been dealt with and that should have been the end of it. But a media witch-hunt quickly blew up, with people like Stuart Barnes (surprise, surprise) leading calls for him to be punished more severely. You'd have thought Johnno had stabbed Russell and eaten his kids on live TV the way they carried on. It irritated us so much that we held a team meeting and decided to boycott Sky; Deano wouldn't let us, but it picked open a sore between us and Sky Sports which festered for a long time. Barnes has been the biggest offender – *Leicester kill the ball, Leicester are boring, we hate Leicester* – though he tried to rectify it by coming into our changing room after one of our titles and congratulating us. 'I've said a lot about you,' he admitted, 'but the best team has won.' After which he was roundly abused by the entire squad, sprayed with beer and champagne and he fled, completely drenched, with insults and jeers ringing in his ears.

Robbie Russell himself was quick to join in, too, bleating on about his little cut and whingeing that it meant he wouldn't be able to play for Scotland in the championship. It was a bit pathetic, really – you expect that sort of talk from backs, because we're all pretty, but when a forward starts to do it you begin to worry. It was a bit poor, too – complaining and trying to get a guy banned isn't the rugby way.

For reasons best known to themselves, the RFU bowed to the media pressure, ignored the yellow card and their own rules and decided to hold a hearing.

They banned Martin for three weeks. It was a disgrace, and it made me really angry. They wouldn't have done that to someone who played 10 games a season off the bench at Newcastle – so why do it to the England captain? They obviously decided to make an example of him, and that's not fair. Rules should apply to everyone, the same way. I felt really sorry for Johnno with all the hoo-ha – it reminded me of the grief I'd been through on the Lions tour – and I felt it typified certain section of our media. One minute, he's a tough, uncompromising legend of the game, the next he's a violent thug.

Johnno appealed, so the ban was temporarily suspended, which meant he could play in Paris. But we lost anyway, and France went on to claim the Grand Slam, a real kick in the guts. Lou had stayed at home with Ellie Mae, so after the game Daws and I went out and got absolutely destroyed together. I remember very little about the evening. I know we spent some time in Club VIP on the Champs Elysee break-dancing with our tops off. I know we had lots of fun slapping Bernard Laporte on the top of his very bald head – and, fair play to him, he was good laugh and bought us a bottle of champagne. I seem to remember Phil Larder doing some strange dance moves there as well. He really did fancy himself as a bit of a mover, Phil, but the only things that actually moved when he danced were his teeth. I got on the bus on the way back with all the wives, and they were all saying 'You wouldn't be drinking like that if Lou was here.' And they were right.

We headed back to Twickenham next, where I played full-back for the first time in my career and we beat Wales 50–10. Afterwards, Clive described me as 'England's most important player'. I hoped he'd remember that 12 months down the line.

After the match and the dinner, Lou and I had a good night out, one of the few she'd had since Ellie Mae was born. She had a bit too much to drink but she wasn't as bad as she was the first time we went out together after the birth. We went for a meal in Leicester, she'd not drunk for a year and she got slaughtered on three glasses of red wine. At about 3am, she suddenly sat up in bed and projectile-spewed red vomit all over our nice, white quilt. I went mental and sent her to the spare room whilst I tidied everything up, like the good house husband that I am. It didn't help my PND but it was quite funny, looking back.

To Italy, where we set a record for the most caps on a bench, with me, Dawson, Jason, Lol, Johnno and Balshaw sitting getting splinters in our backsides. Clive brought us all on and we scored four tries in the last ten minutes. I always loved playing in Italy, ever since I scored my hat-trick there. If you've never been on a Six Nations weekend in Rome, put it in your diary as a must-do. The road to the stadium is lined with bars, the weather's great and the rugby is improving. I scored with the last move of the game and we wrapped up another match and a decent tournament, though one – arguably – we should have won. Clive had been under a bit of pressure since we'd lost to France, so we all went out to Planet Hollywood and had a few drinks together. Some of the lads stayed out late, after Clive gave them his credit card to go for a drink – he was always doing things like that, which made you feel special playing for England. He didn't make that particular mistake again, mind. At 4am, he was woken in his hotel room by a call from American Express asking why he'd run up a £3,000 bill in an Italian lap dancing bar. Balshaw, Tindall and Dawson and a couple of others were in this place – honestly, they were only there because it sold booze till late – and had run up a huge bill on champagne. Eventually, the barman had explained that the card had hit a certain limit and that he would need Mr Woodward's date of birth and password if they were to carry on spending. Tindall, being the ugliest, took it upon himself to be Clive. He took a guess at Woody's date of birth, made up a password and got knocked back.

oOoOo

Back at the club, our focus was on winning the Premiership and on becoming the first club to claim back-to-back European Cups.

It was always strange coming back from England duty, where everything you needed was laid on for you, to the spit and sawdust atmosphere of the Tigers. Deano had a 'breed a fighter' mentality – it was all about hard work and there were very few frills and, to be fair to him, it worked.

The league was ours with games in hand after we beat Newcastle at home. We'd put in some great performances. One of the best was against Harlequins, just before Christmas, the game where Johnno scored two tries. The best of the pair was one of the greatest second row tries of all time – I'm sure he will tell you it's in his Top Five at least. He broke through 20 metres out and side-stepped their full-back Ryan O'Neil and was already wetting himself laughing as he put the ball down. I scored two myself that day, destroying Dan Luger in about three yards of space for one of them. I stood him up and went round him, which felt very satisfying, especially given that Dan was one of my rivals for a place in the England back three.

JP O'Reilly, a back-up scrum-half, was in the squad that day, and had asked Deano if he could be the team mascot for a laugh. Freddy scored a try and JP had started doing his little mascot dance when a load of us ran over and kicked the living daylights out of him. The crowd were horrified, wondering what had happened . . . then his 'head' was knocked off, everyone saw it was O'Reilly inside and horror turned to relieved laughter.

We put a lot of points on a lot of teams that season, with a 48–7 defeat of Saracens at Vicarage Road probably the high point.

The Heineken Cup was looking just as positive. We'd played well in the competition – apart from the defeat away at Llanelli and a narrow win against them at home. My favourite game had been Perpignan away in the pool stages: we were really struggling, Clive was there and I knew he was thinking ahead to the World Cup. I was moved to fly-half after half time and I played well, helping us to a one-point win. I felt that was an important result for me as well as for the team. Woody knew I could play scrum-half, and now, in a pressure game, I'd shown I was a good 10, too.

My personal form continued in the quarter final against Leinster, when I set up a try for Lloydy with probably the best pass of my career and scored one myself.

In the semi we faced Llanelli for the third time. They were the only club to have beaten us in Europe that year, and the aggregate points tally was 33–24 in their favour. They were a really strong team, with Stephen Jones kicking and Scott Quinnell driving them on in the forwards, and Rod Kafer wanted me playing at fly-half. Andy Goode should have taken it on the chins, but he spent the week being disruptive and awkward and it didn't help that we had trouble trying to adapt to Rod's plans to cope with Llanelli's defensive patterns. Kafes would throw this ball over the top and say, '*That's* where I want you to run on to it!' but we spent the whole week trying and failing to do it, which knocked our confidence a bit.

All thoughts of that were banished from my mind when I ran out to warm up at Notts Forest's City Ground to be confronted by several thousand Welshmen all wearing red Afros, pointing at me and singing 'It's a wig, it's a wig, it's a wig' to the tune of *'ere we go, 'ere we go, 'ere we go.*

I'd been receding a fair bit and my agent had done a deal with Advanced Hair Studio – the same people who put hair back on the heads of Graham Gooch and Shane Warne. It involved rubbing special lotion on my head every morning and night and using a laser to stimulate growth. It really worked, though it also earned me a fair bit of stick and this load of Welshmen were certainly not the first to take the mickey. I played along with them, moving my scalp back and forward and pretending to pull my hair off and at the end of the game, when we'd won, I went back to the same corner and started waving at them, just trying to wind them up a bit more. Where opposition fans are concerned, especially the really gobby ones, I've always enjoyed rubbing their faces in it – it's not like they don't try it with you.

I'd played pretty well, defending strongly and kicking us into good field positions in a tight match. They closed me down a bit as the game wore on, and I maybe tried to take on too much myself, doing little chips and making breaks, but I knew I'd be playing fly-half in the final, which was the main thing.

Deano gave a little speech in the changing room afterwards. 'Well, it was a hard game,' he said, 'but we're through so let's enjoy it . . . where are we going tonight?'

We ended up in my local, where Johnno had a minor disagreement with an old farmer who moaned that he was sitting in his chair. I don't think that would happen to the England soccer captain, somehow.

Ahead of the final, we had Bristol at home, and we went down to a surprise defeat. With such a massive game ahead, a lot of the boys were trying to avoid injury and personally, I had a shocker. Dean had overruled Kafer and put me at scrum-half, I'd been mentally preparing to play 10 and the result was I was all over the place and got taken off just before half time.

Deano got the message. I was selected at fly-half for the final, against Munster. I'd got a bit worried about my kicking – it wasn't spiralling very well out of hand and my drop-outs were poor – so I phoned Dave Alred and asked if he'd come up and help me. He met me at Loughborough on the Wednesday and we spent a whole afternoon kicking, which was very unusual for me – usually I hated practising kicks, because I thought it made me think about it too much. But Dave gave me some tips and encouragement and after an hour with him I was booming them all over the place. It just went to show what a great coach he was – and is. In my mind, he was one of the single most important factors in England becoming such a good side over that period. He achieved more than any of the other coaches, with Phil Larder running him close. He had a wealth of knowledge, the eye to pick up exactly where you were going wrong and the ability to communicate what you needed to do to put it right.

Actually, it was Dave, too, who helped me break out of my Post Natal Depression. Although I'd played well with England, everyone knew I wasn't myself. Apart from anything, I looked awful – my eyes were sinking into my head. But I didn't want to admit this to anyone, because I didn't want to show any signs of weakness. I knew Clive would hate that, and that it might affect selection. In the end, I built up the courage to tell Dave. He was a good listener, and his advice was simple: at the end of each day, write down five good things that have happened that day. I did that for a month and gradually I started to get more sleep and things picked up. I still have regressive moments now, where I'll have a bad night, especially if I've got a lot on my plate. But Dave really helped me. Having said that, I always felt he'd mentioned it to Clive because, from that point on, instead of being close to a 'given' in the England squad, my selection became more sporadic.

We travelled across to Wales two days before. On the Friday, myself, Leon and a couple of the other guys went out to play golf – I was just trying to relax, really. Leicester was an edgy club when the nerves were running and people wouldn't talk much. Johnno was a case in point: you could tell when he was feeling the pressure because he'd be very quiet, not that he was ever exactly talkative. One of his greatest assets was knowing when to speak. He never spoke when he didn't need to, and he said just enough when it was needed. Leon wasn't playing in the final – he'd failed a fitness test – so he'd resigned himself to that and was keen to go out in Cardiff that night. He wasn't the only one. Freddy Tuilagi had picked up a virus, so Steve Booth was on standby – he would have come on to the bench and Glen Gelderbloom would have replaced Fred in the starting XV. This was a serious situation; we might well have needed Steve for the biggest day in the club's history. That night, he said he was going out into Cardiff with Leon to meet Jerry Guscott for a few drinks. I warned him not to. 'Whatever you do, don't go out,' I said. 'You could be playing tomorrow and this is a massive game.'

Backy and Johnno told him the same thing. If he'd been out drinking, he'd have a shocker if we needed him.

Despite that, Boothy went out. And he got utterly drunk, coming back in at around 3am or 4am. He stank of booze at breakfast the next morning and I had a real go at him. 'What the hell do you think you're doing?' I said. 'You're playing for the biggest club in the country, we've got our biggest game ever, and you've got no respect for us, your team mates or the club. You're definitely getting the sack for this. I'm telling Deano that you've been out.'

I did tell Dean. In hindsight, maybe I shouldn't have said anything: Steve was a professional rugby player and I could have affected his future. But then our collective futures had a lot riding on a second European Cup win and who was to say he wouldn't have been called in, and wouldn't have missed a crucial tackle, or dropped the ball on the line, because he was hungover?

Boothy came up to me later. 'You told him,' he said.

'Yeah, I did,' I said. 'What are you going to do?'

He couldn't match me physically, so there was nothing he *could* do.

I said: 'You let the team down, and we can't put up with that so get stuffed.'

All through the day, he was crying and saying he was going to get the sack. That wasn't unusual. He was a bad lad who preferred to go out drinking than sacrifice one night of his life to get the team ready.

I'd not been too nervous until the day of the game, but I defy anyone to stay totally calm as a match like that draws near. At 11am, we had our pre-match meal and I sat near our masseurs. One of them wouldn't stop talking. Maybe he was nervous and that was his way, but we didn't want it. Eventually, there were four or five guys glaring at him and I was seriously on the verge of knocking him out at the table. I was squeezing my knife and fork thinking, 'I'm going to kill you if you don't shut up.'

The head masseur, Julie Hayton, twigged what was going on and got him out of there, leaving us to knuckle down and stare at our food. Guys get so motivated and aggressive from the moment they wake up on match day that they're almost different people.

Funnily enough, I quite enjoyed that part of the day, the build-up; it stands out more than most of the game.

I remember arriving at the Millennium Stadium – the best ground in the northern hemisphere, for me, the atmosphere there is second to none.

There wasn't much said beforehand. The previous year, Stade had kept us waiting and then walked slowly towards us and we'd thought 'Yes, let's get it on.' We'd known we were in the scrap of our lives, we were the underdogs and we'd have to fight tooth and nail. This time, we went into the game as favourites. We felt that if we played sensible, controlled rugby, and everyone did their jobs, then we would win. Effectively, that's what happened. There was nothing that flash: a great piece of skill from Stimmo to set up Geordie for the first try, and that was about it. My own score came, basically, from a missed tackle. Nine times out of ten, Ronan O'Gara would have put me on the floor, set up a ruck and we would have gone from there. On this occasion, I managed to break through. Not that I remember anything about the try. Often, I've done things in games that I have no recollection of until I see them later on TV, which is why I'm a firm believer in fate, that it's not really in our hands.

My biggest contribution to the game was probably a tackle on their winger, John O'Neill. He looked certain to score and was right in the corner when I nailed him. It went to the TV ref but I knew he hadn't made it. The Munster crowd were all cheering, shouting 'It's a try, baldy!', I was shaking my head, they were flicking the Vs and, sure enough, I was right and they were wrong. Post-match, Phil

Larder came over to me. 'Oz,' he said, 'that was one of the best tackles I've ever seen.' He shook my hand, and that meant a lot to me because at that time, Phil and I didn't always get on. I'd hated tackling practice since the 1999 World Cup which left me with a snapped lesion in my left shoulder; any big hits, out of a game, when it wasn't strapped up and the adrenaline wasn't there, really, really hurt. Phil spotted that, and thought I was weak because of it. The truth is I needed an operation for five years, but I put it off because it would have meant a nine-month lay-off.

Like the try, the tackle was another moment which felt somehow unreal. Watch it on TV: I'm stood at fly half, and I get past Rod Kafer, Ollie Smith, Freddy and Stimmo to hit O'Neill. Honestly, to this day, I don't know where I found that speed. The last five metres, I suddenly found another gear that I didn't normally have. That used to happen to me quite a lot when I was cover tackling. I'm not sure what it was – maybe the nervous energy associated with knowing you're going to hit someone. I actually preferred cover tackling to scoring tries, which is probably why I haven't scored as many tries as Leon Lloyd, something he'll bore you about if he gets half a chance.

The match will always be remembered, of course, for The Hand Of Back. It soured it slightly for me – not for what Backy did, because any professional player would have done the same. There was lots of rubbish in the papers afterwards about how this was all against the spirit of the game and not to be encouraged, but I defy any of those critics to tell me the difference between knocking the ball out of the scrum-half's hand and lying on the wrong side of the ruck? They're both illegal and they're both done to win your side an advantage; one is easily seen and visible, the other isn't, and that's about it.

Backy's hand didn't affect the outcome – we'd have won

anyway, I'm sure – but it just took the shine off our victory because it allowed people to speculate that it *might* have made a difference.

The ABC boys lifted the European Cup and, fair enough, they'd been at the club long enough so it was their time. We didn't know it then, but the conveyor belt of silverware to Welford Road would grind to a halt after this: it was to be the last prize we'd claim in my time at the Tigers, and my one big regret about playing for Leicester for ten years is that I never got the chance to lift a trophy myself. But I was pleased with my winner's medal and had a rare feeling of satisfaction with myself. I'd played really well but it was one of the few occasions in my life where I didn't feel the need to go round shouting the odds and telling people that. I actually knew, deep down, how much I had given to the team that day and that made me very proud. Of course, a lot of the other lads had done exactly the same, as they did, week in, week out.

The post match is a bit of a blur; it's a shame, but when you win big games, the euphoria takes over and you're left with bits and pieces of memories. I remember walking around the stadium, looking for my family. I saw Ellie Mae up in the stand with her mum, my sister and mum and dad, and it felt great seeing them up there. I remember applauding the Munster fans on the way round; I think some thought that was some kind of mickey-take, but it wasn't. They'd been outstanding throughout the day – their singing and the noise they made outshone our fans, and that took some doing.

We went back to the Celtic Manor, where there was a big party laid on for the whole club, from Sheryl the groundswoman all the way up to Peter Tom. That was great, because it was all Leicester. There was no outsiders, there was no-one coming in to join our celebrations and, even though the bright(ish) lights of Cardiff were just round the corner, none of the lads left. Everyone stuck together and for me that was fantastic.

As the evening wore on, it got a bit out of hand, as it can do. At about 3am, they started playing bar stool jousting: you put a bar stool on your head, with the legs over your shoulders, and charge at each other with the cushioned ends. Richard Cockerill gets a bit feisty when he's drunk, as you can imagine, and he took on Ben Wheeler, one of Peter Wheeler's young sons and absolutely smashed him – laid him out completely. The other son, Joe Wheeler, then stepped up. But as Cockers began his run up, Brace slyly stuck his leg out and sent him flying. Cockers sliced his chin open on the base of the stool and stood there with blood pouring everywhere. He wasn't best pleased, but there wasn't a lot he could do after spending the evening throwing his weight around, so he had to stand there being laughed at while someone went to rouse Doctor Finlay. The Doc usually goes to bed early, because he's not a very good drinker, but he'd have had a few and only an hour or so's sleep. He stitched Cockers' chin up as best he could under the circumstances: next day, a very sorry-looking Richard Cockerill appeared at breakfast with what can best be described as a jigsaw on his face. I think that was a fair comeuppance.

I had a few quiet drinks and went to bed reasonably early. I was mentally and physically exhausted. It was as though I'd reached the top of my personal mountain: I'd played with a broken finger, both my shoulders were knackered, and my knees were giving me trouble. You don't feel these things in games – it's in the training beforehand and the recovery afterwards that the pain comes.

Whenever we won a trophy, the following day was always a Leo Sayer. I got on the bus at 9.30am to go back to

Leicester, Deano brought about five crates of beer on and sat at the back with me and Benny Kay and we started to get pleasantly smashed. I seem to remember everyone was watching Harry Potter on the bus and every time anyone said 'Harry', me and Benny had to drink. For some reason, Deano didn't – that's probably another story.

We got to the club and carried on from there. Most of the girls stayed for about an hour and then went home and eventually it was just the lads and Jo Hollis, our team secretary. She's a great girl, Jo, and she'd held the team together over the years. She mothered us all and saw us as her little children – when she wasn't out on the lash with us. We started to play beer Jenga. You fill a champagne bucket with beer, and stand around it, drinking. There's an empty beer glass floating in the bucket and you take it in turns to add beer to the glass. Whoever sinks the glass has to neck it. Simple enough. But by the end of it there's just me, Jo, Jamie Hamilton and Ben Kay and I introduce a broom handle to the game. The new rule is that you have to pour your beer from above the broom handle and if you get any beer on the handle you get hit with it on the backside.

So Jo pours, and inevitably she spills it all over the broom handle.

The person to her right has to inflict the pain, and that's Jamie. She puts her hands on the wall, bends over and Jamie takes a run up, like a West Indian fast bowler from the 1980s, and whacks her as hard as he can. She's on the floor rolling around screaming, with the three of us wetting ourselves laughing.

After five minutes or so, she minces gingerly back to the table, looking daggers at Jamie. 'That's it, Hamilton,' she says. 'You're getting it.'

It comes around to him and though he doesn't get any on

the broom, someone knocks him and it goes all over the table.

'Right, Jamie,' says Jo. 'Off to the wall.'

By this stage, Jo is so drunk that she goes for him, misses and takes a huge chunk out of the wall in the European lounge. Everyone shouts, *That doesn't count*. So she takes another run up and this time she hits Jamie so hard it snaps the broomstick. Jamie crumples to the floor in agony, with the biggest red line on his butt cheeks that you have ever seen in your life. Now that the stick is broken, we have to play a different game.

So we start to play To My Right. You measure a little finger's length away from the chin of the person next to you and then punch them, as hard or as soft as you like. Will Johnson has joined the game and is next to me, and he hits me relatively hard. I hit Ben Kay relatively softly, just in case someone changes the direction.

Jo Hollis is next to Ben. He absolutely lamps Jo, so hard that she falls off her chair. She's lying on the floor, screaming with laughter.

By this stage, she's fairly paralytic. Someone changes direction, so she gets back on her chair, and goes to wallop Benny with a big haymaker. Only she misses straight over the top of his head and the swing takes her off her chair and onto the floor again, where she lies cackling and unable to right herself, like a dying fly.

The game escalates to To My Right, Head-Butts.

Everyone's thinking, *Benny won't head-butt her too hard, will he? He's a nice judge's son, after all*. But he does, he really sticks one on her. She falls off her chair again, staggers back up, grabs hold of the champagne bucket full of beer on the table, and chucks it over Ben. All hell breaks loose, a huge beer fight ensues and then, because it's 4pm by now, we decide it's time to go to the pub.

We find ourselves in Hogan's, a Leicester bar, having a few beers.

By now, the standard, end-of-season emotions are coming out: a few of the lads have had enough and are on their bikes, so lots of people are hugging each other and crying. It's a common enough sight after a long emotional season – these big, hard rugby players, sitting round a bar and a few of them shedding tears.

It all gets even more blurred after that.

I remember me and Johnno getting cornered by Leon, and him telling us he was going to sign for Harlequins the following day. That would have been a disaster. Players come and go from clubs, and you accept that, but Leicester had started losing too many 'heart and soul' players. People like Craig Joiner had gone, as had Will Greenwood – well, I wouldn't say Will was a heart and soul player but he was probably worth keeping – and the likes of Perry Freshwater, Shorty and Jamie Hamilton were on their way, too. These guys might not have been superstars, big international players, but they kept the team going forward. Leon had been perhaps the single most important factor in the success of the Tigers over the previous five or six years but he'd not had the best of seasons. I'd been partly responsible, having tackled him in training and torn the cartilage in his knee in the process, and I don't think he was getting on that well with Kafer. We started trying to talk him out of it, telling him he'd bounce back and that there was no way he'd have the same feeling playing for Harlequins as he did playing at the club he'd grown up with, ever since his mate Peter Lloyd brought him over from Barkers Butts with Backy, as a skinny little 17-year-old with a ridiculous, stand-up Afro. We spent a few pints and a good couple of hours with him, but he still drove down to Quins next day. Luckily, we'd put doubts in his mind and when Dean phoned him just as he got to The Stoop he convinced him to turn round and come home.

I remember walking back from the bar in the small hours, very drunk after boozing from 9am the previous day. As I weaved along the street to where I lived at the time, half a mile or so away, I sang at the top of my voice, irritating everyone in earshot but feeling really satisfied with what I'd achieved and what the team had done that season.

The next day, I got up at about 11am and got a phone call from a couple of the lads who'd already started drinking again. I was going on holiday that night but I drove down to meet up with them for a laugh and a chat before we went our separate ways. As I arrived, Pete Atkinson was leaving to go to hospital, because Graham Rowntree had just thrown a knife into his head. By now it was about 2pm, so matters had accelerated quite quickly.

Wig does tend to throw things when he's drunk. One time he nearly knocked Dorian West out with a chair.

I looked at him.

He looked at me.

He had another knife in his hand and he was danger personified.

I decided that the best plan was to make a quick exit.

That was the last time I saw the lads until the following pre-season.

Not My Greatest Year

We'd been on holiday to Portugal, a good, long three-week family break, staying with some friends in Lagos. Cozza and I have been associated with an orphanage out there for a number of years; we go over most summers, play a bit of charity golf and then go to a dinner to raise some money for the kids. There are 60 or so of them in the place and it breaks my heart every time I see them. It really makes you think how lucky you and your own kids are.

A week before we went away, Lou went to the doctor. She was really tired, and feeling very low. We'd not long moved into our new house, and the plan was that she'd oversee its restoration, but she was so knackered that she was having to go back to bed in the afternoons. The house was a complete tip, which was bothering her, but the worst of it was the exhaustion – it was like a living hell for her, because she's a very energetic girl, very into exercise and training. She had some blood tests and they revealed that her thyroid gland had stopped working. The thyroid produces a hormone called thyroxine which regulates your energy levels; it's quite a common problem, and it's easily controlled with artificial thyroxine, but if it's not picked up it can be fatal, so we were lucky.

The medication can take two to three weeks to kick in and put you back to how you should be, so the holiday wasn't like a normal trip away. Two days after we arrived, we decided to take Ellie Mae to Lagos for a walk, and Lou

176

couldn't even get her out of the car, which is when it hit home just how serious the illness was. I had to do everything for the first week. We stayed in every night with a glass of wine and a Bolognese pizza – I'd bought about five of them, because I couldn't work out how to use the cooker in the villa. Slowly, as the holiday progressed, Lou's thyroxine began to kick in and she got more energy.

My friend Ade Shannon and my sister came over to stay for a week, and Lou's sister Katie came too; Ade tried to tap up Katie and Ashley, but to no effect. The football World Cup was on and he and I went to watch the England-Brazil game at the local golf club. The match kicked off at 7am and by half time Ade and I had had about six pints of Guinness each; we were absolutely steaming. I remember the drama when Owen scored, and the emptiness when they won with the Ronaldinho free kick near the end. We carried on drinking, staggering out of the bar at about 2pm, really quite smashed. We decided we'd have a forward roll competition down to the tenth, where we found a foursome ready to tee off. In my state, I mistook one of the guys for a mate of my dad's and started jabbering away at him. He must have thought I was a complete raving lunatic, which obviously I was.

We followed that up by going back to the villa, opening a bottle of lager each, putting on our flippers and snorkels and jumping off the roof of the villa into the swimming pool while drinking the beer. The idea was to see how much you could drink in the air before you hit the water.

It was good to have three weeks away, a chance for all my injuries to recover and to have a full break from rugby. My pre-Lions tour wobble aside, I'd always disagreed with the suggestion that modern players needed more time off; my argument was always that we were getting paid a wage to play, so that's what we should do. That holiday changed my mind – I turned up for pre-season fit, refreshed and raring to go, which proves time off is important.

I was keen to get a good pre-season in, because our World Cup was just a year away and the squad was obviously going to be picked on form during the season. Additionally, we were going for our third Heineken Cup in a row, when no-one else had ever won two on the trot. It focused our minds – during pre-season training, you need goals to keep you going because your body is sore all the time from the weights and the running and if you have nothing to go for you might lose your enthusiasm.

I did a lot of strength work with Backy. The good thing about training with Neil was that we always wanted to beat each other, it drove us both on, which was important. Recently, we did a chin up test – he did 30, so I did 31. So he went back by himself and did 33. So I went back by *my*self and did 36. Yes, Backy was the greatest training partner ever. The conversation wasn't that great, though.

I was trying to strike the balance between getting stronger and maintaining my speed. I tended to bulk up with the early weights work – bulk helps in contact, obviously, and you do a lot of weights early in the season – but the downside was that I'd be a little bit slower as a result. My speed usually returned about October, when the weights work dropped off a bit. I was one of the better trainers at the club, one of the guys who would push myself where some were happy to sit in the comfort zone.

Our first pre-season game was against Biarritz away in the Orange Cup. Deano, being about two-thirds French, liked taking us down there. Before the tournament, we had a pre-season camp in Monflanquin, where the famous Monflanquin Seven had one of the major nights in Leicester history. We'd trained hard and been given a day off, so The Seven – myself, Lewis Moody, Leon Lloyd, Adam Balding,

Geordan Murphy, Glen Gelderbloom and Steve Booth — found ourselves in a pizza restaurant (Lewis had a croque monsieur and couldn't understand where the crocodile was) and started ordering red wine. We managed to put away 49 bottles between us, drinking until everyone's teeth were black with the stuff. There was a lot of general messing around and Balding fell asleep in the toilet doorway. The manager asked us to move him but we couldn't wake him up so we just left him there, with people stepping over him to get to the loo.

After about half a bottle of wine, Lewis turned into his usual childish self and started punching people in the testicles. Actually, his greatest attribute is his ability to hit people in the testicles. He finds it very funny. He caught me flush in the balls in the loo with an orange while I wasn't looking. It was agony, and I went down on one knee. 'At some stage during the rest of today I will get you back worse than that,' I said. He just giggled like a girl.

Later, I was fortunate enough to be sitting opposite Lewis and noticed he was sitting with his legs apart, so I grabbed a heavy ashtray and Frisbeed it under the table straight into his groin. He was sick, which was one of the most satisfying moments of the whole trip.

A week later we played Biarritz in front of Serge Blanco and all those guys. We were trying out lots of new players — I'd been training with Danny Hipkiss and this was going to be his first game for the club. The night before, I tried to find out whether he was anxious.

'Are you nervous, Danny?' I asked.

'Well, I am a bit, Austin,' he said, a look of relief on his face. Nice to have one of the senior pros taking an interest.

'Well, you should be,' I said. 'Because you're s***.'

He went on to score a try and win the game for us, so my reverse psychology obviously worked. In fact, Danny

Hipkiss has never looked back, and he owes it all to me, and the sooner he realises that the better.

We played Leeds in our first proper match. I scored a try but we lost. I could have had another: I made a break at the end of the first half, running fully 60 metres from inside our own 22. I remember having to slow down to let Leon or Steve Booth catch up so I could try and put them through a hole, because I was getting pincered into a corner. I waited and waited for them and eventually I threw the pass. But it went to ground and the opportunity was lost.

Gordon Ross hit me, late and in the back, and then started rubbing my hair on the ground. 'You're not that good, are you, son?' he said.

I looked at him. 'I don't even know what your name is, mate,' I said. I know it was an arrogant thing to say, but that's never stopped me in the past. I don't mind a bit of banter, but behave . . . I've just sprinted 60m through most of your defence and if I'd gone by myself I might have scored. I told myself that when we played him at home I was going to beat the living daylights out of him but sadly he didn't play at our place, which was a bit of a disappointment. At Leicester, we always had lists of players we wanted to intimidate, shall we say, and he was on mine. Most of the others were Newcastle mutes who had always generally wound us up. The thing with banter on the pitch is you've got to be winning to do it properly, which is one major reason it was so good playing for Leicester all those years. We knew we were going to win, so we could give people stick for a bit of fun. When teams like Leeds and Newcastle gave us stick, it was usually pointless. We'd look at them and think, 'What are you doing that for? At the end of this game, we're going to be the ones doing the smiling.'

Unfortunately, that day at Leeds it didn't turn out that way and they enjoyed their victory, big-time. To them, we were their Man United or Chelsea – to beat the Tigers would make their season for them, even if they ended up finishing ninth or tenth.

I picked up a bit of a groin strain against Sale away. You'd always start thinking, '*Is this the start of something major?*' I'd had lower back problems and groin strains previously, and fortunately this one went away after a couple of weeks after I went back to my old groin routine – no weights, just a lot of exercises in the swimming pool, twice a day. That was a massive relief, because the sense that this was going to be a huge season for all of us was really starting to build.

In mid-October, we played Neath away – going there always felt like going to a different part of the world, rather than just another part of Britain – on a wet, grey Friday night. I was trying a new pair of boots which I'd worn in training a few times, a mixture between blades and studs designed to give me a bit of extra grip in the rain. By half time, my Achilles was really sore. We'd been training on new vibration platforms developed by NASA as exercise aids for astronauts on long trips. You stood on it and the movement worked your leg muscles in different ways. I got on the platform in the changing room in the break, thinking it was probably just a tweak.

Little did I know that my season had just been wrecked.

I went on in the second half and scored a good try, a dummy switch with Kayfs under the posts right in front of their crowd, who immediately started spitting at me and throwing things. Naturally, I rubbed their faces in it. Well, it was the 79th minute and we were going to win, weren't we?

They kicked off, we caught the ball, a ruck formed, one of their guys dived over the wrong side and Frank Tournaire shoed him, quite legally. Unfortunately, the referee saw it differently and they scored from the penalty with the last kick of the game. I felt very aggrieved at the unfair ending to what had been a good Leicester performance.

The Achilles kicked in from there and got progressively worse – playable, but hard to train on because it took so long to warm up, even wearing heat patches, and it was incredibly sore. Before we played London Wasps, I pulled out. It didn't go down well with Deano and Wellsy, who thought I was trying to save myself for the internationals. To a certain extent, they were right – I was on 47 caps at the time and I was desperate to get to 50; additionally, with the World Cup on the horizon, and games against Australia, New Zealand South Africa coming up, I wanted to stay in the squad. If you're in, you can have the odd average game or be slightly injured but when you're left out it's really difficult to get back in.

Anyway, I'd given a lot to Leicester, it was only one match and the fact was that my Achilles needed a rest. If I just kept playing it was going to get worse and worse. Already, I was only about 80 per cent fit. Wellsy, in particular, had a go at me: not being an international, he had a chip on his shoulder about players seeming to put country before club. (By the way, we beat Wasps 9–6 in the pouring rain and I wouldn't have touched the ball anyway.)

With a little time off, I needed to get some proper physio. The treatment I was getting at the club wasn't the best, perhaps because they didn't think I had much of an injury. I spoke to Greg Mortimer and we established that a little bone spur was rubbing on the tendon and causing the problem. It's not an uncommon injury – Martin Johnson suffered with the same thing, and so has Freddie Flintoff – so I had my boots modified, with a hole put in the back to relieve the pressure on the bone, and that seemed to help a bit. I still didn't know how serious it was.

We met up with England ahead of the Australia game, the first of the Autumn internationals.

Clive came up to me at training. 'Austin,' he said. 'These Australians. They know about your speed, they know about your pass, they know about your side step. They know about your cover tackling and your work rate. They also know about your mouth. But what they don't know about you is that you're not playing.'

Clive and his funny ways, eh? I came off the bench and did a couple of good things, played not too bad, set up one of the lads for a try towards the end of the game and made a couple of tackles on the other side, so I was quite happy with my performance. I wasn't happy with the Achilles, though: it was burning, unbelievably hot to the touch and terribly sore, and I had to sit with my foot in an ice bucket for ages to try to reduce the inflammation. I should have stopped playing then. If I'd held my hand up and admitted I had a real problem, I'd have been sent away to get it right. With treatment and rest, I'd have made the Six Nations and who knows what would have happened. Instead, I kept quiet about it. Well, we all do stupid things, and I've probably done more than most. In my defence, I was on 48 caps, now, and desperate to get those last two. Meanwhile, my form was obviously suffering and the management were developing an opinion of me and my play without that important knowledge.

I was on the bench again against New Zealand and I struggled to warm the heel up, even with the luxury of being able to stretch and warm it up with the adrenaline pumping through me.

I came on for the last couple of minutes, which was a bit bizarre – what can you do in that time? You're better off leaving the guys who are up to speed out there. We were three points ahead. The Blacks had the ball and looked like they were going into a move I'd seen them do earlier in the game, so I came out of the defensive line with the intention of hitting Doug Howlett. But the ball went across him, they were around me and it was only a fantastic cover tackle from Ben Cohen that saved us in the corner. Thanks, Benny. That would have been 49 caps and goodnight otherwise, I would have thought.

Afterwards, the Achilles was just so bad that I had to tell the physios, and the message got back to Clive. Even then, I got them to doctor the message, and tell him it wasn't too bad, and I managed to get on the bench again for the SA game.

Midweek, we had a meeting of The Bitter and Twisted Club. Me and a few of the other senior players who'd found themselves demoted to the bench for one reason or another – at the time, guys like myself, Lawrence, Jason, Daws, Mark 'Ronnie' Regan and Danny Grewcock – formed the B&T as a way of venting our frustrations. We'd meet on Wednesdays in a restaurant near the team hotel at Penny Hill Park and go though all the problems with the coaches, putting the world to rights and getting it all off our chests before the weekend. It actually wasn't a bad idea; negative feelings are always around when you're on the bench, because while you want the team to win human nature says you'd quite like the man playing in your position to have a bad game and maybe pick up a mild hamstring pull, and this was a way of dealing with that negativity.

It was always a good laugh. We used to take Ronnie over for comedy value. He's one of the funniest guys you'll ever meet – a weird combination of very thick and very sharp. I remember winding him up on the back of the tour bus in 2000. He said he was clever. I said, 'No, you're not, Ron, you're stupid.'

'No, I'm not, bab,' he said, in his West Country accent.

'I'm clever. I'll prove it to you . . . ask me a question . . . anything you loike, bab.'

By now, most of the lads on the bus have stopped what they're doing and are tuning in. They can sense something's coming.

I said, 'OK, tell us your seven times table.'

'That's easy, bab,' says Ronnie, and by now you could have heard a pin drop.

'One times seven is seven,' he starts, promisingly. Then it all goes rapidly downhill. 'Two times seven is seven, three times seven is seven, four times seven is seven . . .'

The rest was drowned out in howls of laughter and abuse, with Ronnie going 'What? What? That's roight, that is . . . isn't it?'

I didn't gang up on him too much, though, because he was really quick with his own put-downs and it was always better to have him on side.

That South Africa match turned out to be one of the most astonishing games of rugby – in inverted commas – ever seen at Twickenham. Having seen us beat the Wallabies and the All Blacks, the Springboks had obviously decided that their best hope of victory lay in kicking the crap out of us.

The game started pretty well but when one of their forwards was sent off the whole thing descended into mayhem. It was bizarre, sitting there watching Daws getting his head kicked in – I actually found it quite amusing at the time. Corne Krige dropped an elbow on Johnno, which was probably like a little tickle to him, and Jonny took some big, illegal hits too. He went down a couple of times and then had to come off, which was when I went on. I remember stripping off and Phil Larder sprinting down, looking really worried. He started telling me to do this and that, watch out for so-and-so, and I found that strange. I'd played fly-half against Munster in the Heineken Cup final not long ago and he'd told me that it had been one of the best fly-half performances he'd seen. His worried face now suggested he had no confidence in me at international level, which annoyed me. It was a bit of a Moody, in fact – a kick where it hurts.

Anyway, I just nodded and before I knew it I was running on for my 50th cap. Strangely, though it was a massive honour and something I'd dreamed of, it was very anti-climactic, and a really big disappointment. I'd love to have been in the starting XV, so I'd have led the team out, which would have been the high point of my playing career. But I never got that opportunity.

The first thing that happened was, I was on one side of a ruck and they broke through and I got across and cover tackled somebody who was about to reach our line.

The second thing was, they had a scrum from there, and I tackled their number 8 and stopped him dead.

The third thing was, one of their flankers came in and stamped on the top of my head. Like you do.

That's when I stopped thinking it was funny seeing Daws getting battered. Their violence wasn't being reserved for him and Johnno and Jonny – they were dishing it out to whoever was there, and seemed actually to want to injure people, rather than just giving them a clout. Watching the video after the game, I realised how serious some of the hits were. It was pretty disgraceful, frankly, and it was highly satisfying to put 50 points on them.

I set up two tries, one for Richard Hill with a kick and another from a pass to Jason Robinson, so I'd played my part, made a contribution to the cause, done something good for the team. I suppose the adrenaline from reaching my 50th cap had masked the pain in my heel for however long I'd played.

Post-match, all the boys used to run out to the tents to do

some hospitality or see their friends, and I limped off to see my mum, dad and Lou. They were all beaming, really big smiles, looking really proud of me, which was a great feeling. At the dinner I was presented with my 'silver mushroom', a tiny silver cap on a plaque marking my 50th match, and I made a speech. They didn't want me to, but it had been an emotional year, with Ellie Mae being born, and then my post-natal depression and Lou's illness, and no-one was going to stop me. I thanked my parents, my wife and all the players I'd ever played with; my dad's an emotional man, and he and my mum both had wet eyes. It was a good day in a pretty bad year.

After the internationals, I was back playing for the club again. Deano wasn't happy that I'd turned out for England. 'I thought your Achilles injury was so bad you had to miss the Wasps game,' he said. 'You didn't miss the England games, did you?'

So I had to carry on playing, to save face as much as anything else.

We had Beziers away on a Sunday in early December, and I hadn't trained all week. Deano picked me to play at fly-half, and I remember sitting with my Achilles in a boiling hot bath before we left for the stadium, and then running another when we got there, trying to keep it warm and relieve some of the pain. I had an injection in my backside before the game to try and take away the pain, but it was killing me, though I played well. I owed Deano a big performance. The following week, we played them at home in the return, and I had another really good game, setting up a couple of tries before going off with about 15 minutes to go.

But that was that. I sat next to Deano on the bench as the lads finished the French off and said, 'I can't carry on any more. I've got to get this sorted out, otherwise it's going to snap and that'll be the end of the whole season.'

Thankfully, Dean saw sense. 'Take as long as you need, mate,' he said. 'I won't pick you until you're 100 per cent fit.'

My long road to rehab started.

I went to see the physio and doctor and took as much advice as I could, as well as doing a bit of research of my own. There seemed to be two options: have an operation, and have the spur stripped away, or undertake a strengthening programme which involved doing hundreds of calf lifts a day. I took the latter option, and really threw myself into it, with no weights to begin with and then in the gym on the bar.

It can get lonely, working on your own much of the time, and you miss the *craic* of training and the changing room. Earlier in my career, when it was just me and Lou, I'd go home and mope and get really down if I was injured. But once we'd had Ellie Mae, that changed. We held her first birthday party at Brewster Bear's, and seeing my little girl and 20 of her friends in one room, crawling and toddling around, took my mind off my problems. Being able to come home and play and mess about with her, and just be a dad, did clear my head and help me deal with the uncertainties of life as a professional rugby player. I don't think it's an exaggeration to say it helped me stay sane.

It didn't get better quickly and there were times, even with Ellie Mae's smiles and Lou's support, where I feared the worst. I remember telling Leon in February that I was finished, I just couldn't get this thing to go away. I couldn't run or even cycle, but I could box and use a grinder, so on the upside my upper body was in terrific shape. I did my best ever bench press of 155kg, I did my best ever squat of 250kg – I just couldn't do any movement exercises or run.

I worked for the BBC on the Six Nations, and it was torture standing pitch side and watching the boys play, and get progressively better and better. Josh Lewsey had burst onto the scene and, given that most of my international rugby was going to be played in the back three and he'd taken one of those spots, that wasn't great. He'd struggled to get in the squad until this point but he was a good player, and a very good physical specimen, who I respected despite begrudging him playing a little. As a proud Englishman, you want the national side to play well, but this was also my livelihood. Imagine you've got a unique job that you love, you're off sick and someone comes in and does well in your position: you'd be worried about it. And you'd have employment law and job security backing you up, too.

England beat France at home and I stood there in the freezing cold, my Achilles still sore, doing TV, wearing silly coats and scarves, trying to keep warm, whilst Jerry and the rest of them were all nice and warm in the box in the studio.

Before the Scotland game, I'd made a breakthrough and was starting to jog again, and Clive rang me and said if I played for England A against Scotland A then I'd have a chance of being involved the following week in the full Ireland game. I had to give that serious consideration, because it was heading the way of a Grand Slam and obviously I was desperate to play a part in that: Scotland were never going to beat England in this form, and I thought we'd win in Dublin as the finale.

In the end, the thing that stopped me getting back in time was the way that Deano had been so good about it all. We'd made a target date of playing against Munster in the quarter final of the Heineken cup on 13th April as my comeback game and I didn't feel I could undercut that for a Test match, so I had to tell Clive I wouldn't be fit. It was a hard call to make, but I started to feel much more positive. Physically, I was in unbelievable shape in terms of weights and strength, and I was obviously in Clive's thoughts. It looked as though

I'd be going on the pre-World Cup tour to Australia and New Zealand in the summer and, with little rugby in my legs, I'd be fresher than most of the other guys.

England duly beat the Scots and I went to Dublin to commentate on the game for the BBC. The night before, I went out with some of the TV guys and the place was crawling with England fans. It was clear this was going to be a massive occasion: people were coming up to me and asking me if I had tickets and offering me £2,000 a pair. I didn't get involved in any of that. I always preferred to give them away. As it happened, I had four and, annoyingly, I passed them on to an Irish guy I knew who sold sportswear wholesale. The deal was that, in return, he would send a loads of kit to the orphanage in Portugal, which the kids could wear or sell to raise funds, in return for the seats. He sent over one box of adidas t-shirts – one box, for tickets worth £6,000-£8,000. Disgusting. We don't have a lot to do with each other any more, that's for sure.

You could tell as soon as you arrived at the stadium that England were going to win. I chatted with the coaches and the back-up staff beforehand, and they were all really nervous but all looking forward to the game.

I was out next to the camera, and the President of Ireland Mary McAleese, when the famous Johnson Red Carpet Incident occurred. England had lined up in the wrong place, the president couldn't possibly walk on the grass, so would England move? Not a chance. It was hilarious and it said one thing very clearly: England were an immovable object. They certainly were in the game. It was the best performance from England for a long time, as they thrashed a pretty decent Irish team.

The English fans went mad at full-time and I joined in, clapping and laughing. But inside I felt completely empty. Standing so close to what had just happened but not having been a part of it was horrible. I watched the boys do their lap of honour and celebrate on the pitch, and then I went inside, out of the cold. I was standing near the changing room, listening to them singing inside, when Clive came up and shook my hand.

'I want you to come in and celebrate with us,' he said.

'Thanks Clive,' I said. 'I can't, but thanks.'

The offer meant a lot to me, and I wanted so desperately to take him up on it. It would have been fine – they would have soaked me and covered me in stuff, but it would have been great. But there was no way I could. The players hate cling-ons, and I didn't want to be one of those. I was an outsider, so I stayed outside, waiting by the door to congratulate them as they came out in dribs and drabs. It was one of the worst feelings ever – not being able to go in and see my mates because I didn't feel I deserved to. A horrible situation. But I could just tell from the smiles on their faces that I'd done the right thing, and I was quite proud of myself for not going in. I hadn't contributed: all I'd done was commentate on their achievements, put a few sentences together here and there. It was their Grand Slam, not mine. They went off for a good night out and I got the late plane home.

As soon as I landed, I tore down the motorway and went straight to the gym, at about 9pm, to do some more exercises on my Achilles. I was keener than ever, desperate to get as fit as I could.

Not long after, I made my comeback, ahead of schedule, in a Premiership game against Northampton. The rehab had stepped up and I was still struggling with soreness when I tried to accelerate but at least I had a ball in my hands again. I came off at half-time and started against Sale the following weekend, getting 60 minutes in before Deano brought me off.

'You look OK,' he said. 'I want to play you at fly-half against Munster.'

Those were great words. I'd recovered in time to play, potentially, a pivotal role in our attempt to win three Heineken Cups on the trot. If we beat Munster, it was all mapped out: Biarritz or Perpignan in the semis, whom we knew we could beat, and then the final.

It was quite a tight game, I remember. Backy scored a try and as we came back to our own half-way line for the conversion, the chat was all about cracking on from there and really putting pressure on them.

Then it all went wrong for me. Harry Ellis – on for Jamie – threw a pass my way from his first scrum. My plan was to pull a move designed to send Freddie or Leon up the middle where they'd set up a ruck from which I could kick us out of our half. But Harry's pass was a little short and I had to wait for it, which slowed me down in my sideways movement and meant I was slow off the mark getting to Fred. It all went pear-shaped from there. Rob Henderson scragged me, I couldn't offload and Leon – whose timing was off because mine had been – ran straight into the side of me, bashing my head, knocking me out and snapping my knee at the same time.

At the time, with the concussion, I didn't really feel the knee. I went straight down and had no idea what had happened, though seeing it TV you can see how badly the joint wobbles. I remember lying there worrying about David and Hayley Liepins. David had supplied me with a sponsored car for years, and this was the first time they had ever come to see a game. *'I can't be injured in a big game like this,'* I thought. *'I can't go off. I've just had a load of time off. There is no way that I am leaving this pitch. I'm just a bit concussed.'*

Then – after two or three minutes – I started to feel the

pain in my knee and I realised I must have banged it as well.

The referee came over. 'Make a decision,' he said. 'Are you staying on or going off?'

'There's no way I'm going off, sir,' I said.

One of the physios was looking at the knee. 'You're going to have to, Oz,' he said.

But I shook my head. 'I'll be fine,' I said, pushing them away.

I just had this feeling that I couldn't be injured in this game. It wasn't supposed to happen. I stood up, and that's when I realised I had a more serious problem. The pain was excruciating.

'*Oh, my God!*' I thought. I hobbled into position, still thinking that maybe I could run it off.

Straight away, Henderson ran at me and I managed to tackle him, but I realised that I wasn't able to move and that the game, for me at least, was over.

Deano signalled, and they ran on with a stretcher. I waved it away: I'd always said that I'd never leave a pitch on a stretcher, it was just one of my rules. So I got dragged off, holding on to someone's shoulders, and taken to the physio room. Munster scored a try as I was being carried around the corner. My knee was in bits. I had torn my anterior cruciate ligament, partially torn my medial cruciate and knocked all the cartilage off the bone. At that point, I didn't know any of that. I certainly wasn't thinking about the World Cup, and whether I would be fit in six months' time. Surely, that was too far away to worry about? The doctor came and examined me. 'You'll have to see a specialist tomorrow morning,' said. 'I don't like the look of that.'

I got dressed, slowly, and hobbled outside on crutches with Lou and my sister, who was carrying my bag for me. We'd lost, the Heineken Cup dream was gone, and the fans were melting away. We were making our way through the car park and a Tigers fan walked over to me. 'What do you think you were playing at today?' he shouted. 'You cost us that game.'

'What do you mean?' I said. He was beered up and really aggressive.

'Well, you didn't play very well, did you?' he said.

The majority of Leicester fans are fantastic, but this one wasn't. Here was I, in agony, with my wife, pregnant with our second child, and the idiot was starting on me. He had no concept of what I'd gone through just to be able to take the field today. And he was wrong, anyway. I'd played fine.

'Sorry,' I said. 'I got injured.' I was trying to stay polite.

'It's not good enough, is it?'

You're right, mate. We've only just won back to back European titles and Premierships galore . . . you're spot on. We're all useless.

Hang on. No you're not. You're a tosser.

'If you don't go away, right now, I'm going to shove this crutch up your backside and smash you over the head with the other one,' I said.

He started to walk towards me, so I dropped both the crutches and headed for him. I was willing to fight anyone, with or without a leg.

Luckily, Lou stepped in between us. 'What do you think you're doing?' she said to the guy. He said something back, the moment was gone and he walked away. I hope he sobered up later and realised what a fool he'd made of himself.

I was pretty emotional. We'd lost, we were out of the Heineken Cup, I'd badly injured myself and now I was being abused by one of our own fans. It was unbelievable, one of the strangest occurrences of all time.

I had an awful night. My knee was locked solid – I couldn't straighten my leg or bend it from the position it was in, I couldn't sleep and I was in a lot of pain. We'd moved out of our house so that it could be renovated and we were living in a two-bed flat down the lane, so getting up those steps with Ellie Mae was quite interesting. She kept asking me what was wrong, and that made it worse. Until that point, I'd felt pretty strong. Now I felt utterly fragile and my 18-month-old daughter's big eyes and worried face made me feel quite emotional.

Next day, the specialist confirmed I would need an operation as soon as possible: I had it on the Monday at Nuffield Hospital.

oOoOo

When I came round from surgery, I saw the specialist there.

'How did it go?' I asked.

He looked pretty grave. 'The operation went well,' he said. 'But I think it would be in your best interests to retire.'

I was still woozy from the anaesthetic so I wasn't sure whether I'd heard right. I've always been a bit odd after operations – one time, I came round and called everyone I knew, said 'Where's my presents?' and put the phone down. I had no idea I was doing it. Another time, after I'd had my shoulder done, I woke up and saw the consultant, Angus Wallace and shouted 'You big fat porn star!' at him. Apparently, I repeated it over and over again. He came into the room later and said, 'I'd just like to inform you that I'm not actually a porn star, I'm a surgeon.' I wondered what the hell he was talking about.

With all this in mind, I grabbed the doc's sleeve. 'What did you say about retiring?' I asked.

I'd heard him loud and clear and his words sent me into overdrive. In fact, I became a gibbering wreck. I started crying, my mind racing with thoughts. 'What am I going to do now? How am I going to feed my family?'

When I calmed down, I phoned Lou and Doc Finlay, the Tigers' team doctor, and they were both soon there, with Mark Geeson, our physio. The sight of a few reassuring faces helped, and Finlay and Geese eased my mind. Players had come back from serious setbacks like this before, and I would be able to do the same, they said – though I'd never be quite the same player again. I only heard the first bit, naturally.

I turned my mind to overcoming this latest setback.

Before the op, I'd told the consultant that if he found the ACL was torn he shouldn't bother repairing it. If he'd replaced it, I'd have had no chance of getting fit in time for the World Cup. Instead, I'd asked him to patch me up as best he could to give me a fighting chance of being able to run on it by the late summer.

To be fair to him, he must have done a bloody good job because I'm still walking around. I've got pain, and I will have forever, and it does still dislocate sometimes, but he got me through a lot of rugby afterwards.

However, word had got around. Dave Reddin phoned and said he'd heard I'd torn my ACL. 'Sorry you're out of the World Cup, mate.'

'Hang on,' I said. 'I'm not yet.'

'OK,' he said. 'We'll see.'

But I could tell from his voice that he thought I was.

I needed some time to rest and recuperate and we headed off to Barbados for the wedding of my mate Si McKee. I had a good time, all things considered, but poor old Lou had the holiday from hell. I was on crutches, Ellie Mae was 18 months old and running around like a lunatic and Lou had to watch her and carry all the cases. And she was six months' pregnant.

We'd flown out there First Class with Virgin so I could lie down flat because I was still in a splint: I had a bed on one side, Lou was on the other and Ellie Mae was asleep in the middle. Lou and I fell asleep, and I was woken up by one of the stewardesses holding Ellie Mae in front of me and saying, 'Can you control your child please?' She had been running up and down the plane, shouting and making a nuisance of herself – a typical Healey.

We eventually got to the hotel and everything was fantastic, though we had our moments. On the beaches out there they have trees which drop poisonous fruits. Lou was having a swim in the sea one afternoon and I was looking after Ellie Mae. She'd toddled off to play in the sand 15 or 20 metres away from me and she picked up one of these fruits and went to take a bite of it. I jumped up and sprinted over to her with not an ounce of pain, grabbing this thing out of her hand before it went into her mouth. And then I fell to the floor, in theatrical but genuine agony. Mind over matter, obviously. Lou ran out of the sea and stood there dripping wet. 'If you can run like that, why can't you carry the bloody cases?' she said.

We got back from the break to find the season was going pretty badly for the club. We lost a few games – Gloucester, Newcastle, Harlequins – and things went from bad to worse. It was quite difficult to take, especially from the sidelines, on crutches – I was non-weight-bearing for about eight weeks. We scraped through to qualify for Europe by beating Sarries in the play-off for last place, only getting to that match by beating Quins by one point on aggregate over a two-leg semi, which brought home how bad things were.

It was the first poor year for Leicester and it signalled the beginning of our decline.

In our great years, our pack were unbelievable: the only gap was at blindside, and then Cozza came along and filled that one. Backy was probably the best of all of them: I don't think people understand how good he was. It pains me to say it, but I think he was the best player in the world for a long time and his retirement and the decline of Leicester and England are not a coincidence. Playing alongside him, he was awesome to watch – the places he put himself and the strength that he showed were quite remarkable and his understanding of the game was amazing. Because we were both small, we could do things together that other players couldn't. People would come through my channel, Neil would take them low – not to cut them down but to hold them up, to let them get an extra two or three metres in the tackle, so I could get there and rip the ball away.

Johnno was a world great, too, obviously, and an outstanding leader. Where Backy knew what the opposition were trying to do to us, Johnno had a brilliant general feel for the way the game was going. I could see opportunities and gaps and between us we could read a game very well.

It wasn't all down to the pack. They won the ball and held onto it but we had some magical players behind the scrum. Someone like Leon, or Geordie, or myself would always produce something different, something that no other team had.

As we aged and developed injuries, inevitably we began to fade – it happens to everyone but it wasn't great going from being undeniably the best team out there to also-rans scrapping with everyone else.

On the day of the Sarries final, I met my surgeon for a review of the operation and my recovery.

'Things have gone better than I thought they would,' he said, as he pored over scans and x-rays. 'You can come off the crutches now. But my advice is still that you should retire from rugby.'

It was great to get back on my own two feet, because, for a sportsman, there is nothing worse than being on crutches for a long period of time.

Now I faced one of the toughest decisions I'd ever had to make.

Regardless of the specialist's advice, I still wanted to get to the World Cup.

Why can't I get there? I thought. I'd come back from the Achilles when I'd thought I might not, and I'd had other injuries which I'd managed to work past. I had three months or so: could I do it in that time?

Against that, I had to think of my family and their financial security.

If I played on, my insurance would no longer cover me. If I took the insurance now, I would write myself a nice, fat cheque – £600,000 in cash, a waiver of contribution on my pension, which was a lot of money, and a waiver of contribution on my mortgage. All in all, it would add up to well over a million pounds.

What if I turned that down, tried to play on, found I was knackered, and then couldn't play again? My income would have disappeared down the toilet overnight.

I wrestled for a long time with it.

The bottom line was, did I play rugby for the money? The answer was No. I played the game because I loved it. The money was great, but it wasn't the be-all and end-all. I wasn't alone in this: I think that if you took the dough away from rugby now, 95% of the guys would carry on playing. They'd all go and find another job and there would be a bit of whingeing, but they would still do it, would still put their bodies on the line, still go through Monday to Wednesday being hardly able to walk, just for the buzz of chucking an egg around.

If I came back and the knee went again, I could always get a job and do something different. My family could move out of this house into a smaller place. We'd keep going and at least we'd be together.

What's more, I had faith in my ability to beat the injury.

My mind was made up. I turned the insurance down and vowed to play again.

I was heartened at Franklins Gardens, on the day of that match against Sarries, when I walked in front of one of the stands without my crutches for the first time in a while. I remember a lot of our fans clapping and shouting that it was good to see me up and about as I hobbled by, and that was a real lift for me.

I also remember watching the game and seeing the lads running around at pace and feeling real fear in my heart – fear that I'd never be able to do that, at that level of intensity, again. Had I made the right decision?

Another thing that sticks in my mind from that day is the sight of Rod Kafer sat up in the stands, watching the game from afar. As backs coach – and as a player – Kafes had been an inspired signing, as far as I was concerned. He'd taken us to the 2002 Heineken Cup final, had a good feeling for the game and had moved our game plan on a lot. I'd really enjoyed his company, too, as well as playing alongside him when he wore the 12 shirt and I was at 10. He weighed in at around 110 kilos, a big man with a big jaw, and we made a good team when people ran into our channels: he'd hit them and I'd turn them over with a few little judo flips. But towards the end of the season, they'd lost faith in him and gradually edged him out, he'd taken the hint and was actually joining Saracens the following year. So the management had banned him from our ground in the week leading up to the match and now they'd banished him to the bleachers and forbidden anyone from talking to him. It was a pretty disgraceful way to treat a solid guy; we didn't know it then, but it also hinted at things to come and showed how quickly life could change at a big club like Leicester.

My thoughts turning to my knee, I spoke to the England

physios and doctors and they mentioned a specialist in America called Bill Knowles. He'd worked with a lot of skiers and Charlie Hodgson, who'd suffered a similar injury himself a few months earlier, was going to see him for a month. I spoke to Deano and asked if I could go with Charlie. Deano agreed, and said the club would chip in a pay part of the bill, which was good of him.

The pair of us were to spend a month out in New Hampshire together. I met Charlie at the airport. I didn't really know him, he was new to the England squad, but we got on well and did the usual thing of trying to get upgrades as England Internationals, which worked on the way out there, but didn't on the way back when they'd hardly heard of England, and certainly not rugby.

We met Bill and then the long process started, and I can't remember ever being so focused in my life. The decision to risk the financial security of my family to play in the World Cup drove me on like a possessed animal, despite the pain – I was only a few days off the crutches.

England were on tour in New Zealand and Australia and though we weren't getting to see any of the games we found the results on the internet and heard reports in phone calls; they were winning games, which made it even more important for us to get fit quickly. Bill took us through a whole new programme of training, things that we'd never seen before, and we both worked like mad.

We'd get up, have breakfast together, and then have an hour's swimming with exercises and CV work. We'd go and have a snack and then do a weights session, before having some lunch with a lot of protein and glucosamine and various other tablets. We'd maybe sleep for an hour before going back in the afternoon for a CV work-out, either on a trampoline, a ball or a cross trainer. I remember one particular session on the cross trainer where I pushed myself really hard – probably too hard. I built a mental tunnel in my head where all I could see at the end was Lou, Ellie Mae and my mum and dad's smiling faces after a game, and I tried to reach them through this never-ending tunnel. I completely blanked out any pain I was feeling and for 40 minutes my heart rate never dropped below 175bpm, which was pretty strenuous going. At max, it was up into the 200s. It's the toughest training I've ever done in my life.

That session alone proved to me that I'd made my decision for the right reasons: I'd done it because I wanted to play in the World Cup and I liked playing rugby more than I liked seeing lots of zeros in my bank account. That was one of the greatest feelings I've known; the awareness that I'd made the right decision for the right reasons.

Charlie and I lived together in a log cabin. I did most of the cooking, because Charlie was limited in that department, and he did the majority of the tidying up because I was limited in that department. One night, we'd put some bags of rubbish outside and were just turning in when we heard a banging noise. I thought we had burglars, so I got up and went down and opened the front door to find a big bear staring at me. I froze until it started to move towards me and then I slammed the door shut and legged it upstairs to my bedroom, yelling to Charlie to have a look. The wildlife was pretty amazing. We used to ice our legs in the river after training and one day we were walking back and a moose plodded past just where we had been.

We had a good time. Bill really looked after us, as did a lot of the American athletes. We met up with some skiers, who obviously suffer with their knees, and a girl called Courtney, who was on the American ski team, took us under her wing and showed us around. One of the guys was a rugby fanatic, and he knocked on our door one night to invite us out to dinner. Charlie and I had been given pairs of compression tights to wear every night, to aid the removal of lactic acid, and it was really hot out there so we'd usually sit around in these things without tops on. I went to answer the door, followed by Charlie, both of us wearing nothing but tights. We must have looked like a right pair of weirdoes but the guy didn't bat an eyelid. He obviously thought, *That's how those crazy Limeys dress*.

It was a great month, and meeting Bill Knowles saved my career. In Leicester I wouldn't have been able to channel my energy. Over there, I had no distractions – we even had to buy phone cards to call home.

It was incredibly hard for Lou, of course. She had about ten weeks to go before giving birth to Daisy, and Ellie Mae to look after, and we had just moved back into our house. She was still struggling with her thyroid problem, but she never mentioned that she was tired or complained, not once. We had a lot of help from both mums, but it must have been as tough for Lou being at home as it was for me being away and training my nuts off.

At the end of the month, the knee was a million miles from where it had been. Sharp bits of bone and cartilage were floating around in it and causing pain, and it wasn't right, but I was on track.

Now: could I make the World Cup squad?

World Cup Dreams

My greatest achievement in rugby was getting back to play against France in one of the pre-World Cup friendlies in the summer of 2003. I say 'friendly': there's not much friendly about France in Marseille.

I'd been back two days, Clive was about to announce his 40-man squad and a piece appeared in the *Daily Mail*. The name on the piece rang no bells – I think it was Peter Jackson writing under a pseudonym. It harked back to the Lions tour of Australia and revealed that I still hadn't paid my fine. Well, that was true enough.

Clive phoned me from holiday in Portugal and had a massive go at me down the phone. 'I don't need this,' he shouted. 'I'm on holiday. I don't expect to be reading this about you the day before I'm due to name the squad. It's not about you, it's about the squad.'

Well, yes Clive. But don't look at me. I had no idea that this was about to appear in the newspaper – I've spent the last month in America, remember?

He raged on and slammed the phone down, saying, 'If you don't pay this fine, then you're not going to the World Cup.'

The call really deflated me. I'd left my young family and spent four weeks working like a lunatic over my summer break to give myself a chance, a small chance, of being able to run. I just didn't need this rubbish.

I'd been getting solicitors' letters from the Lions saying

they were going to take me to court. I'd reply, saying, 'I know your fine wasn't lawful, you know it wasn't lawful, so if you want to take me to court, feel free.'

Apart from anything else, I'd been sent the letter of notification of my disciplinary hearing the day after the tour agreement ended so, strictly speaking, I hadn't even had to turn up for my bollocking, never mind write them a nice fat cheque. I wish I'd stuck to my guns and made them sue me. It would have cleared everything up – especially the fact that I had not actually written the article, or said the words, about which everyone was so upset. I even had a letter from Eddie Butler admitting that.

But the way Clive laid it on the line, I was left with little choice. I wish now I'd told him to shove it, because I think my selection chances probably ended there and then anyway. From that point, I always felt there was uncertainty about my selection and that continued even more when I got to our Rugby World Cup camp.

Anyway, I paid the fine and phoned him back to tell him that I'd done so. I got a terse text back saying, 'I heard. I don't need this s***. You will be playing against France in Marseille and that will be your last chance to prove your fitness.'

He wasn't being very endearing at the time, and I wanted to kill him. I needed someone to look after me – I was quite fragile.

When I turned up at the camp in early July, I still wasn't running and everyone else looked in good shape. It was so frustrating watching them and I had plenty of time to ponder what had gone on.

Why was Harry's pass a little bit low in the Munster game? Why had I made that call? If Harry had fizzed it into my hands, or I'd called something different, or just booted it off the pitch, everything would have been different. It's like

Sliding Doors – your whole life can turn on one seemingly insignificant moment.

I was really getting down – so much so that I went and bought myself a new car, a BMW M3 convertible. I thought it might cheer me up. It didn't.

I was still training incredibly hard, mainly on a bike and a rower. We had a rowing competition at the end of each week – my team was Julian White, Danny Grewcock and me, and the challenge was to see how far we could row in 12 minutes between the three of us. It was a good team, those two guys are great trainers and very strong, and we won it every week, sometimes by quite a long way. That was good, because it helped me to feel more involved in the stuff we were doing. I spent hours every day in the swimming pool, trying to get the movement back in the knee and slowly, day by day, it improved. I would train when the team trained and then I would book in two extra rehab sessions a day on top, training five times a day in all. My strength was going through the roof – I was beating all of the forwards apart from Julian and Grewy on any upper body strength tests. I remember training with Lawrence and striving to beat anything that he could lift. I was bench pressing ridiculous amounts – 65kg dumbbells in each hand – so it wasn't all bad. I was in serious shape, and I thought that would serve me well. Ultimately, it was between me and Gomers. Daws was in and so was Kyran Bracken, and I wanted to be named as the third scrum-half.

In the early days, Kyran and I had been quite good mates, though our relationship tailed off when I was selected for the Lions in 1997 and 2001 ahead of him. Me being me, I'd given him a bit of banter about it. Now the roles were reversed and he wasted no time in sticking the knife in and twisting it. There was an edge to his jibes, though: I'd always been jokey, he seemed to really enjoy upsetting me. I don't think I'll ever forgive him for that. Everyone else was being really good: Daws was helping me along, Johnno had time for me, lots of people were doing their best to help keep my spirits up, because they could see that it was difficult for me not being fully involved. But, deep down, I feared Bracken was right. Physically, I wasn't up to it. In the previous world cup in 1999, I'd won all our CV, strength, speed and fitness tests . . . absolutely everything. Now, I couldn't run. They were playing practice games and I wasn't. I spent eight weeks of training camp working by myself, which was like being in a dark room. The knee was swelling up like mad after every session and I had to summon up serious amounts of motivation.

I used to spend quite a lot of down time with Lewis. I've mentioned his weird fixation with testicles before. We spent hours playing his favourite game, Nadger Ball. We'd sit at opposite ends of the room with an orange, or a melon, or any large, spherical fruit we could lay our hands on. You open your legs and put your hands on your head while the other lobs the fruit at your balls. That's how boring it was, but it entertained Lewis no end. He thought it was the best game he'd ever played in his life. He caught me on one occasion but then I got him back with a perfectly floated orange, right into the nuts. For anyone who fancies playing it, there's one other rule: if you move or put your hands down to block the missile, the other guy gets to throw the next one overarm.

The first day I was able to run properly was the Monday before we played Wales, away in Cardiff. Clive put me on the bench and he told me I would get on. I didn't, and I watched Gomers have a fairly good game. He did his basics well, his passing, kicking and decision-making was good, which wasn't great for me. I managed to drive home afterwards, stupid quick, to spend one day with Lou and Ellie Mae.

I headed down to London on the Monday for the meet-up ahead of the trip to Marseille. I was highly motivated, now, and desperate to play rugby again and I threw myself into team training. We had a non-contact practice game; Daws was putting the ball into the scrum and it was my job to pressure him at the base. Of all the stupid things for someone to do, Backy kicked me on the side of the knee, right where I'd done it.

I was very angry. I couldn't believe that a team-mate of mine would do that to me, knowing exactly what I'd been through and how hard I'd worked to get back. He could have ended it there and then, one bad shot on that knee and I was done for. I almost kicked off at him but just managed to rein myself in. Clive's watchword at the time was TCUP: Thinking Correctly Under Pressure. If I'd punched Backy it would have gone down as a black mark against me. After all, would I snap in the World Cup Final? Retaliate, and you could cost your team the three points that lost you the game. I was mad keen to make a good impression, motivated and controlled in training, constructive in meetings. I wasn't messing around at all and I couldn't throw all that away even for the satisfaction of smashing Backy.

I made it to the Marseille match, and Clive called me in for a pre-game chat.

'Just get through this game,' he said. 'Don't try and do anything extravagant, don't do anything that you don't have to do, just make your decisions, pass well and take control of each situation. All you have to do is be solid and steady and prove your fitness, and I'm 99.99% sure I'm taking you to the World Cup.'

Looking back, it was a strange thing for him to say. He'd never tried to control my play before – quite the reverse. 'I want you to play like Gunter Netzer,' he'd always said to me. I hadn't had the faintest idea who that was, but I looked him up on the internet and it turned out he was a famous soccer playmaker for Germany from about 20 years before I was born, someone who could do anything and pop up anywhere. I'd always felt proud, even elated, whenever Clive said that. Now he was telling me the reverse but I was so happy I didn't stop to analyse his words. I just nodded – when I should have ignored him and gone on to play my normal game – and left the meeting floating on air. Fantastic. At last . . . I almost wanted to cry with joy: all that work and sacrifice had paid off. Thank God I'd not taken the insurance.

During the game, I proved my fitness to a good enough degree, and my passing was spot on, probably the best out of the three nines who'd played. I put Tinds through on the pass for the try and supported him well. On the downside, we had problems around the base of the scrum – for some reason, they played Corry at No 6, when he's a better No 8, and they played Alex Sanderson at No 8 for the first time. Alex really struggled with the ball at his feet, which put me under more pressure – I couldn't keep Galthie, one of the world's best pressurising scrum-halves, off him. Still, while Daws was probably the best at handling pressure at No 9, I wasn't far behind so I didn't think it was too much of a problem. I knew, too, that I wasn't 100%, though I was getting there. I remember a ball squirted out the side of a ruck, and it was between me and Galthie to dive on it. I hesitated for a second, I had to *think* about it rather than just diving on it, and he beat me to the ball. I also missed a cover tackle on Dominici which I'd normally have made: I missed him by three or four metres, I just didn't have the cruising speed. *Sliding Doors* again: had I been fit I would have got across and put him into touch, we'd have had a line-out and cleared it.

We lost, by a point and I was terribly disappointed; we

hadn't been beaten in over a year and I hated being part of a losing team.

I didn't know it then, but that was my last England cap. My 51st.

I'd done a pretty good job and post-match I went up to Clive. 'Thanks for the chance to show I'm fit,' I said. He nodded and looked happy enough.

I had a quick drink with my dad, met some of the Leicester lads who'd moved out to France – Shorty and Perry Freshwater – and just chilled out for a bit. I was confident I'd be on the plane Down Under. I knew I wasn't completely fit, but I also knew I'd worked hard enough so I could run around and make it look like I was OK and that I'd get better in the coming weeks.

We returned to England and played France at home in the return friendly. I wasn't even in the squad for that, and neither was Daws. Kyran played, with Gomers on the bench. I thought they'd picked me and Daws, and Clive just wanted to see who to take out of the other two – until Phil Larder came up to me during the training session before our midweek day off.

'Whatever happens,' he said. 'Keep your chin up. You've had a bad injury, but keep your chin up.'

It's obvious, in retrospect, that he was giving me the nod and telling me I wasn't going, but I didn't see it. Unlike me, that. I sussed it later, on the drive home for the day off, like a depressing light bulb appearing over my head. For some reason, I didn't bother trying to speak to Clive.

I think now of all the things I could have said.

'Look, Clive . . . the semis are two months away. I'll be so much fitter by then and you know for a fact that if we are two points down and you can choose me or Gomers to send on off the bench to change things and try something different you're more likely to get that from me.'

Maybe I might have changed things. But I didn't. I went home, watched us batter the French, and waited.

Clive had said in a meeting before everyone left that he would text you if you were in the squad and phone you if you weren't. There were 40 of us in with a chance, and ten had to be chopped.

I sat there on that Saturday night, hoping for a text, dreading a call. Everything I'd planned for, and worked for, in the two years leading up to this had gone wrong. I kept thinking, '*Why couldn't I have had this preparation in 1999, when we didn't have much of a chance, and had 1999's preparation for this World Cup?*' In '99, I'd been one of our best players, certainly one of the best-prepared. More *Sliding Doors* and what ifs were going through my mind. I veered from the knowledge that I was out to moments of hope. Clive had usually been a man of his word with me, he'd been relatively straight. But then the old, 'I'm 99.9% sure I'm taking you' . . . that 0.1% suddenly looked like a very large doorway, with the World Cup bus heading through it at speed.

The phone didn't go, the night went really slowly and I struggled to get to sleep. I'd waited four years, since we'd been beaten by Jannie de Beer's boot, and I really, really wanted this.

I'd had two serious injuries in the year when I didn't need them. Things had been going pretty well up to that point. There was all the other stuff off the field with Lou and Ellie Mae, but I was raring and ready to go. I was desperate.

I finally fell asleep and woke up on the Sunday morning, the 7th of September with my phone ringing next to the bed. I leapt for it.

It was Johnno.

'Has Clive phoned you?' he said.

Something in his voice told me I hadn't been picked.

'No, why?' I said. 'What's the score?'

'You're not going.'

I felt myself fall through the floor.

'Did he say why?'

'He just said he wants specialists in the 9 position.'

'Alright mate, thanks for ringing me.'

I put the phone down and told Lou the bad news. On the strength of what Clive had said earlier, Lou's mum had taken three months' leave from her job so she could help with Ellie Mae and Daisy, when she was born, while I was away. It was even worse for Graham Rowntree when he was left out; he'd been told he was going, too, and had already booked his family flights to Australia. Poor old Wig lost about £5,000, which he couldn't get back, and I felt even worse for him. That would have been another knife in the side, the icing on a really nasty cake.

When I'm depressed about something, I end up sleeping and I'd gone back to bed after speaking to Johnno and telling Lou.

Half an hour later, my phone went again. It was Clive. I think he expected me to argue with him, maybe have a Gazza moment, but I didn't. Apart from anything else, I was clinging to my last hope – that someone would get injured and I'd be called up. You *cannot* go through a tournament like that without injuries. (Unfortunately England did, apart from Grewy's busted toe, and even I'm not that versatile.) Maybe it sounds selfish, and I'm sorry, but it's true, I'm human: I'd have loved it if someone else had dropped out and given me a chance, and anyone who says they'd feel differently is a liar.

I asked for a reason and Clive didn't really give me one. He just said he thought it was the best way to go. One day I'll get the truth out of him, probably when he's in a head lock and squealing for mercy.

So I just accepted it, and wished him good luck. 'I'm really disappointed,' I said, 'because I know we're going to win it.'

I know I would say this, wouldn't I, but it was a bizarre decision. Yes, I wasn't totally fit, but I could cover wing, scrum-half, fly-half and even full-back if pushed, and Andy Gomersall was just a scrum-half. And, no disrespect, even in that position, even at 80%, I think I was the better player. Daws phoned Clive after the squad was named and asked why I'd not been picked and Clive gave him the same thing about wanting specialists. Well, I had more caps at scrum half than Andy, so that didn't make sense either. I couldn't fathom it out and I still can't.

One thing I do know is there were members of that coaching staff who didn't want me there. Phil and Dave I'm not sure about, Andy Robinson I absolutely am. If I knew who didn't like me, I soon found out who my friends were. They were the people who rang me and Wig and sympathised. People like Shaggy, Lol, Daws and Jase Leonard . . . the players I'd been through the wars with in the last four or five years.

oOoOo

Clive's call was the start of my serious drinking. I'd said to myself beforehand that if I didn't get selected I would just get on with it – I knew I'd never be the same again, but I'd try and bounce back and continue to get fitter so that I could make my comeback with Leicester.

Unfortunately, it didn't work out like that. I put the phone down, went to the local pub and had a few. It's one of my traits, going out and getting blotto if I'm feeling low. At least I managed to break myself out of it that day and not go totally mental. Lou was pregnant and, to a large extent, that's what stopped me. I had three or four and then came home because she was due to give birth any day.

I went back to training at the club, and asked Deano to let me play against Irish. Because I'd been with England I'd missed our pre-season, but he agreed to put me on the bench, which I was grateful for.

I trained on the Monday and Tuesday in a bit of a blur and then on the Wednesday – 10th September, I remember it clearly – I kind of woke up and reality hit me. Some of the papers were saying that it was a massive mistake not to take me, because I'd always performed in the big games. Others said I'd been a liability in Australia with the Lions. The conflicting views started to mess with my head and I began dwelling on it all.

I wanted to believe I'd been left at home because of the knee, and because I'd been slightly below my own standards in the France game. But were some of these stories right? Was the knee just an excuse? Was it that, or was it all the stupid rubbish I'd been saying off the pitch all these years? I'd always walked a tight line, trying to be truthful and honest and sometimes ending up saying unfortunate things because they'd just come into my head. Some of the other players like to suck up to the management, but I couldn't do that. I've always preferred to take the mickey out of someone and then give them a cheeky smile and hope that they take it on the chin as a bit of a laugh. I didn't generally mind copping it back, after all.

Had the coaches finally washed their hands of me? I could imagine them in the selection meeting: 'Look . . . why should we take the chance with him? You know what he's like.'

'*Have I not been picked because of my big mouth?*' I'd ask myself. '*Have I been judged on all the off-the-pitch stuff? Has my personality put paid to my international career?*'

If that was the case, I only had myself to blame and I couldn't help but beat myself up over it. These were very dark days, when I tortured myself and reflected over all the things I'd said and done. I wondered whether, if I had my time all over again, I'd have been the same gobby, cocky joker? I wasn't sure. I don't think I'd have been the same person if I hadn't, that's for sure.

At training, my knee was like a balloon. Leon pulled me to one side and said, 'Why are you here?' We did one speed session and I was running as fast as I could but I couldn't get near anyone because the joint was completely surrounded with fluid. But I felt I *had* to train – I *had* to play and get back on that treadmill.

I came home from training on the Wednesday and Lou and I were watching *The Games* – that celebrity game show on the TV – and she started to get a load of contractions. She'd been having a lot of Braxton Hicks – false contractions – so I was pretty blasé. 'We'll just finish watching this,' I said, 'and if you've still got them then we'll go to hospital.'

The contractions started to get closer together, and stronger, and we realised this was the real thing. We jumped in the car and set off for the hospital, a fair drive away. By now they were getting really close and I started to think she was going to have the baby in the car so I hammered it all the way, not even stopping at red lights and cutting a half-hour journey in half. Lou was in a lot of pain by now, and we went straight into the delivery suite. It was too late for her to have an epidural, so she had to go through the whole thing with just gas and air.

She was amazing: she'd shown such strength and character all through a horrible year, never thinking about herself, just about me, and I realised how much I loved her when I saw her going through labour, without proper pain relief, to give us another child.

It made me step back, realise that rugby is only a game. I'd been exceptionally privileged with my sporting career and the World Cup was a blow, but not being selected was as nothing compared with seeing my second healthy baby daughter born.

It gave me a boost that I really needed.

I was keen to name her Louise after her mum, but Lou insisted on Daisy. I sent a badly punctuated round robin text out, saying 'We've had a baby girl Daisy Lou was amazing', and everyone thought the baby's name was Daisy Lou. We started to get cards to 'Daisy Lou', which I liked, and I managed to get 'Daisy Lou Healey' on her birth certificate. I think Lou was quite keen to get it taken off. Sorry, love.

I sent a text, too, to everyone in the England squad, and to Clive, saying we'd had a baby. It was meant more as a statement of fact, just to let the boys know, and to show things were going well and there were no hard feelings. When anyone in the squad had a baby, he'd be given champagne and everyone would clap and cheer. Clive texted me back and said, 'The champagne is on its way.' He was good at that, Clive; he was good at making you feel special.

We're still waiting for that champagne, though.

Not receiving it made me realise that I wasn't in the squad anymore, and I wasn't an England International any more. I was finished. That was it. More than anything, it was a lonely feeling. England had been part of my life for so long, and I suddenly felt very distant from it, and from the lads, and that was such a hard thing to take. Playing for England had been a massive goal in my life and a massive brick wall had been erected between me and that goal. All the years of focus, of tunnel vision – like when I'd been on the stepper in the States – and it all just seemed to have slipped through my fingers like a handful of dust.

Later that day, I drove Lou's mum and Ellie Mae over to

see them both. I'll remember the moment Ellie Mae saw her sister for the rest of my life. She's a bit of a tomboy, a bit gung-ho and she likes to throw herself into things, but she was unbelievably gentle; she held Daisy and gave her a little kiss on the forehead. That brought tears to a few eyes.

Lou stayed in hospital overnight, but came out with our new daughter the next day and it was great to have them home, and great to be a family of four in the house.

Deano said I didn't have to train until the Saturday, which was good of him. He knew when to tell me off, and he knew when to help me and this was one of those times.

I spent the next few days helping Lou and working on the knee. I was still swelling up a lot, and I was using a machine that sends electrical impulses through your legs and helps pump out the fluid from your joints. I'd also had an ice maker installed in the house so I could have regular ice baths and I bought a compression unit which packed my leg really tightly in ice to further assist the dispersal of the fluid. Without those three things, I wouldn't have been playing. I was self medicating, doing the things that would have been done for me at England.

I was also boozing: despite the lift that Daisy's birth had given me, I'd been getting fairly smashed on a daily basis to deal with it all.

I came off the bench against London Irish – it was something like 19–19, and a close game. I got an incredible reception. I'd never had an ovation like it, even after coming back from Heineken Cups: the sound was unbelievable, a roar of noise that sent the hairs up on the back of my neck and choked me up a bit. I felt like I was home, among friends, and it gave me a massive lift. I'd like to thank everyone who was there that day, actually. You gave me a huge boost.

I owed the club some good performances because Dean,

especially, had been good to me during my injury woes and supportive when I wasn't selected for England.

With my first touch, we scored a try, Ollie Smith, right in the corner. I just felt, 'Let's go, I'm back!' Without wanting to sound arrogant, I always felt as though the team got a bit of a lift whenever I came on. I know that does sound arrogant, but others have said it, too. We scored another try not long afterwards, through Henry Tuilagi, one of the most powerful men I've ever seen in my life, and that was that.

The England squad hadn't left yet and I was getting phone calls from people like Cozza and Johnno. A lot of the calls were filling me in on Kyran Bracken's situation. Kyran was in pretty bad shape, they said, with his long-standing back injury having flared up. He was keeping it secret from the management but, obviously, it might get to the point where it became obvious. 'Keep your chin up, you never know,' was the message. As things happened, I wish they'd not told me because it gave me false hope: Kyran was able to play, albeit with a number of injections in his back and mouthfuls of pain killers, and he went on to put in the best scrum-half performance of the tournament for England when he stood in for Daws against South Africa in the group stages.

They flew off Down Under, with KB and without me, and we carried on at Leicester. We embarked on our worst run of games of all time, losing five on the trot to Sale, Gloucester, Leeds, Northants and then Bath away. We weren't playing that well, half our pack was missing and there were a lot of young guys in the team. Morale was low, and it was lowest for me in the match against Gloucester. I'd been having a bit of a problem with my back – if it's not one thing, it's another – and I felt my calf go as I hit a tackle bag in the warm-up. It hurt like hell – I couldn't stand on it and thought I'd torn the muscle, or pulled it badly at best. I withdrew from the game, with a number of people, Wellsy in particular, thinking I was faking it. I couldn't believe they would accuse me of that.

And how bad is this? I was at home that night, feeling sorry for myself, when the phone went. It was Clive, phoning from Oz.

'Austin?' he said. 'Daws is injured and Bracken's back's bad. I need someone to come out as cover. Can you fly out?'

I could have cried. I almost had to force myself to get the words out, to be honest with him. 'I can, Clive,' I said. 'But the truth is I've pulled my calf today.'

'OK, mate,' he said. 'Keep me posted.'

His next call was to Martin Wood, and he flew out instead. Mind you, he was sent home four days later after Kyran miraculously recovered. It's amazing what you can do if you get enough painkillers inside you for a fitness test.

At the time, I thought this had to be the lowest point of all. An injury to someone, and the call to go out as a replacement, had been my fall-back; now that had gone, too.

I went in the next day to see the Leicester physios to get my calf looked at. They said it was a pull, but that now felt wrong to me: I was able to stand on my toes, which you shouldn't be able to do if your calf has gone. It was just tightening up straight away if I ran. Fortunately, I took a second opinion from a guy called Mark Buckingham. He invited me down to see him – I arrived at the same time as Paula Radcliffe, so I knew straight away I was in good hands. He took a look at me, poked me around a bit and said my calf was fine. In fact, I had sciatica, which was related to my recent back twinges. He gave me the most painful bum massage I've ever had in my life and sent me on my way, almost fully fixed. Amazing. So amazing that some at the club now thought I *must* have been faking the injury; they couldn't understand how I'd recovered so quickly.

I'd really upped the drinking at this point, hitting the booze much more heavily since Clive's call. I'd come home from training and open a bottle of wine, neck that, and then open another and neck that, too. My excuse to Lou was that I was trying to keep my back relaxed so that it didn't tighten up again. What a load of tosh that was.

I sat out the Leeds game in the stands but played against Northampton, our fourth defeat on the trot. Deano had us all in at 9am the next day for a clear-the-air meeting.

Essentially, the thrust of it was, *Let's buck our ideas up . . . now I want you all to go out and get drunk.*

Steve Booth always knew somewhere that was open 24/7 so he made a couple of calls and we found ourselves in a bar watching England vs Samoa, and getting the beers in. At 9.30am on a Sunday. Well, it was my 30th birthday.

Our Samoans were there – Freddie and Henry – and all the boys, and we were all cheering for Samoa. That was amazing to see. I was drunk and had my own selfish reasons why I wanted Samoa to do well – if someone played really badly, or got hurt, maybe Clive would ring again – but I still felt guilty and, deep down, I wanted England to win. Wig was in a similar boat, but there was no reason why the rest of the English boys should have been cheering the islanders: after all, a lot of our mates were out there wearing white. I couldn't fathom it: only Will Johnson was cheering for England.

I got absolutely smashed. We finished at the bar after the game and I suggested that we go to my local, purely so that I could walk home which was fairly selfish, too. We got taxis over there and started drinking again. The worst of it was that my family and some friends had driven all the way down to see me. I nipped home at one o'clock and said hello; my mum and dad and people were all trying to give me my birthday presents, but I was absolutely blotto and could hardly see straight. I mumbled some thanks and then said I was going back out.

'But we're having your birthday lunch,' said my mum.

'I'll be there in a bit,' I said, and left, walking back to the pub and carrying on drowning my sorrows with Freddie Tuilagi, George Chuter and my mate Ade.

In the end, they ate without me. I kept popping back for five minutes here and there but the lure of the pub was too strong. I feel pretty guilty, and embarrassed, about that now, though I think they knew what I was going through so no-one said anything. The Healey family are very up-front and will tell someone to their face if they're really out of order.

I carried on through the evening, going out for a night in Loughborough with Ade and getting back at goodness knows what time in the morning.

The following day, I got up, went out and started drinking again, which had never been like me really. I'd never been a massive drinker – I could put it away when I was with a group, and in the mood, but it never had a hold on me. But now I was in a mess, and I was on the verge of becoming an alcoholic.

Fortunately, I realised in time that it wasn't the right thing to do. I was jeopardising my job, and possibly my family, and I needed to stop being such a soft arse. It was an easy way out and I've always seemed to take the easy way out and make excuses when times are hard; it was time for me to front up and just take it on the chin.

We played Bath – and lost again – at the beginning of November, and I watched the England game against Wales and did some commentary on it for ITV. I'd seen Balsh get stretchered off and there'd been lots of chat in the studio about how I'd be going out to replace him. I felt sorry for Balsh; he's a good lad, it was his first World Cup and he's never had a lot of luck. Things were going well for him at this point, too. But at the same time I was still desperate for the call. Even if I'd been there for one game, and been involved in it, I would have felt like I was part of it and I wouldn't have felt like an outsider.

I thought there was a fair chance I'd get a call, but it never came and I assumed Balsh was fine, or Clive was happy with the cover he had, or he'd phoned someone else and I'd read about it in the newspapers. Lou's mum was starting work again, and I'd said I'd drive her back home to Leeds with Lou and the girls.

We'd just got past Sheffield when my phone went.

It was Clive. 'I want you out here on stand-by,' he said. 'You've got to be at Heathrow for 6pm to get the 8pm plane.' It was then 4pm.

There started probably the worst journey of my entire life.

I turned the car around at the next M1 exit, drove back to Leicester like a maniac, changed cars, picked up my gumshield and one pair of boots which was all I could find and was back on the motorway south by 5pm. The road was chocker and I must have put the fear of God into a lot of innocent motorists. All the time, my mobile was going with people saying, *I told you so, I told you you'd end up going, good luck, make sure you get involved, it was meant to be*, and all that sort of chat.

I got to Heathrow just in time. A girl from the RFU met me and gave me some kit, which was obviously meant for someone else because it was XXL and the shoes were size 10 – I've still got those in a box, if anyone wants them, those horrible brown designer ones they wore for the tournament.

Because I was the last person to check on to the plane, they'd downgraded me from business to economy.

'Can you please get me back up to business?' I said. 'Only, I'm flying out to the World Cup to try and play for

England, and if I have to sit in a little seat for 12,000 miles by the time I get there my knee will be so swollen I'll have no chance of playing whatsoever, even if I spend the next four days draining it.'

There was lots of shaking of heads, and pursed lips, and sharp intakes of breath, but just as I was about to get on the plane they did get me re-upgraded. In some ways I wished they hadn't, because they sat me next to some Australian who just talked about Australia all the way there while I pretended to sleep for 24 hours.

I landed in Sydney at 6.30am: really boisterous, feeling on a physical high and hoping against hope that this was it. I'd not drunk on the way over and I was raring to go. Clive came and met me and as we walked out past a load of photographers I felt part of the squad again, fleetingly. It didn't last all that long.

'You can't stay at the team hotel,' said Clive. 'It's Rugby World Cup rules . . . you have to go to another hotel till we officially call you up.'

Fair enough. I arrived at my hotel and Dave Reddin was there five minutes later. He took me for a fitness test, a load of nice, heavy weights at 7.30am after a day-long flight halfway round the world, which was pretty unnecessary. I passed and Clive asked me to meet him outside the team hotel – I wasn't even allowed inside.

'You're free for the rest of the day,' he said. 'We're holding fitness tests tomorrow on Lewsey and Balshaw; if they fail, you're on the bench against France.'

In the World Cup semi-final, that was, in case you've forgotten.

'Of course, if they pass, you're on a flight back to the UK at 5pm.'

Just over 24 hours after I'd arrived.

A few of the lads said they were going to play golf, and

asked if I wanted to go. I was jet-lagged, so I needed to stay awake to try and acclimatise as quickly as possible. A few holes sounded like a good idea, and I went out and thrashed about a bit with Mark Regan and one or two others. I fell asleep in the buggy a couple of times but managed to get through. That evening, I went for a pizza with Daws and Shaggy, and then Tinds and Cozza joined us and we had a beer with Zara Phillips and some of her friends at a local bar. If I closed my eyes, I could half feel I was really there, as of right – I could almost fool myself that I was part of the squad. I could also fall asleep again. By 8.30pm I was snoring into a bottle of Corona.

The following day I got up early. I knew the fitness test was at 9.30am and, like a sad little school kid, I walked around just talking to myself, hoping one of the guys failed. I actually hoped that it was Josh because I felt like he'd replaced me in the squad after my injury all those months before. I mooched around Manly for an hour, just looking at the sea, buying a smoothie and a doughnut, and waiting, killing time.

At the appointed hour, I snuck over to where the tests were being held and watched them, through the fence from miles away, so no-one could see me. I wasn't hopeful. You pretty much have to have a broken leg to fail a test if you can take enough painkillers in the morning to get rid of the niggle and, with a place in the 22 for the World Cup semi at stake, Josh and Balsh would be pretty motivated to pass.

I saw them strip off their tracksuits, stretch a bit and then start running.

And they were running fine. It was clear to me watching that they'd both passed.

I walked away, at rock bottom, knowing my final chance had gone. I'd flown all the way over there and I'd just seen it vanish before my eyes.

It was incredibly cruel.

Then my phone went. It was Clive. 'I need to meet you,' he said.

'What happened?' I asked.

He paused. 'Look,' he said. 'I'll come and see you.'

Five minutes later we met up.

'It's like this,' he said. 'They both passed. I've spoken to Deano and he wants you back in England by Thursday. You've got a Tetley's Cup match against Sale. Personally, I'd like you to stay out here. Someone could get injured in the semi and you could end up playing in the final. But you wouldn't be allowed to be part of the squad.'

I hated hearing those words: *you wouldn't be allowed to be part of the squad*.

'Thanks Clive,' I said. 'It just wasn't meant to be. I need to get home and play for Leicester. That's what Deano wants.'

I remember him saying goodbye but most of the rest of it is lost now. I got in a taxi at about 1pm and was on the flight back that night. The plane was empty, because everyone else was flying the other way, and I got upgraded to seat 1A; that was about the only decent thing that happened to me in those 48 hours.

I felt for a while that things changed in that plane. I thought I'd experienced 'closure'. Deep down, I knew that was the end of it. My last hope was extinguished, and I wasn't going back. In my head, finally, I wished the lads well.

I turned into a fan again. I was on the outside. I sat there at 35,000 feet feeling low as hell; but at least that was the end of the bad part. Now I could move on.

Except I couldn't.

I arrived back home on the Thursday night, and turned up at the club to be told I was playing full-back against Sale, a

225

position I hadn't played in for Leicester before. I hadn't had much sleep, I had jetlag and it wasn't my best game. Or ours. We were rubbish, and I went absolutely mental in the changing room at half time, throwing things and screaming at the guys, trying to start a fight to gee them up.

'Why can't we put in a decent performance?' I shouted. 'Haven't any of you f***ers got any heart? If we lose this now, you shouldn't play for the club ever again.'

It was real anger and I was on the verge of tears. I saw Deano's face as we walked back out; he had a wry, almost wistful, smile on his face. At full time we were drawing, and in the last minute of extra time I stopped somebody on the line, they recycled the ball and scored in the other corner. We'd lost, and there was a terrible feeling of lowness. I felt awful for Deano. There was a lot of talk in the papers about him not producing the goods, but what did they expect? Half our squad was away in Australia. There was only really me, Josh Kronfeld, Leon and Wig of any age and most of the rest were youngsters. Good youngsters, yes, but you can't win hard games without experience, and coaching can't give you that.

I went out, had one beer with the lads and fell asleep in the bar before jacking. I got a taxi home and slept for two days, non-stop – a mixture of depression and straightforward tiredness, I think.

I watched the France semi-final, a great performance by the boys, especially Jonny and Johnno, and I was cheering like a nutter. I was pleased, and really happy for them, and for England, and it was clear at the end of the game that they were going all the way. The Aussies had gone on a lap of honour around the pitch after their win over the All Blacks but the lads had noticeably avoided that. There was no celebrating, just a few nods and handshakes. They were in the final but they weren't happy with that, they wanted to win. The mental strength showed through, together with all the work they'd done. You could see all the pieces of the jigsaw fitting together, which made it even harder. Once, I'd been one of those pieces.

We had Rotherham away on the day of the final: not the most glamorous of fixtures by comparison. We were due to kick off at 4pm and the club delayed the bus departure time so we could watch the whole final in the morning. It was still going to be tight, so I packed my kit the night before – something I never did – and flicked through the papers in the morning. All were carrying variations on a theme: *This was going to be England's greatest day*. I had to stop reading them, though I had no doubt that they were right. I didn't think Australia had a hope of winning. Not a hope.

I watched the game in bed. A wry grin crossed my face when Lote Tuqiri out-jumped Jason Robinson for the first try. It had always been one of Phil Larder's reservations about me playing on the wing, that I wasn't big enough to cope with the high ball. Jase is a couple of inches smaller than me. I'm not knocking Jason, by the way: he's one of the greatest players the world has ever seen and I'm sure Tuqiri would have beaten me to the ball, too.

That's one of the few memories I have of watching the final. I remember Jonny's kick and the celebrations when we won but most of it is gone, locked somewhere in my memory. I can't actually describe how I felt. I had tears in my eyes, I know that. Some of them were from seeing my mates win the damn thing. People like Johnno, Benny Kaye, Daws… guys I'd been through a lot with over the years. Seeing Will Greenwood so happy and jumping around – Shaggy had had an awful year, with the loss of his baby son Freddie – brought tears of happiness. At the same time there were tears of jealousy, hatred towards the injury I'd suffered and resentment of the people who I didn't think deserved to be there as much as I or Graham Rowntree did. Even my own team-mates, like Dorian West. Nobby was a great player, but he'd come into it late, almost by default. I don't resent him now, I just did at the time. I just needed someone to hate, I think.

Even worse, Lou and my girls weren't there to be with me. They'd gone to Lou's parents for the weekend to get away so I left a quiet, cold, lonely house behind me as I drove to meet everyone to catch our bus. We had a lot of foreign players in the team at the time, and they were more supportive than a lot of the English guys. People were clapping me on the back and saying, 'I can't believe they won. Hard luck.'

Wig was sat at the back of the bus, just looking out of the window and shaking his head; he was clearly in a bad way as well.

I actually can't remember much of the drive up or the match. I felt like I was concussed, and I wrestled with weird feelings – a bizarre combination of pride and jealousy.

I scored two tries in the game and the ref denied me a third, even though it was a definite try and he was looking straight at me when I was lying on top of the ball over the line. He didn't give it and I swore at him, bitterly, though I don't know what I said. We won but the game was a blur.

I came off the pitch and saw my mum and dad there. They clearly felt as upset for me as I felt for them: they would have loved have been in Sydney instead, celebrating having watched me play for England in a World Cup Final, every bit as much as I'd wanted to be there. I could see that it was difficult for them, and I did pull myself together a bit. '*Stop thinking about yourself so much,*' I thought. '*There are people on your side, helping you, like they always have. Stop being such a soft b******, and get on with it.*'

For a few moments, a jumble of memories raced through

my head, memories of the support I'd had from my family through my whole career, from the day when my dad bump-started the car down Shamrock Road to get me to Rhyl to play for the under-9s when we were late one day, to the time when he ran with me to the ground because it wouldn't start at all.

I went back to Leicester and, instead of going out drinking with the lads, I stayed in.

Then the messages started to come, players texting and phoning me. A few of them taking the mickey: 'Where's your World Cup winner's medal?' is one I vividly recall.

My real friends were different. I took a lot of calls from Australia saying, *This was for you and Wig, Oz, we're thinking of you both.*

Clive said afterwards that there were two players he hadn't taken who were as much a part of the squad as those he did, and they were me and Graham. That meant a lot. But I can't swap that for the reality of having been on that pitch.

I can never swap that for being stood next to Clive and Johnno and the boys on that podium, chucking water over everyone and slapping them on the back.

I'll never have that, because I wasn't there, and for a long time that hurt me more than I thought possible.

Tasting My Own Medicine

The red carpets were rolled out and the champagne started flowing as the World Cup winners got home and the dinners started in earnest.

The first do I went to was Matt Dawson's, part of his testimonial, on the Wednesday after they arrived back. You always invite internationals along to sit on tables as part of the package for your guests and I came into the room alone and was introduced by myself. And then I heard, 'And now . . . please welcome the victorious World Cup winning team.'

A familiar empty, hollow feeling took hold but I stood up and clapped with everyone else and I was glad I did: I felt a lot of pride for the guys, especially my close mates.

We had dinner and Matt stood up and made his speech. He thanked the England team for turning out for him and finished by saying, 'I'd also like to thank Austin, who didn't get a World Cup winner's medal, for coming, too.'

He grinned, everyone laughed and I sank in my seat. He carried on taking the mickey for a while, and speaker after speaker followed suit. Fair enough, we rarely missed an opportunity to have a laugh at each other's expense. But this was slightly different, slightly bigger than somebody knocking on or dropping a high ball. I'd missed the chance of a lifetime.

Steve Wright was hosting the dinner and he called me up to respond. Everyone started cheering and laughing, so I went up to the podium, making sure I was biting my tongue.

'There's nobody in this room who was prouder than me when my friends won the World Cup for our country,' I said. 'Although I am a rugby player, and I was desperate to be there, I am also a very proud Englishman and what you've achieved is monumental and makes me feel very proud. By the way, I think you're all w*****s.'

Well, at least it got a few laughs.

It was the first of many such events. The mood was great, people couldn't get enough of it and they kept rolling them out.

There was a dinner for Martin Johnson's Testimonial Year, the Cup was there and I was MC. After the dinner, I announced one of the fund-raising stunts. 'Ladies and gentlemen,' I said. 'There will be an opportunity later in the evening to have your picture taken with the World Cup for a £10 donation to charity.'

Will Greenwood was the first person on stage: he pulled a tenner out of his pocket and handed it over.

'There you go, Oz,' he said.

I was genuinely wrong-footed. 'What's that for?' I said.

'So you can go and have your picture taken with my World Cup.'

That was a real dagger to the heart, for Will to do that. I'd lived with him, we'd been best mates throughout our rugby careers and even he couldn't resist laying into me. I didn't have a comeback. Normally, I'd have ripped him to shreds – I'm loads wittier than that lanky, big-nosed pillock – but my brain was empty. Then Jason Leonard came on stage and did the same joke. Well, that's forwards for you. Again, Jase was another a close mate and I could see they found it funny. I just don't remember them doing it to Wig and that rankled for a while.

Another dinner was held in honour of The Magnificent

Seven – our players from the tournament. Graham and I were asked to attend and I was placed next to David Jones, the previous chairman of Next, a key sponsor of the club. We were having a nice chat and a drink when Nick Mullins, the BBC journalist and MC for the night, got up on stage to kick things off. 'I'd like to welcome the Magnificent Seven from Leicester Tigers,' he announced, to a roar of approval, as the guys walked over to the stage with the Cup. 'Oh, and by the way, all is not rosy. Austin Healey is here as well.'

Without thinking, I picked up a bread roll and skimmed it at him from about 15 or 20 metres. It caught him square in the eye. I've done a lot of spontaneous things in my life, but that was probably the most emotionally driven thing that I've done. Nick's presentation stopped as he spluttered and clawed breadcrumbs out of his eye. I sat back down and waited for someone to berate me but David Jones leaned over. 'He deserved that,' he said, which made me feel a lot better.

I know it sounds like I'm whingeing and I know I've dished it out to enough people over the years to deserve plenty back. I just felt that people were taking it too far. I could accept any amount of chat about being little, or gobby, or even no good. I could take stick for the mistakes I made. This was something else. This was something permanent. I couldn't undo it. Nick's remarks really got to me. He didn't know me from Adam at the time, he had absolutely no idea of what I'd been through to try to make it to the World Cup and he didn't seem to care a jot that my professional career was going to end in disappointment. To him, I was just a joke he could use to kick a speech off. But I had a young family and a very uncertain future. To me, all this was very serious.

That period took away a huge chunk of my confidence, of my self esteem, and, though I didn't fully appreciate it at the time, it was really the beginning of the end of my rugby career. I wasn't going to get back to where I'd been voted into the World XV for three years on the trot, where I'd won two Heineken Cups with Leicester, where I'd played for England and the Lions, and won Premierships. That was a big nail in my coffin. That's it, you're finished, you've had your moment in the sun, it's all over. I became particularly bitter and twisted about the whole situation. I remember driving home from club training sessions thinking, 'What's the point in carrying on? I can't be bothered.'

I had people coming up to me in the street and saying, 'Well done in the World Cup... you were fantastic.' I had to put them right, sadly, though I always claimed I didn't play because I was injured. That way, I thought they'd have more sympathy.

There were some great stories coming out of that time.

I loved the tale of Daws trying to go through the metal detector at Sydney Airport, and it keeps bleeping. The Aussie security guard makes him empty all his pockets, then take off his shoes, and finally his belt, and still it keeps bleeping. In the end, the guy scratches his head and says, 'I can't work this out, mate.'

So Matt lifts up his t-shirt. 'Maybe it's this, mate?' he says. 'That's a World Cup Winner's medal, that is.'

Great banter, I'd have been proud of that myself.

The boys went down to Trafalgar Square, met the Queen and Tony Blair and got driven around in a bus. Tetley's, being a sponsor, had put some of their beer on the bus, a few of the lads decided to endorse it and Jason Leonard got a bit more enthusiastic in his endorsement than everyone else. He'd had a few dozen tins when he suddenly realised he needed the toilet. Except there wasn't one on the bus. So, somewhere down Oxford Street, he grabbed an empty champagne bottle and weaved to the back and weed into it.

He thought no-one was looking – and he was right, except around a thousand TV cameras, a million people and everyone else on the bus. He must have been desperate because he overflowed the bottle and dribbled several further pints of urine down the back of Lewis Moody's leg.

One of the funniest tales, told by Johnno, involves Dorian West. They're waiting to see the Queen and one of her flunkies comes in to address the lads. 'When you meet the Queen,' he says, 'you will first address her as 'Your Majesty' and then subsequently you will address her as 'ma'am'.'

Everyone nods their heads earnestly. Everyone except for Dorian, a working class hero in his own mind. 'I'm not doing that,' he says. 'My taxes pay for all of this.'

Moments later, the doors open and in walks the Queen, a small lady with a huge presence according to Martin. He took her along the line, introducing everyone in turn. 'This is Jonny Wilkinson, ma'am . . . this is Will Greenwood, ma'am . . . this is Mike Tindall, you might have seen him around the place,' and so on. Eventually they get to the end of the line, where an apprehensive Dorian is waiting.

'And this is Dorian West, ma'am,' says Johnno.

Whereupon a sweaty and very nervous Nobby says a very timid 'Thank you' and becomes the first ever English rugby player to curtsey to the Queen. The rest of the squad just wet themselves laughing.

After the medal and just being there, it's these things I miss most. The endorsements and the extra wedge would have been nice, but it's the banter and the *craic I* really wish I'd been part of.

I wish I could tell these stories in the first person.

Things weren't great at the club. Leicester were performing poorly at the time, and Deano was under pressure. The lads came back for their first game, which was Bath at home on November 29th. I think that was the day Johnno announced his retirement at the end of the season and the seven of them came out to a huge welcome which was well-deserved and nice to hear, though most of them were on the bench. We lost 13–12, a shocker, and I missed a drop goal right at the end.

We were 10th in the league and we'd lost six of the first eight games of the season, which was a huge thing for us, literally unheard of. From a personal point of view, it was a nightmare. If I was getting lots of mickey-taking at dinners, I took 10 times the amount on the pitch. I couldn't do much about it: before the tournament, I'd dished out eight or nine years of serious stick; I always had a good put-down handy and if someone tried to come back at me I could always rub their noses in it with the scoreboard. Now I was getting a taste of my own treatment.

None of it was particularly clever – 'Where's your World Cup winner's medal?' or 'Did you watch the final? Wasn't it good?' – but I really hated it. I just had to take it on the chin; you make your own bed in this game and I had it coming. It was a chastening experience, though, and my own levels of lip subsided dramatically.

I chatted to Graham Rowntree, and he was going through much the same thing. The only difference was that people felt sorry for him and didn't try to wind him up. It helped to have Wig; we'd crack jokes to each other, have a bit of banter between ourselves and retain some sanity.

It didn't help that the knee still wasn't right, or anywhere near. It was absolutely killing me, swelling up every week no matter how much ice and compression I used. Lou was still struggling to get her thyroid condition under control, and she had developed chronic fatigue syndrome as a side effect. She was shattered, I was battered and life wasn't great.

I just needed a bit of time off, I guess, but professional rugby isn't the sort of job where you can go away for a couple of weeks when you fancy it. I ended up playing most of the games in that season, although I was injured for one crucial encounter, Stade Français at home in the Heineken Cup.

The pressure on Dean was really building now and the atmosphere at the club was turning dark and bitter, with rumours of plots to oust him, even involving some of the players. We were nowhere in the league – people were even whispering about relegation – and the Cup was a possible lifeline. We'd played Ulster away – I had a shocking game, one of my worst ever, in the strongest wind I've ever played in – and were smashed 33–0, but we murdered them at home in the return, and it seemed we'd turned the corner. The following week, we faced Stade. They'd beaten us at their place and at stake was a quarter final place.

We lost, 13–26, missing most of our kicks.

I remember sitting in the changing room afterwards, before the rest of the players came back in. Deano walked in; he was rarely buzzing with *joie de vivre* but he looked like a man who'd reached the end of the road.

'Whatever happens,' I said, 'I haven't said anything about you and I still think you're the right man for the job here. And I hope that we can keep our friendship.'

He looked at me. 'I realise that you've had nothing to do with it,' he said.

That was the Saturday evening, and something was clearly on the cards. The following Monday we were called in and told that he'd left the club. The story they sold us was that the board had wanted to change the coaching structure, but that Dean had resisted these plans. As I've said, one of his greatest strengths was his stubbornness, the fact that he was uncompromising; now, some felt that was his undoing.

It was still a shock. The most successful club manager in

the history of the professional game, gone, after a few bad results.

Dean had achieved tremendous things at the Tigers and I still think it was a mistake to lose him. He was one of the best guys I've ever worked with at club level. He certainly got the best out of me; I know there are some people who didn't like him, who felt he didn't help the team or he didn't do much coaching, but I'd put his rugby brain right up there. The drop in form was inevitable – no-one can go on winning forever. We'd had world class players at the club, five or six each season, for years, but age was starting to take its toll on even the greats like Backy and Johnno. The question is, would Deano have got the club back to where we'd been? It's impossible to answer that but I like to think he would.

In the short term, John Wells would take over and be assisted by Andy Key, which was disappointing. I'd always liked and got on with Kiwi but he never stimulated me or pushed me. Whether that was down to me or him, I can't tell, but it was a fact. As for Wellsy, he was like Andy Robinson, a safety-first man, someone who would rather not lose a game than win it. Perhaps I'm too romantic about my sport in an age when it's become a business, but that was something I hated. For me, it was about winning in an entertaining way. That's what thousands of Tigers fans paid good money for each week. Being able to play professional sport in front of big crowds is a very special opportunity in life. If you accept the adulation and the money and the fame, you must try to make people smile and enjoy their day out. Rugby's perceived as a game for the posh but it's certainly not like that in Leicester; a lot of our supporters had hard, mundane jobs and the weekend was their release. They don't want you kicking to the corners and playing the percentage games every week.

I'd realised that was Wellsy's way when I first joined

Leicester. We were playing West Hartlepool away in 1996 and we were leading about 27–0 at half time. Will Greenwood and I had just joined the club and were playing pretty well. Bob Dwyer was away at the time so Dosser Smith was in charge. Dosser gave a bit of a team talk at half time and then turned to me and Will. 'What do you reckon, lads?' he said.

'I think we should try some of the things we've done in training now, things that we don't know whether they've worked or not, and really try and put this side away,' I said.

Wellsy turned to me. 'Shut up,' he said. 'We won't be doing that. We'll close the game out and make sure we win it.'

I looked at Will and he was just shaking his head. '*Should have gone to Bath*,' I thought.

Obviously I'm glad that I didn't, but you take my point.

Don't get me wrong, Wellsy's a good guy and we've had some good banter together over the years. Mainly it's been me taking the mickey out of him and him floundering around and trying to come back, but failing because his brain's not quick enough. We were always at opposite ends of the rugby spectrum; he saw me as a flash Harry just because my jersey wasn't mildewed and my boots were clean. No word of a lie, he had cobwebs on his, and he used to train in a Christmas jumper when I first joined, literally a pullover with little red deer on it. How could you *not* take the mick?

Anyway, I just didn't need him as a coach. I wanted someone who would inspire me, not slow me down.

The changes didn't stop there and they weren't all bad. Mark Geeson was removed as the head physio and in came Paul Stanton. I'd not always seen eye to eye with Geese, though we'd developed a much better relationship in recent years, but Studley Stanton was a class above. He was a very well-respected physio from BUPA in Leicester who'd seen a lot of the lads privately. He had a great manner, really jolly, and he enjoyed his job. The fitness coach John Duggan went, too, a great guy who was replaced by my mate Darren Grewcock. Grewy is a stern motivator, very confrontational, but really good to train with. He gets the best out of most people and for me his arrival was great. It gave me a bit of a kick-start. I started to train harder and get more involved in stuff and I'd say Darren's arrival was part of me starting to break out of the depression of not being part of the World Cup.

Maybe I'd been wrong about Deano going, because we won the next 13 games on the trot and qualified for Europe. The knee was starting to feel a bit better as the sharp bits inside it were gradually being ground down and everything started looking up. I scored two tries against Wasps when we battered them towards the end of the season, which was a really good result against the coming force in English rugby at the time. We'd had to do it without Daryl Gibson, too, after he'd managed to break his toe with a paving slab while laying his patio the day before. Instead of going out on the lash afterwards I came home and had a couple of quiet ones with Lou. I'd started boozing less by now: things were brightening up, I no longer spent the drive to training thinking, 'Shall I crash my car into that tree?', I was going to train, and train hard.

A lot of that was down to Grewy. He'd told me to stop being so miserable and get on with it, and eventually I started to realise how fortunate I was. I was still being paid well to play sport, I had two beautiful daughters and a beautiful wife and I was still being stopped in the street by people who thought I had played in the World Cup. Maybe, eventually, I'd somehow morph into the squad in everyone's minds anyway.

The day after the Wasps game I was woken up by a call from Matt Griffiths from the BBC.

'How would you fancy presenting *Rugby Special* today?' he said.

I'd enjoyed my flirtations with TV and had always hankered after the chance of fronting that show. I'd also fancied being a captain on *Question of Sport*, too, but somehow they gave that job to Matt Dawson instead. God knows why, he's painfully bad – Ally McCoist toys with him every week, like a cat with a really thick mouse.

I asked whether the show was recorded and Griffiths said it was.

'What time do you need me?' I said.

'Just get to Worcester Rugby Club as quick as you can,' he replied.

I raced over after training and arrived about 11 o'clock and found the producer.

'Goes out tonight this, does it?' I said.

'Er . . . no,' she said. 'We're on live at 12.10pm.'

Blimey. I had an hour to learn a 60 minute show, which was nerve-wracking to say the least.

The guests were Cecil Duckworth and John Brain from Worcester, Andy Gomersall and Craig Dowd of Wasps.

During the rehearsal, I turned to Duckworth. 'Right,' I said, 'I'll come to you first, Cecil. I'll say, "*Congratulations, it's been a long time coming but finally you're in the Premiership. How does it feel?*" What sort of answer will you give?'

He trotted out this long-winded spiel, about a minute and a half in length. 'Perfect,' I said. 'That'll give me time to settle in and we'll lead into something else.' We filmed a few recorded links and then went live.

'Welcome to *Rugby Special*,' I said. 'As you may or may not know, I'm Austin Healey. John Inverdale can't be with us today, he's not well, one of the bulbs burst on his sun bed, so you'll have to put up with me. Here we are at Worcester, who've just been promoted...' – big cheer from the Worcester faithful in the audience – 'and our first guest is the owner of Worcester, Cecil Duckworth.' I turned to him. 'So, Cecil – how does it feel?'

'It's great,' he said.

And that was that. He just sat there, looking at me.

I thought, *'You absolute b*****d ... this is my first live TV show, I've had no training, no practice and you just throw that back at me.'*

'With those kind of answers, Cecil,' I said, 'I don't think I'll be asking you any more questions today,' and turned straight to John Brain. The show went OK: I got a few things mixed up, ran things in the wrong order, but no-one seemed to mind. I went to Andy. 'Gomers,' I said. 'Have a look at this from yesterday's games and look at my two tries. Seeing that, don't you think Clive made the wrong decision in taking you to the World Cup instead of me?' There was a bit of laughter and cheering and I started to build up a bit more banter and get into the swing of things, gently abusing people and having a laugh. We finished up and I just felt a huge sense of relief, and immediately wanted to do it again. It gave me a great buzz.

We played Newcastle Falcons away, drawing on a freezing northern day, and when we came in John Wells was already in the changing room. He'd made it plain that he wasn't keen on doing the job by himself, he needed some help, and the club had been searching far and wide for an assistant. Peter Wheeler and Peter Tom came in and made the announcement: Pat Howard was coming back the club to coach the backs. Pat was already in my top five least favourite people of all time. We'd never liked each other when we'd played together – when I played fly-half I was always shouting out 'miss one' to miss him out and annoy him – but I think he'd started it, to be fair. Just after he joined the club, he went up to Lou, drunk, and asked her why she was married to me. The same night he asked my best mate Ade why he was my best mate. I put up with him for the benefit for the team but this wasn't great news. Oh, and Richard Cockerill would be the assistant forwards coach while still playing. That made me chuckle. They'd scoured the nation and come up with Cockers. Admittedly, Paddy had a bit of a pedigree but Cockers was unproven, apart from doing mini rugby with the 5–12 year olds where, apparently, he was very good.

We got to the play-off final against Sale, winning 27–48, a great game which earned us a place in Europe. We did it without Jaco van der Westhuyzen, too, who'd joined that season and played magnificently all through. Jaco was named our Player of the Year, an award all the guys want to win. There've been some great names on there down the years, the likes of Garforth, Johnno, Backy and, of course, myself. The dinners are always great fun, full of supporters and sponsors, and I always made a big thing about booing and pretending it should have been me, which I found quite amusing. I'm not sure about the rest of the lads. Jaco made a speech and afterwards I got up and said 'I must apologise for Jaco... he doesn't speak very good English.' He didn't seem to see the joke and, fair enough, it wasn't actually very funny really. Maybe it's the sheer volume of stuff I come out with; some will work and some won't.

I knew that Paddy was going to arrive the following season but I decided to forget all about it by going on a massive holiday once rugby had finished. We had a huge break this time – seven or eight weeks off – so we went to Spain, hiring a lovely villa in Puerto Andratx and rotating friends and family through the summer. I did loads of swimming, a lot of relaxing and started to get more confidence in the knee.

I've noticed, by the way, that I keep referring to 'the knee' as if it is some kind of external thing when obviously it's part of my body. I think it's a psychological thing.

We had a fantastic time, eating in some great restaurants and I wangled my way on to Tom Cruise's boat which was a big thrill for him. We returned fully refreshed and I turned round and flew back, this time to La Manga with the Professional Rugby Players' Association (PRA).

La Manga is the PRA's annual, fund-raising golf trip, where 20 players go out with 60 or 70 paying guests from companies like Mercedes and Guinness. If you get the chance, go – it's probably the best trip you'll ever go on.

Leon and I went out together the night before. We met a guy from the PRA and went out for a few drinks, ending up in a Spanish nightclub playing spoof, not for drinks but to see who was going to go and break-dance on the empty dance floor in front of all these cool Spaniards. Unfortunately, I lost. I'd only had two or three pints so hadn't lost my inhibitions but that was tough: I stood there, break-dancing and body popping on my own for about ten minutes while the other two wet themselves and the Spanish stared at me like I was a raving lunatic. We played again, Leon lost and he bottled it. That sums him up – he'll let you do it, but he'll never do it himself. He won't risk his reputation or his street cred for anyone. He's also a secret tipper; go out on a session with him and before long he'll be slyly pouring his drinks into plant pots or 'forgetting where he put them'. He'll wander off to the loo with a full pint and come back with an empty one.

'Where's your beer, Leon?'

'What . . . this? Oh, I just necked it in the bogs.'

'Yeah, right.'

The guests arrived in La Manga the following day and we were introduced to them all. They were a really good bunch and it was great for us, as players, to mix with people other than other players. There was a big ginger guy there called Kevin Lanane who works for Laboursite. We immediately took a shine to each other and whiled away the morning on a bombing contest in the swimming pool. I think he won. He displaced a bit more than me. It was good to see people enjoying themselves. I was asked to look after one of the older guys, a chap of about 60, and he had the time of his life: and I'll never forget him standing on the piano singing.

At the end of the night Leon and I coated ourselves in sun cream and played a game of Cocoa Butter Luge on the marble floor in reception. You push off the wall, run a few steps then dive onto the floor and see how far you get, leaving your beer bottle as a marker. I won, naturally.

I flew home on the Sunday night, having been drunk for effectively 48 hours, and got to the club at 8am on Monday to be introduced to our new fitness coach, Phil Mack. He'd just taken over as Head of Athletic Performance; Grewy was still there, but now just as an assistant and I think that put his nose out a bit. The first thing we did was a bleep test. We all had to get above a certain level – I think it was 12 – and I just made it, dropping out at about level 12.8. Leon dropped out at 10. We were both still full of booze, you could smell it on us.

Not a great start, but at least my knee wasn't hurting too much. I'd made a conscious effort on holiday to stop using it as an excuse and, while I wasn't looking forward to Pat Howard's arrival, I was keen just to play rugby again and let that be my enjoyment.

Pre-season started and we formed different teams: Green, yellow and red. I was in the green team, who got to wear t-shirts with 'Catch Up Fatty' on the back, miss some extra sessions and finish early on Fridays. My main focus was to keep my head down and not be argumentative with Pat, to listen to him and take on board what he had to say. He'd immediately tried to single me out, and I was already getting disciplined for things I shouldn't have been disciplined for. He was making the point that he was in charge, which was fair enough because he was.

Paul Stanton, the physio, spent an hour and a half a day working with me to increase the flexibility in my knee and I managed to get some speed back, although not all of it which was a shame because Tom Varndell had turned up and was burning everyone off.

We played some drinking games towards the end of the first four-week cycle of pre-season. One was introduced by John Dams; there were 30 of us and he covered a table with 160 half pints of beer – a full keg. We had to walk around the table and then around a cone which was about 10 metres away and by the time you got back you had to have finished your drink. It doesn't sound much between all of us, but it catches up with you and by the end the lads were quite drunk. At which point, he produced a second keg and I dropped out. It just turned into a free-for-all, with spew everywhere and a fight between some of the big guys.

Then they brought out Sumo suits and we spent a while battering each other in those. I'd just knocked over Michael Holford and was on top of him, when suddenly there was a massive pile-on and about 15 guys jumped on top of me. It was a horrible moment; I felt so claustrophobic and thought I was going to be crushed to death, an awful feeling. I was yelling at them to get off, shouting that they were hurting me, but when they're drunk they don't listen, no matter what you say.

Those drinking games were mad, really. Daryl Gibson introduced another one involving half pints. Everyone puts his mobile phone in the middle of the table and whenever one of them rings you all have to down your half.

The whole squad was there, so there were about 40 phones in the middle and we'd just played so all our friends and family were calling. You can imagine the mayhem. We did 20 halves in about an hour, which wasn't brilliant as I had to go off to dinner with Lou and some friends afterwards. That was another night where I came home and slept on the bathroom floor – the comfiest place in the house when you're drunk.

oOoOo

The new season started off pretty well, though we lost our first game to Sale away, which was a kickback from the final. They'd signed a few new players, Sebastian Chabal among them. Steve Hanley tried to rough me up, which was funny because he's about the softest winger I've played against.

We followed that with a good sequence and I was looking a bit like my old self, scoring a few tries and setting other people up. I didn't have the same acceleration and power I'd had before but I was feeling a lot more buoyant.

With England, Clive had gone and Andy Robinson had taken over. I knew that was probably it for me, internationally. I thought then that it was a crazy appointment and, as a fan I hate to say it, I think I was proved right. When the boys lost to Argentina in the autumn of 2006, making it seven straight losses and plumbing new depths for England . . . well, in my mind he should have quit there and then instead of clinging on. Everyone else – Phil Larder, Dave Alred, Joe Lydon – had been fired and not the top man, which wasn't right. I said as much to the press, which perhaps wasn't all that sensible.

It was not – and is not – a personal thing. Pat Howard and I never got on, but I did respect his knowledge of the game. He was opinionated, but his opinions were usually spot on, in the early days anyway. He was very innovative, and he had the ambition and nerve to try new things. By contrast, whenever you were with England you always felt Robbo was holding you back.

Clive was obviously a very difficult man to replace but Robinson was essentially a good forwards coach and no more. He's a whip cracker, he's good at driving the forwards on and I'm sure his technical knowledge in that area is excellent. I just wouldn't have let him near the backs, or near selection.

To me, his knowledge of the game is not wide enough, and he's not as open-minded as someone like Woody or Brian Ashton.

Still, I did ring him and congratulate him on the appointment, out of courtesy and also to let him know I was still available to play for England. I could tell by his voice that he was enjoying the conversation, that he thought I was begging to be back involved, which wasn't the case. It wasn't that deep: I'd have loved to be selected but it was no longer the most important thing in life to me. He never picked me, of course. He'd say it was because he didn't think I was up to it, I'd say it was because he let his personal animosity towards me get in the way of his thinking. But that's life. I've got 51 caps, of which I'm very proud. I can't remember how many Andy got. About five, I think.

I watched his reign get underway, with England playing poorly and getting beaten, and, while I had no desire to see Robbo on top of the world, I hated seeing it: as an Englishman, I wanted the team to do well.

To be fair to Andy, while I think a lot of it would have been down to him – picking Matthew Tait against Wales and then immediately dropping him, pulling Charlie Hodgson off halfway through the game against the Pumas, stuff like that – he didn't start with the best of hands. We'd always found in harder to motivate ourselves at Leicester after winning our Heineken Cups – what else is there to play for now? – so it must have been doubly hard for the England boys who'd been involved in the World Cup. And he lost a lot of really great players: Johnno, obviously, but people like Shaggy, Backy, Jonny Wilks, Phil Vicks and Trevor Woodman, Lol, Hilly, Jason Robinson and Ben Cohen either retired (or were close to it), declined or were injured over the next few months, and no coach can deal with that.

We had our Christmas party after we lost to Gloucester at home. It was due to be a fancy dress affair but got cancelled because Wellsy wasn't that keen on people having fun. Like most of our Christmas dos, it ended up with a few friendly fights – just a bit of punching and head-butting, no biting or kicking.

My problems with Pat continued, and I spent a lot of time on the bench. It wound me up but in March I was smacked in the face with some much-needed perspective.

I was sitting at home and happened to be flicking through the rugby pages on Ceefax when a headline caught my eye: 'Hampson has serious injury.'

Our young prop, Matt Hampson, had been hurt with England U-21s, it said. But there was very little detail and I assumed they meant he'd done his knee ligaments or something and thought nothing more of it.

It wasn't until I got to the club the next day that I realised it was a good deal worse than that: he had broken his neck while scrummaging.

The magnitude of the injury was unbelievable and the Tigers were in shock. It was hard to take in. Matt is a great bloke, well-liked by everyone and a really promising player:

a lot of people, tragically, suffer this sort of injury in all walks of life, but it doesn't happen to one of your own, does it?

At that stage, they weren't even sure whether he was going to live.

Oval Park was very quiet that day; no-one wanted to train. We just thought about his family and friends.

He pulled through, though he was left paralysed.

My kit was stored next to Hambo's in our cubby holes, so I couldn't help but think of him every day. Others did far more than just think: people like Matt Cornwell and James Buckland have done so much with their time and commitment. They'd drive down to see him at Stoke Mandeville after training, when they were completely shattered, just to see their mate, and to me that is what rugby players are about. Hambo's own spirit is immense and he's recovered a lot of his old humour and banter.

Our supporters were brilliant. He needs ongoing care and the costs are projected at three or four million pounds. People did unbelievable things to raise money for him – one girl who had lovely long hair had it all shaved off in the middle of the pitch, people with asthma walked up mountains, others sold things at auctions . . . the response was awesome and I think it will be ongoing; the Tigers, the whole family of the club, can feel proud of themselves for how they've helped Matt. (If you'd like to help yourself, go to www.leicestertigers.com and follow the link to Matt's page.)

It all put me in my place. Here I was, worried about being on the bench, moaning about my knee, and there's a young man deprived of his mobility by rugby. It was scary, really scary, and I don't know how I'd cope if it happened to me. I'd like to think I'd show Matt's bravery, but I don't know.

Typically, I soon re-immersed myself in my own comparatively petty troubles.

The season carried on, with Pat constantly nibbling away at me. I knew what he was doing but he was very clever and would pick on my weak points so occasionally he was right.

'You're the worst high ball taker I've ever seen,' he said, one day.

I wasn't great at it, so whenever their scrum half was about to box kick I'd move to full back and let Geordan or Sam Vesty come across and take them.

He tried to undermine me by leaving me out of the team for Sam. Pat had made it his goal to turn Sam Vesty into an England player. Don't get me wrong, I've got respect for Sam, and he's got a lot of guts. But he's not an international player yet. Pat would say, 'I'm leaving you out for Sam, he needs a game.'

Well, so do I. He'd come back with the fact that I wasn't great under the high ball. 'Yes,' I'd say, 'but I can do everything else and I'm miles quicker than anyone else we've got. So what's your problem?'

It came to a head in the Heineken Cup quarter final against Leinster. The week before, we played Leeds. Historically, I'd always played badly the week before a big Heineken game, with my mind on the match round the corner. I didn't play that badly, mind – I missed one tackle and dropped one high ball. But that was all Pat needed.

On the Monday, he and Wellsy called me in.

Wellsy said, 'We're thinking of leaving you out this weekend.'

'What are you talking about?' I said. 'You know my reputation in the Heineken Cup. I've never let the team down in a big game ever; in fact, I'm one of the main reasons we've done so well in Europe over the last few years.'

'Well, you didn't play very well last week,' said Pat.

I'd been concentrating on the quarter-final for weeks, training towards it, looking to peak at the right time, and I told them so.

'Well, we're putting you on the bench,' he said.

'Whose decision was it?' I asked.

They looked at each other. 'It was our decision,' they said, together, so I couldn't single one of them out, though I've no doubt it was Pat's call.

In the lead up to the game, I was well and truly hacked off; that one decision had plunged me back into a miserable low.

Wellsy took me on one side. 'Look,' he said. 'Don't say anything to the press.'

I swore at him and walked away.

Sure enough, I got approached by a load of reporters when the news got out. How did I feel?

'Obviously, I'm not very happy,' I said. 'I'm quite distressed about it all, actually. I was really looking forward to playing in this game and I feel like smashing Wellsy's car up with an axe.'

This was laughed off as another crazy Healey saying but the truth was, I really did feel like it. I'd even put an axe in the boot of my car for that very purpose. I gave myself time to calm down and ended up putting the axe back in the shed. It would have been giving them the excuse they needed to sack me and I didn't need that just at that point. To be honest, if I'd been booted out then I'm not sure what would have happened to me. I'd been racking my brains to come up with something I could do after rugby – TV? Coaching? A whole different career? – for a week or two.

Wellsy had recently announced he was stepping down as head coach and leaving the club. He was off to join the RFU Academy, where Dorian West had already, miraculously, got a job. He must have thought, if Dorian can get a job there anyone can. It wasn't exactly a disaster, because I didn't think that much of him in terms of coaching, but we'd always got on OK. The problem was, Pat would almost certainly be replacing him as head coach and I only spoke to him when I absolutely had to.

In fact, it was a seriously worrying time for me and brought on a lot of sleepless nights and tetchiness. (Sure enough, Howard was later confirmed in the post: the club claimed they'd searched high and low before announcing he and Cockers would be the new coaching staff. Cockers would step down as a player, which he'd actually done about five years earlier, to become the head coach of the forwards, which was very funny. Backy would become the defensive coach, which was a good move given that he probably has more defensive knowledge than most people in world rugby; as long he could transfer that knowledge he'd make a great coach.)

We got to Dublin and I cricked my neck in training, funnily enough; it was touch and go as to whether I'd be on the bench. I think Wellsy thought I was faking that as well. It was exacerbated by a spot of Leon Lloyd bed-flipping. Leon and I had been sharing rooms for the past eight years or so and we always played this game: you sneak up to the end of the other guy's bed when he's in it, pick it up and flip them over. The only rules are that you can't bed-flip someone when they're asleep, or when you're drunk. Obviously, both rules get ignored when you're drunk, so the last one is irrelevant, really. I'd just had my neck clicked back into position by the physio when Leon came in to our room, snuck round the corner and flipped me. Immediately, my sodding neck clicked back out again. I was in agony.

'I can't believe you've just done that,' I shouted to Lloydy, as he skedaddled, cackling down the corridor. I had to go and have an injection on the morning of the game but I was just about OK.

Bed-flipping was a common occurrence when the lads had been drinking. I remember in Scotland on a pre-season tour, we found Graham Rowntree asleep so Leon and I flipped him. He spent the night with a double bed on his head, but was so drunk he didn't even realise. He came into breakfast in the morning looking really puzzled. 'I must have been really smashed last night,' he said. 'Somehow I got the bed on top of me.' Me and Leon just looked at each other and giggled. Then we went and bed-flipped Steve Booth, who was injured, and he started crying like a little girl.

Anyway, I sat on the bench, seething, thinking of all the things I'd done for the club in that tournament. I know that doesn't guarantee eternal selection, but I'd been playing well and having a good season up until the Leeds game. I found it really hard to take.

They played Geordan on the wing in my place, which Geordie wasn't very happy about, either. He's one of the best full-backs in the world so why play him out of position?

Essentially, it was so they could fit Sam in at No15. To be fair to him, he played really well. I hadn't moaned at Sam during the week; I just wished him all the best. It wasn't his fault.

The lads put in a fantastic performance, and I got my usual abuse from the Irish fans which I enjoyed and which lifted my spirits. It's a great place, Ireland, it was always one of my favourite places to play. With two minutes to go, Wellsy came over. 'Warm up,' he said, 'you're going on.'

'There's two minutes to go,' I said. 'We've already won the game. What's the point?'

'You're going on,' he repeated.

'Are you serious, or are you winding me up?' I asked.

'Are you trying to get me back for what I said in the paper about the axe?'

'You're going on,' he said, a third time.

I stripped off, slightly bemused. Just as I was about to run on, Wellsy grabbed me. 'Don't do anything stupid,' he said.

I couldn't believe my ears. 'Wellsy,' I said. 'The score is 29–13, there's two minutes to go and you're telling me not to do anything stupid? You cheeky b*****d.'

I ran on, half expecting him to sub me straight back off again. I was fuming – how petty did he have to be? Mind you, how petty was I? I should never have responded like that. 'Thanks very much, I'd love to play' would have wound him up more, anyway.

Seconds later, the whistle went and I walked back off swearing to myself. My attitude to being dropped was, if I could work it out logically, I'd accept it. If I couldn't find logic or reason, I found it very hard to take. I had a shower and was out of the changing room in ten minutes flat. I put my bag on the bus and went straight into town to meet a few mates. And spent the night drinking myself into a stupor. As I say, that's a weakness: turning to drink when I'm down, and I'm not a sociable drinker. I got back to the room, smashed, and found Leon had locked me out and put the chain on. You see, to Leon that would be the height of wit. I had to kick the door in and promptly fell asleep. I woke up in the morning with the bed on top of me, so obviously I'd been flipped in the night. Probably for snoring.

The semi-final came around quickly, and we were playing Toulouse. The mood was good; as well as being in the latter stages of that competition, we were in with a good chance of winning the Premiership. It was Johnno's and Backy's last season, and everyone wanted to finish with a trophy, or even two, for them.

I'd heard from some of the guys that they'd been to Pat

and said they thought I ought to be playing. I'm trying not to blow my own trumpet here; I'm not undroppable or anything. But I had been playing well. Plus, I was integral to a lot of the moves so leaving me out meant a lot of work to fit other people in. Pat came to me and said he was going to give me a chance.

I thought, '*Thanks very much! Nearly ten years here and you're going to give me a chance?*'

Like I say, Pat was technically a good coach, and I know he didn't like me. But a blind man could see I still had a lot to offer so surely he'd put the personalities to one side for the good of the team? Coaches are always talking like that, though. Rarely do they have the sense to think, '*These guys have been through the mill for this club. We owe them a bit of respect.*'

We played at the Walkers' Stadium for the first time and there was a fantastic atmosphere, with well over 25,000 supporters there. The pitch was a little bit hard for rugby and you certainly wouldn't want to play there every week – you'd get a lot more injuries. We dominated the French in the first ten minutes and Darren Morris and Ollie Smith dropped two scoring passes which would have put us 14 points up. Then they got back into the game, scored quite early on and before we knew it we were out of the competition.

It was a bummer, but there you go. What really wound me up came later, when Paddy blamed me for their first try. I found that bizarre. Andy Goode kicked for touch on the left hand side and missed touch. They threw two wide passes and ran back at us. I'd stayed back covering the corner for the return kick, which was the right thing to do.

'Why didn't you come forward?' he said.

I couldn't win. If I had and they'd kicked it – which nine times out of ten they would have – he'd have blamed me for that, too. He was just undermining me and setting me up for a fall in the Premiership final. We thumped Wasps at home in the play offs and were teed up to face them again in the decider.

I got the call to come in and see Pat and Wellsy. I said: 'You're putting me on the bench, aren't you?'

'Yeah.'

'Why?'

'Sam's better at taking high balls, and we think Wasps are going to kick a lot.'

Brilliant, incisive game-planning, that. Wasps hardly kicked at all.

It was a downer. The knee was starting to hurt again after a long season. I know I said I wouldn't use it as an excuse, but it was agony at times. I'd been having an injection every week to enable me to play from about January onwards. I also had to have it drained every week – they stick a needle in the side of your leg and suck all the excess fluid out. It's not particularly nice. I was also on pain killers every day to train, taking Volterol and Brufen in cocktails I mixed myself. I hate to think what it has done to my innards over the years, but you need to train if you want to play and you need to play if you want to pay your mortgage. It's the downside of playing a hard sport like rugby, and it makes it all the worse when you're getting undermined by your coach.

But more than anything, I wanted to play because I wanted to play in Johnno's and Backy's last game. They were my mates, these guys, people I'd have died for if it came to it and, though they might have found me irritating at times, they'd have done the same for me, I know it. I'd seen the emotion in them both when they bowed out at Welford Road; they were awarded their changing room pegs and they and the rest of us got very emotional. They'd had two absolutely fantastic careers, had been the best in the world in their positions for a long, long time and, with the help of a few others, were the reason why we'd won so much in the last five or six years.

I'd sat there feeling a mixture of pride and sadness for Neil and Martin, and a bit of uncertainty for myself; with them gone, I'd be one of the last of the old guard, a bit on my own.

We got stuffed by Wasps in the final. I sat on the bench in the pouring rain, watching the boys get smashed, which was fantastic, very enjoyable. That's sarcasm, by the way. It was horrible. I went on with the intention of trying to start a bit of a fight, to get Wasps to try to rough us up so they'd get pinged. Purists will harrumph and sneer and say that's not the spirit, old boy, but it felt to us like we were in a battle for our lives. I couldn't face losing, I didn't want Johnno and Backy to finish on a low, I was absolutely desperate for us to win. I started trying to rile people, to put pressure on Daws and maybe niggle him into giving a penalty away. I almost succeeded with Joe Worsley – he took a big swing at me but sadly he missed and the ref didn't see it – but Daws was on him in a flash, shouting 'Stay focused, stay focused.' That's what made him a great player, he had the mental edge, and I knew in that moment we'd had it. They were so controlled and we just couldn't get at them. We lost by around 20 points, and I watched Lol and Daws lift the trophy at the end feeling like I'd been knifed in the guts.

We came back to Leicester on the bus. Let's describe it as pretty hectic. There was a lot drunk on the bus and we broke it up with a stop at Toddington – not the service station, the village – to visit the boozer there. Then back on the bus, and more drinks. Everyone went out to celebrate the two retirements, and I think even Backy had a few, which was very unusual for him.

And that was that.

Me and My Mouth

Lou and I took to kids to Portugal for three weeks and had a fantastic family holiday.

Away from work, I felt human, and relaxed, for the first time in ages.

I Used To Be A Rugby Player

I got back from Portugal and headed straight off to La Manga again for another PRA weekend. Again, Leon and I battled it out in the Cocoa Butter Luge Championship of Europe and, again, I won, with a distance of 35.3m. It's all about power and technique and I've always had more of both than him. We made a bit of noise and left a greasy yellow stain on the floor so hotel security asked us to knock it on the head at about 5am. I pulled Leon to bed, on his chest, by his feet. A quiet night out. (I did La Manga again in the summer of 2006 and got absolutely smashed with a guy called Nick Dite, who was pouring vintage Dom Perignon down my arm and drinking it out of my armpit and then stuffing champagne and vodka into me in a dentist's chair. By about 3am I realised I was in huge trouble so I went back to the room where I fell asleep in the bath with the shower spraying on me. I woke up in the morning stinking, bizarrely, of tooth paste. Wondering why, I went into the room to find Leon giggling like a kid.

'What are you laughing at?' I said.

'Go and have a look in the mirror,' he said. He'd come in after me, filled my hand with toothpaste and spent a merry half hour tickling my face. With each tickle, I'd brushed my hand against my face, with predictable results.

'Don't worry,' he said, when he got his breath back. 'I've got it all on video.' He got the camera out to show me and then realised he'd been so drunk he'd forgotten to put a tape in.)

I was looking forward to getting back to pre-season. I was fairly confident that this would be my last year. My contract was ending and I couldn't see Paddy rushing to renew it. Simon Cohen had just been employed by the club to oversee financial matters and he was one of my old agents, a great guy, always up for an argument, which was good. I went to see him and got down to the nitty gritty. I had a clause in my contract where, if I was on the bench, I got paid the same as if I was in the team. I could see me getting a lot of 20 minute cameos, so I wanted to ensure that clause was adhered to. Simon approved it, so it was just a case of sorting my knee out one last time. It was hurting more than ever and now wouldn't bend properly.

I'd arranged for Bill Knowles, the guy who had saved my career in America, to come over to Leicester in the summer. The idea was he would train with me and Leon, who was also struggling with his knee, for a month.

Bill stayed at my house; he'd go out and work with me and Leon during the day and then teach my girls how to do stupid things on the trampoline in the evening. Leon and I just trained with each other, while everyone else was outside, running and doing stuff which we weren't allowed to touch because of our knees. Two weeks into the month, the boys came back from the ill-fated New Zealand Lions tour. Among them was Lewis Moody, and he decided to join me and Leon in the pool where we were quietly minding our own business and working on our rehab. We'd just finished up and I was trying to get out when Lewis thought it would be hilarious to pull me back into the pool from the steps and hold my head under the water. I was knackered, I couldn't fight back and I honestly thought I was about to drown. Imagine that: my last moments, being held under water by that gurning lunatic. I kicked out to try and free myself and connected with the ladder, splitting the webbing between my second and third toes right down to the bone. Finally, the gimp let me go, I got out of the pool with blood spurting from my foot and hobbled to find Dr Finlay. I'd had a phobia of needles since my unfortunate hospitalisation as a kid, and had been terrified of having stitches my whole career. I'd been lucky, and had played for years and years without having any: it helped that I was always careful not to put my head in the ridiculous places that people like Backy used to put theirs. I also had a mantra I used to chant which I felt kept me safe; it sounds mad, but I'd shout, 'I am iron, I am Andy Northey' before I ran out. It was something the real Andy Northey used to say, and it seemed to protect him from injury so I started copying him. It had worked until the previous year against London Irish, when I'd been kicked in the chin and sliced open. As the Doc sewed me up, I realised that stitches weren't that big a deal, the rest of the year was a breeze and I didn't play with the fear I'd had for a decade or more. So I wasn't that worried about having these ones done, either. Big mistake: it was agony. The worst part was the alleged anaesthetic he jabbed me with first – that made me howl. I'd rather he'd just sewn me up.

Sod's law, the Doc said I couldn't train for at least ten days – even in the pool – which was an absolute disaster with Bill there. I managed to grab three last days with him at the end, and things weren't looking great.

'I'm still in a lot of pain, Bill,' I said. 'Any suggestions?'

'Well,' he said, 'there's this guy in Munich called Dr Hans Müller-Wolfhart. He's worth a go.'

I'd never heard of this Müller guy, but I checked him out and found the internet crawling with testimonies, tales and thank-yous.

I went to see Pat. 'My knee's shattered,' I said. 'It kills

and now it's not bending properly. I need to do something, and I want to go and see Müller-Wolfhart in Germany.'

'You can go,' said Pat, 'but you'll have to pay for yourself.'

That sentence probably made me more angry than anything he'd ever said to me before. I'd damaged my knee playing for the club in the Heineken Cup, I'd gone through two years of pain playing with it and all I wanted was a little of bit of help to get it fixed. I'd like to have told him to stick it there and then, but I needed this last year to make it to a decade for the Tigers, which was a personal target. Additionally, I'd get to my testimonial year and finish my contract, which were both important financially. So I bit my lip and paid for myself to go.

The club's physios and doctors didn't particularly approve of me going, I don't think. I think they viewed Müller as some sort of quack: he hadn't published any research and his methods seemed miles away from anyone else's. When I got there and walked into reception, the nurse told me to take a seat in the waiting room. Inside were Kelly Holmes, Paula Radcliffe, several other world record holders and a string of well-known German footballers. I phoned the club and said, 'I think I might be in the right place.'

The first thing Müller said to me was, 'Are you paying for this yourself?'

I said I was, and he slashed my bill to bits; I think he charged me three grand, which was virtually cost-price for the nursing and medicine.

Then he sent me for some scans. They showed that the cartilage on my knee had been knocked off again, leaving a big hole.

As he examined the scans, I said, 'Look, if you need to use steroids, that's fine. I won't be tested for another two months.' I'd never used steroids, and I never would have for training, or just to get bigger, but I was prepared to go that far with my knee if it meant saving my career. I'm against drugs in sport for performance, but as a means to continue playing, when your mortgage is on the line . . . that's a tougher call. I had a family to feed.

Müller shook his head. 'We use nothing like that,' he said. 'Everything here is legal and natural and quite safe.'

He put me on a programme of chiropractic work, his unique injections and even radiotherapy. The chiropractic work was designed to rid me of the painful sciatica which had returned and was burning right down into my calf and becoming more and more of a problem. Müller managed to deal with that in one treatment. He needed longer to work on my knee, though. I phoned home to Pat. 'He thinks he can do something with me, but I need to stay until Friday,' I said.

'OK,' said Pat. 'Stay until Friday, but then you have to come and meet us in Scotland for pre-season.'

I went through a series of around two hundred injections in five days, with Müller injecting all sorts of things I'd never heard of like activegan, ostinil, trauneal and a lot of vitamins into my knee and the base of my spine. The ones into your back don't sound the nicest, but you don't actually feel the needle going in that much. It hurts a bit, but the worst part was the amount of fluid going in around your spine. He put a lot in the first time, particularly, and you could always recognise the guys who had just had their backs done by the way they waddled out.

I'd met Kelly Holmes before out in South Africa and knew she was a good laugh. On that first morning, I'd been sitting in the waiting room when she came out. As soon as she saw me, she shook her head and winced theatrically, obviously trying to wind me up about the pain of the treatment I was about to face. I stored that one away in the back of my head.

Two or three days later, I happened to get in ahead of her. I had all my jabs and at the end I borrowed one of the little white plasters they used to cover the injection sites to prevent infection and stuck it on my forehead. I'd heard on the grapevine that Kelly was there for an Achilles problem so I staggered out of the consultation room, holding my head and looking like I was in agony, and plonked myself down next to her with a groan.

'Crikey, Austin,' she said, pointing to the plaster on my head with a look of horror on her face. 'What's that one for?'

'Achilles, Kelly,' I said. 'New treatment. Hurts like hell.'

She turned pale and I burst out laughing – she slapped me on the leg for that one.

Joking aside, the effect of all those jabs was startling, almost electrifying; when I'd had a shower before I left, I just felt myself getting wet. When I got home, I could feel every single droplet of water hitting me. I became so responsive, just in the course of a week, it was amazing. It lasted for a good six months.

The effect on my knee was equally incredible. When I'd left, I could only bend it to just below 90 degrees. When I got back, I could bend it all the way up to the top – I had full flexibility, which I hadn't had for two years. I'd spent the whole of the previous summer working my backside off, trying to get through the cramp in my hamstring and trying to get some flexion in my knee. Müller sorted it inside a week. If it sounds like he's a miracle worker, I have to say it felt like a miracle to me. I wasn't the only one. During the week, he took us all out for dinner – a lot of footballers and athletes, some world-renowned people were there (and me). People kept coming up to him to shake his hand, trying to buy him bottles of champagne and wine, and nobody paid the slightest attention to the sports stars sitting alongside him. It was like he was some sort of messiah, and it was a real eye-opener. He'd obviously helped an awful lot of people in that area and they had the greatest respect for him. I quickly developed the same respect.

I would recommend anyone with any ailment, anything Müller can help with, to go and see him. He is an unbelievable guy. You just need to be prepared for a lot of pain but as long as you have a goal you're willing to fight for you'll be fine.

I arrived back better than I'd been for some time and joined the boys on the pre-season trip to Scotland. I was still fuming about having to pay for the treatment myself, and it still annoys me to this day. It didn't stop there. Müller had told me not to play for at least ten days to two weeks because he'd given me a deep injection in my calf and contact could rupture it. A week later, Pat wanted me to play against Edinburgh. I said I couldn't. Pat said, 'I want written con-firmation of that, by tomorrow, from your doctor.'

I had to phone Germany and get it faxed over, something which really angered me. I'd been at the club for ten years, Paddy had been head coach for two minutes and he was making me do rubbish like that.

I'd laid off the booze at this point; while I was in Munich, they'd run a lot of blood tests and found that my liver wasn't working very well. They put it down to the amount of Volterol I'd been taking to be able to train and play but told me to get myself on the wagon too. I fell off at least once when one of the lads had his stag night in Edinburgh. I'd worn the wrong shirt at training – I was only supposed to be watching, but Paddy made me join in – so he forced me to wear a chicken suit: I looked like Big Bird, only shorter, with feathers, tights, a yellow beak and everything. I wasn't that pleased, bearing in mind everyone else was just dressed normally. We went into town and got absolutely destroyed, finishing off by buying almost everything for sale in a local chippy. Harry Ellis had his usual five portions of fish and chips and we gave up trying to get Darren Morris to leave… the wind must have been blowing in the right direction because the big old hot air balloon landed at the hotel sometime the following morning.

The season started with me on the bench, strangely enough. My knee was pretty good, Cozza got injured and they made me captain for one of the games. It was the third time I'd been captain, and I got the impression it was an olive branch from Paddy. We hit a bit of a losing trot and I went back to Germany in early October for a quick check-up and top-up from Müller. Again I had to pay for myself, though having seen the benefits Leicester did at least agree to pay half. I don't think I've had the cheque yet, mind you.

Müller drained it off and showed me how to do it myself and then told me I should check out the Oktober Fest. If you like your beer and your partying, give it a go: it's an unbelievable event, seven or eight massive tents with about ten thousand people in each one, all drinking big litre glasses of lager, getting smashed and eating chicken and pretzels.

The following day I turned up to see Müller. 'Did you have a beer?' he said.

'Yes,' I said.

'How many?' he asked.

'Eight,' I replied.

'You English rugby man,' he said, grinning. 'You are crazy.'

He ought to see some of the lads if he thinks I'm crazy.

I'd been playing mainly scrum-half, which had a nice symmetry to it – it was where it had all begun with Birkenhead Park Minis all those years before, and it was like I'd come full circle – and, as the autumn internationals approached some pundits were saying I ought to be back in the squad. Harry Ellis was struggling a bit and Daws was now an old crock of a has-been who'd rather record *Question of Sport* than play for his country so I thought, what the hell, nothing to lose, and phoned Andy Robinson to sound him out one last time.

'Look Robbo,' I said. 'I just wanted you to know, whatever you've read in the press, it's all water under the bridge as far as I'm concerned. I'm still mad keen to play for England and if I was involved I would come with no baggage and be fully committed.'

He sounded very vague and distant – like he was pulling the phone away from his ear and flicking the Vs at me for the amusement of someone else in the room.

'Yeah, yeah,' he said, 'you're still in the running, we're still looking at you.'

I put the phone down, knowing there was no chance. But I'd made the call, so I'd done my bit.

I wasn't selected, but I was made captain for the club games when the boys were away and we came away with a lost two, won two record, which wasn't too bad, considering.

I was enjoying leading the team, but my thoughts were turning more and more to retirement. I wasn't 100 per cent ready to quit and I had it in me physically to carry on for another year, with injections and painkillers and draining my fluid away. The problem was, my bottle had gone. In my heart of hearts, I didn't think I had the guts to carry on. Dave Alred once said to me, 'All the best trainers are the bravest people, the ones with the courage to put themselves through the pain for the end goal.' Those words resonated with me: I'd put myself through a lot of pain for a lot of years and I'd reached the end of my road. More than anything, it was the training I couldn't face; any player will tell you that's worse than the games. Leicester wanted me to re-sign and I'd come up with a compromise – I'd train two days a week and be available for games at the weekends, but that was it. They were making the right noises but dragging their heels a bit and I was going through a lot of worry, fear even, about my future. Imagine you have two young daughters, you're in your early 30s, and your job, the only thing you're really qualified to do, the only thing you've really known for 10 years or more, is about to go pop? And you won't just be losing your job – your routine, your support network, your timetable, even lots of your mates . . . you'll be waving goodbye to them, too. It was really tough.

I'd got involved with an organisation called Careers After Sport. They give you a mentor – mine was Alan Dickinson, a great guy – and take you through potential future jobs. It turned out that three banks were interested in talking to me. One of them was Credit Suisse. I went to a series of interviews and really hit it off with them – my direct boss, a guy called Richard Elgar, was another Scouser who was very down to earth and bright – and they offered me a position. As Leicester dithered, I took it and with that a huge weight lifted off my shoulders. Just having a job was an awesome feeling, but having one where I would still meet interesting people from around the world and have flexibility and prospects was fantastic. I can't tell you how much of a relief it was. I've made a decent amount of money from playing rugby, but we're not footballers, and I've also spent an awful lot, mainly on doing up my house. I call it the sieve - it just sucks money out of my bank account into its walls. Working for Credit Suisse wasn't going to be easy: I had to be there on merit and I needed to study for and pass a series of testing exams. For someone who's been out of the classroom for 10 years and more, that's hard. But it was a challenge and it's one I'm throwing myself into at the moment.

Funnily enough, around then I started playing really well,

and went on to have one of my best seasons in recent years.

Not long after that, it got back to me that Andy Robinson had been taking the p*** out of me for ringing him, and was saying I had bugger all chance of playing for England again under him.

That was irritating, and I said so in *The Mirror*, also questioning whether he should be England coach.

Things went from bad to worse after the final autumn international of 2005. The England guys had hired the bottom floor at the Orange Tree pub in Richmond for a private party. I was doing Sunday *Grandstand* so was staying down in London, and arranged to go out for a beer with Daws.

He called me and said, 'Why don't we meet at the Orange Tree?'

So I headed over and was hanging around upstairs, just chilling out with a few mates. Daws and Charlie Hodgson came up and said, 'Why don't you come down for a beer?'

So I did. I'd been there five minutes when Cozza walked over to me.

'Do you want a beer mate?' I said.

'No,' he said. 'I need to have a quick word.'

We went into the toilets. 'I'm in a really difficult position, Oz,' said Martin. 'Robbo's just come over to me and told me to tell you to get out.'

'No worries, mate,' I said. 'I don't want to put you in a bad spot. I don't want you to stick up for your mate of ten years. I'd rather you kept the England captaincy. I'll just leave.'

That was a bit mean of me: Cozza's a great mate and he was in a difficult situation.

'I'll come up for a beer with you in a minute,' he said.

As I was leaving, Andy Robinson was outside the bog door. I just walked past him, said nothing and walked up the stairs. At the top, Tom Varndell was throwing up. He'd just won his first cap and was in pieces, so I crouched down with him, checking he was alright. Robbo and Joe Lydon followed me up and came over.

'You have to appreciate you can't come into this party,' said Robbo.

'That's fine,' I said. 'It's a private do.'

'No,' he said. 'Anyone else could, it's just you. You've disrespected this team. You've made comments about them.'

I stared at him, open-mouthed. 'Look, Andy,' I said. 'I haven't. I've made comments about you and Joe and the other coaches, and I think that they were valid comments. If you want to talk about where you're going wrong then give me a bell. As for not coming to the party, that's fine, no worries.'

Joe Lydon stared at me like there was steam coming out of his ears: I honestly thought he was going to attack me. That's the same Joe Lydon, by the way, who was eventually fired because England had barely scored a try in his reign as our country's supposed 'attack coach'.

The boys came out in twos and threes and we all went into town together, which kind of showed that nothing I'd said in the newspapers had affected any of them in the slightest. It was all about the management.

Leicester beat the Ospreys in Europe, getting out of jail with a last-second try by Danny Hipkiss, and had a hell of a party on the way back. The following Monday we had our Christmas do in Leicester. We met at the Varsity pub and the only two things you had to bring with you were an eye patch and a die. We were drinking Turbo Shandies – Smirnoff Ice and a Budweiser in a pint glass – and I worked out a game around the table with two of the dice. If I threw a double, I had to down my pint. Anything else and the other boys had to neck a half. The first three throws were doubles, so I had to throw back three pints. The swines were also spiking my drinks with vodka so I was wasted within half an hour.

Matt Cornwell lost at spoof and his punishment was to get on a bus and go at least three stops, so that was him out of the way for an hour. Matt was always losing at spoof – earlier he'd had to eat all the condiments in the little bowls on the table . . . mayonnaise, ketchup, salt, pepper, vinegar, brown sauce. He was sick but he got it down, which was in the spirit of the evening.

My mate Charlie Fowler turned up late for a few beers and was presented with the contributions bucket – a pail full of the remnants of everyone's drinks, which a few people had also gobbed in. To be fair to Charlie, he drank the lot. The day went on long into the night and ended with a little bit of fighting. Darren Morris got punched in the face by someone. He fell down. He went home. Cozza got me in a headlock so I punched him in the bollocks. He got drunk. He went home. It was like dominos. We finished at midnight, and most people were in absolute bits.

I spent the following day in bed with the shakes. I was in a bad way and vowed to mend my ways, to the point where Lou and I had a quiet New Year's Eve with friends and ended up drinking tea at midnight, just about staying awake.

I played in the Powergen Cup semi-final at Cardiff, and was really delighted to get back there one last time. We lost to Wasps but I had one of my best games for a long time before being taken off after 60 minutes, exhausted.

Not long after, we had the debacle of the Heineken quarter-final against Bath at the Walkers Stadium.

Pat said, 'You're on the bench. How do you feel about it?'

He was smiling and clearly looking for a reaction. I'd done enough to warrant a start at 9 or 10, but I knew they felt Goodey's goal kicking was needed and I didn't want to give him the satisfaction. I was too knackered, apart from anything: I'd started my new job and was feeling the pressure from that.

I just said, 'Fine.'

In all my years, that was probably my best comeback to a coach, and it took me a decade to get there.

We'd spanked Bath away the week before – I'd come off the bench again. I actually played 34 games that season, more than anyone else, which was good going in my final year, particularly for my bank balance.

The game went poorly, Goodey had a nightmare and we lost when we should have won. That was a really big disappointment for me. I'd been dreaming of finishing my career in the Heineken Cup final again and the defeat shattered that. I had a bit of a go at Andy, but there were other people who didn't perform as well; the trouble with playing fly-half is you take the plaudits when you win so you have to take the criticism when you lose.

The following week was bad. Nobody wanted to train. It was as though our season had ended there and then and a lot of people went into their shells. I lost it a few times, culminating with me going AWOL for a couple of days midweek. I was skipping in the gym and John Dams told me to go and skip somewhere else.

I threw my rope at him. 'Get lost,' I said. 'I built this sodding gym with those bloody Heineken Cup wins.'

It was just a cheeky little thing I used to trot out from time to time – invariably followed by Leon butting in and saying, 'You built the foundations, mate, but my tries put a roof on and bought the equipment.' Usually when he'd been drinking too much and it had gone to his head, to be honest.

I threw in a few swear words, too, and John was pretty annoyed. 'You'd better go home,' he said, so I did. I went and packed my stuff – everything, because I didn't anticipate going back. It was a real toys out of the pram moment – I was done with it all, I'd had enough, though in my defence a lot of people felt the same way. It just all burst out at the wrong time. I went home and Pat phoned me.

The steam had subsided a bit, so I told him I'd be back in a few days.

'Fine,' he said. 'Come back when you're ready.'

Obviously, I turned up in time for the Friday and our local derby against Northampton. We won, and went on to beat Wasps, Saracens and Bristol in the run-in.

The Bristol game was clearly going to be my last home start of the season, so Pat made me captain for the day, which was good of him, all things considered. Ellie Mae and Daisy were our mascots. I'd always wanted to walk down the Welford Road steps with my two little girls. Lou and I have always kept them out of the limelight but this was the one day when I thought I'd put that to one side, because they weren't going to get a chance to walk onto the pitch with their dad again.

What no-one else knew was that it wasn't just my last home start of the season, it was my last home game, full stop. I didn't tell anyone that, I just kept it to myself. If people asked, I'd say I was going to play part-time the following year.

Partly, I think I was too scared to admit it; I couldn't face saying the words, 'I'm not playing anymore . . . thanks, goodbye.'

Partly, I didn't want the ceremony that would have followed – the announcement, the bottle of champagne, all the little rituals of the end. After all those years of me gobbing off and being the centre of attention, I actually just wanted to go quietly.

The girls were very excited and they looked great in their little Tigers' kits and new trainers, walking down ahead of me. I'd prepared myself for feeling very emotional, even for tears, but when I saw them, all that went; I just couldn't stop smiling, and I knew I'd accepted, mentally, that my career was over.

I'd bought a load of tickets, so there were 25 or 30 members of my family there. I would have liked more, and to have had a party with them and the players afterwards, but then everyone would have known I was finishing. My mum and dad were quite emotional and had probably guessed the truth; I think they half-wanted to be mascots themselves.

We murdered Bristol 32–3 and I played well; we'd gone unbeaten in the league at home all season again, which was a nice way to round things off at home and a memory of times past.

I took the extended family for a quiet meal afterwards at Pizza Express, our usual haunt after games. When I'd first started at Leicester, the families used to stay in the Crooked Feed, the European lounge. We'd all drink together and socialise with each other's folks: you really got to know your mates' mums and dads and brothers and sisters, and it turned us into a very close-knit community. Now most of that has gone. Our families weren't even allowed in there until after half time, and even then the room would be full of sponsors and their guests which ruined the family side of things. You were constantly bombarded by people who wanted to talk to you and pull you this way and that; I know that comes with the territory but, for me, the most important thing about playing for Leicester in the beginning was the family atmosphere and that is slowly going down the swanny for the want of a bigger profit margin at the end of the season. Maybe when they move or build a bigger stand there will be a designated area just for families and members of the club, the board, and the people who are there day to day, people who give their time and passion to the club. I would love to see that happen again.

The week after the Bristol game we had London Irish in the Premiership semis. I was relegated to the bench again, despite having set up two tries against Bristol. It was a strange, endless situation with Pat but a lot of the fight and fire had gone out and we'd finally reached an accommodation. We weren't going to be the best of mates, and he was never coming round for dinner or Christmas tea, and I don't think I'd say that about anyone else at the club (except the front row – they'd eat too much food), but there was a bit of mutual respect there. I accepted he was a good coach, and he knew I was a good player, and that was enough.

We'd ended up with the bizarre situation where I'd pretty much decide when I was coming on. One of my skills has always been the ability to analyse the ebb and flow of a match, to look at people, spot their natural timing and see what they're doing wrong. Watching matches is like watching the sea to me: if a team's playing well, the waves break evenly. If they're not, you get one wave and wait ages for the next. I'd say, 'Harry's dropped off the pace a bit' or Scott's gone' or 'Goodey's not doing so well, you need to put me on now,' and Pat would say, 'OK, on you go.'

I came off the bench against Irish, we gave them a good beating and that was it, we were all set up for the big finale against Sale.

It seemed to have been written somewhere by some higher being: my last game at Twickenham, in front of a big crowd, and hopefully I'd be finishing with another trophy for the club. That was certainly how I planned it, after seeing Backy and Johnno finish in defeat the year before. Desperation. That's what I felt. I was absolutely *desperate* to win.

During the week, I'd told the coaches I'd like to say the last word in the team huddle in the changing room. I spent the whole week planning what I was going to say and had a great speech lined up.

'Today, above all days, we share each others' talents,' I was going to say. 'Twenty years from now, you will remember whatever you do today, and you'll remember what your team-mates did.'

There was plenty more, and it was Churchillian stuff, but when it came to it I got a bit choked up, so I just said, 'Lads, it's a big day. Let's not f*** it up.'

I was more emotional that day than I'd ever been. Inside, I knew that this was it: after those 80 minutes, it was all going to melt away into memories. Leon, probably my closest mate at the club, sensed that, and wrote me a good luck card with a poem in it. That was a nice gesture. Crap poem, mind.

I'd been dropped again – it was always the big games Paddy left me out of – and it was pouring with rain. I knew how to play in the rain – you have to when you come from the north – and I always looked forward to those conditions. I sat there, getting soaked, and watching us get beaten. I went to Paddy at half time. 'You need to put me on now,' I said. 'We're in trouble.'

I went on and made virtually no impact. With my very first touch, I made a break right up the middle and, as I ran, I tried to press the accelerator. I had nothing left in my legs, there was no gas left in the tank. In my mind's eye, I saw myself speeding through the gap, swerving to the outside and then cutting back across to dive under the posts. Five years earlier, that's what would have happened. Now, my body was 20 metres behind my mind, and I got scragged. All I had left was my experience and knowledge and that can only count for so much. In that moment, I knew I'd made the right decision. I could feel myself fading away. Before, I could run round people and they couldn't touch me. Now guys would say 'I'm going to get you' and they'd be able to. Where I'd always been able to get the other side of the tackle to offload or fall in a safe position, with my pace gone I was being hit in front of the tackle and taking the full force. That's not much fun when you're my size.

I wanted to be able to beat everybody, and I no longer could. I couldn't be a winner anymore, I had to be the same as everyone else and I didn't want that.

We lost.

Post-match, the cameras were zooming in on me to see whether I'd have a bit of a weep. I was certainly crying inside but I didn't want to do it on the outside. I was very disappointed. Again, I blamed some of the players in my team and unfortunately told them later on that night, when I was drunk, what I thought of them. I compounded that by saying the same later in the press. Sorry, lads. In my defence, it was difficult to take, losing the final game of my career like that.

I'm definitely going to have to play in a charity game and make sure we win somewhere if I can.

Just like we always had, we stocked up on booze for the journey home, me trying not to think that this would be my last time on the team bus, everyone else fighting over what colour vodka to buy. Cockers settled that one by buying all the colours: he clambered aboard with about 15 bottles and passed them round the bus. We started with a game of 21 – it's simple enough, but hard to explain and very difficult to play when you're drinking – and vodka shots. Then we started snorting vodka and before long the usual fights had erupted. I remember Cockers, who'd drunk a whole bottle of black vodka by himself and was in bits, slapped Goodey on the back of the head and got slotted for his trouble, which made me smile. When we got back to the club, he fell off the bus into the road, spewing, we hauled him into a taxi and sent him home. He spent the night sleeping in a chair in his kitchen with Serge watching him in case he died.

Me, I grabbed my bag, got myself a cab and went home without looking back.

oOoOo

People always said I'd never be able to retire, that I, the arch-baiter, would miss the banter in the changing room. Strangely enough, I don't miss that at all. I remember it, like I remember the smells of Deep Heat, massage oil and vomit, the sound of guys chucking up with nerves, or roaring with aggression, even the simple clack-clack-clack of studs on the tiles.

The thing I do miss is the playing. I miss running out in front of a crowd on a Saturday and hearing them cheer, feeling that burning sense of pride inside when you've done something great in a game and excited people. Oddly, I also miss people groaning when you've made a mistake. I was never afraid of making mistakes.

In a less emotional way, I also miss the structure of professional sport, where everything is planned out for you by others, and I miss the sense of achievement playing brought me. Even if we lost, I did something in every game that felt like a victory to me – a clever little reverse pass, a good step to wrong-foot a full-back, a big tackle. In my new job, I don't have the structure and I'm searching for the sense of achievement. It's very early days, and I'm only just starting out, so I imagine – I hope – that those moments will come when I do actually achieve things . . . pulling off a deal, working through the night on something really interesting, whatever it may be.

Physically, I'm finding it hard to get into the gym. I must've been in 20 times since I quit playing, lifted a dumb-bell, put it straight back down again and just walked out. What's the point? There's no drive or passion there, and I was one of the biggest trainers the sport's seen. I'll have to do it, mind you: I'm very vain and I'm getting fat. I eat chocolate and rubbish, whatever I want, I drink coffee and even have a beer or two – though a lot less than I did in my depressed years, or when we'd just been out and smashed Quins or whoever.

Without Credit Suisse I think I might have gone mad. It's hard, retiring from sport, whatever anyone tells you and whatever I tell anyone else.

How am I getting on? Fine, really busy at work, seeing a lot more of the kids, doing family stuff . . .

I can hear myself now. And inside I'm thinking, *But I just want to play.*

It's been the love of my life since I was six and it's just not the same any more. I was asked to join smaller teams, like Orrell and Coventry, but I couldn't do it. It was the fear of not being the best: the fear of going there and watching some young kid running round me, or some big guy running over me, or feeling someone smashing me in the back of the head because he's getting the chance to batter someone who played for England. Physically, I probably wouldn't last anyway, even at the pace of lower leagues.

I've not been back to the club much. It doesn't feel right, maybe because of the way things are between me and Paddy. When he leaves, I'd love to go back and do stuff, if they want me to. It was my home for 10 years, after all. There's no guarantee they would ask, of course. The way they let a man like Dean Richards leave on bad terms showed how what you've done for the Tigers is very much viewed as being in the past.

There'd always be that horrible feeling of being an outsider, too. Leon rang me the other day and said the team was going out paintballing. 'You ought to come, mate,' he said. 'It'd be great, like old times.'

Me and My Mouth

'Thanks Leon,' I said. 'I'll give it a miss, but thanks.'

I'd love to have gone, really, but if you don't feel part of it, it's not right.

Recently, I dug out my mum's old scrapbooks. She's kept them religiously, right from my early days. You look back and think, 'I didn't actually achieve all that much,' and, compared to some, I didn't. But then you read what people wrote about you when you were younger, and it's amazing. It makes the hairs on the back of my neck stand up. Everyone has their moment, and for me it was two or three, maybe four, years where I was at my peak. I can at least be proud of some of that stuff.

But that's all in the past, now.

'I used to be a rugby player.'

The hardest words I've ever had to say. It's been a long journey, but the sooner I admit that it's over, the better.

Wasting Police Time – The Crazy World Of The War On Crime
PC David Copperfield
A disgruntled uniformed PC blows the lid on the fiddled crime figures, huge
waste of time, money and manpower and political interference that are
paralysing Britain's police.

Shocking, very funny and critically acclaimed (and written about
extensively in *The Daily Mail*, *The Daily Telegraph*, *The Sunday Times*, *The
Sun* and *The Observer*, among many others), this a unique book will appeal
to all who worry about crime and the government's failure to deal with it.
'Entertaining and sobering' – The Observer
'A sensation' – The Sun
'Lifts the lid . . . a very un-pc PC' – Daily Mail
'A very revealing book' – The Daily Telegraph

Road Trip To Hell – Tabloid Tales Of Saddam, Iraq And A Bloody War
Chris Hughes
Chris Hughes is a tabloid journalist who has spent the last five years
travelling to and around Iraq. The result is a dry, moving and frightening look
behind the scenes in this ruined country. Hughes doesn't pretend to be an
expert on Middle Eastern politics and he often bumbles and fumbles on his
travels – he unwittingly joins mercenaries on a gun-running trip, accidentally
rearms a looter and discovers the gruesome fate of Uday Hussein's prized
Arab stallions (curried). But he was also the only Western reporter present at
the second massacre of Fallujah, the first into Saddam's hidey-hole and the
first into Iraq post-9/11. He escaped death several times, made friends with
ordinary Iraqis and writes sympathetically about their troubles and fears.
'Five stars . . . a brilliant read' – The Daily Mirror

It's Your Time You're Wasting – A Teacher's Tales Of Classroom Hell
Frank Chalk
Frank Chalk is an ordinary teacher in an ordinary British school . . . a school
where the kids take drugs, beat up the teachers and give birth in their
classrooms – when they can be bothered to turn up.

It's Your Time You're Wasting is his bleak but blackly humorous diary of his
final year in the modern education system. He battles the tearaways, worries
about the few conscientious pupils and muses on the shortcomings of the
staff (including his own), recording his experiences in a dry and very
readable manner. His book will horrify (and amuse) millions of parents and
will become a must-read for many of the country's 400,000 teachers.
'Addictive, ghastly and engaging' – The Times